John Stuart Mill and Epistemic Democracy

John Stuart Mill and Epistemic Democracy

Ivan Cerovac

LEXINGTON BOOKS
Lanham • Boulder • New York • London

Published by Lexington Books

An imprint of The Rowman & Littlefield Publishing Group, Inc.

4501 Forbes Boulevard, Suite 200, Lanham, Maryland 20706
www.rowman.com

86-90 Paul Street, London EC2A 4NE

Copyright © 2022 by The Rowman & Littlefield Publishing Group, Inc.

All rights reserved. No part of this book may be reproduced in any form or by any electronic or mechanical means, including information storage and retrieval systems, without written permission from the publisher, except by a reviewer who may quote passages in a review.

British Library Cataloguing in Publication Information Available

Library of Congress Cataloging-in-Publication Data

Library of Congress Cataloging-in-Publication Data
Names: Cerovac, Ivan, author.
  Title: John Stuart Mill and epistemic democracy / Ivan Cerovac.
  Description: Lanham, Maryland : Lexington Books, [2022] | Includes bibliographical references and index.
  Identifiers: LCCN 2021054907 (print) | LCCN 2021054908 (ebook) | ISBN 9781793636768 (Cloth : acid-free paper) | ISBN 9781793636782 (paperback) | ISBN 9781793636775 (eBook)
  Subjects: LCSH: Mill, John Stuart, 1806-1873. | Democracy--Philosophy.
  Classification: LCC JC423 .C4447 2022 (print) | LCC JC423 (ebook) | DDC 321.8--dc23/eng/20220105
  LC record available at https://lccn.loc.gov/2021054907
  LC ebook record available at https://lccn.loc.gov/2021054908

∞™ The paper used in this publication meets the minimum requirements of American National Standard for Information Sciences—Permanence of Paper for Printed Library Materials, ANSI/NISO Z39.48-1992.

It is the duty of governments, and of individuals, to form the truest opinions they can; to form them carefully, and never impose them upon others unless they are quite sure of being right.

John Stuart Mill (1859a: 36)

Contents

Acknowledgments	ix
Introduction	1
Chapter 1: Two Criteria: Education and Competence	17
Chapter 2: The Epistemic Value of Political Conflict	41
Chapter 3: Democracy and the Quality of Political Outcomes	55
Chapter 4: Political Representation and Filtering Mechanisms	81
Chapter 5: Plural Voting Proposal	113
Chapter 6: The Epistemic Role of Partisanship	137
Chapter 7: Filtering Mechanisms and Antipaternalism	161
Conclusion	181
Bibliography	183
Index	199
About the Author	205

Acknowledgments

The work on this book was supported by the Faculty of Humanities and Social Sciences at the University of Rijeka and the Department of Humanities at the University of Trieste. Although the book was written in a reasonably short time, it systemizes and builds upon the research conducted within the past eleven years. While the initial work on this book started during my affiliation with the project "Well-being, Affiliation and Social Justice" (UIP-2017-05–3462), the final version was completed during my collaboration within the research project "Responding to antisocial personalities in a democratic society" (IP-2018-01–3518), both funded by the Croatian Science Foundation.

I would like to thank my colleagues at both universities for their continuous support and inspiration. Special thanks go to the members of the "Fellowship of Public Reason," an informal group of researchers based at the University of Rijeka. The Fellowship proved to be a valuable platform where my work was discussed, scrutinized and substantively improved. Furthermore, the Fellowship organized over thirty workshops, summer schools, international conferences and author-meets-critics symposia, thus giving me the opportunity to discuss my research and learn a lot from many philosophers whose work I address in this book. I would like to express immense gratitude to Elvio Baccarini, my mentor, good friend and the head of our Fellowship, for the continuous support in this project. His insightful comments and wise suggestions have greatly influenced my entire philosophical work, and this book is no exception. Snježana Prijić-Samaržija, Nebojša Zelič and Ivan Mladenović have provided valuable feedback both at the early stages of this project and in its very end. Their prominent work in social epistemology and political philosophy constantly inspires and stimulates my own. Finally, Luca Malatesti, the leader of the research project I am currently engaged in, provided valuable support is the latter stages of my work.

The book benefited a lot from philosophers and participants of various conferences and other events organized all around Europe, where I had a pleasure and a privilege to present my work. I have learned a lot from Richard Arneson, Richard Bellamy, Giulia Bistagnino, Thom Brooks, Emanuela Ceva, Simone Chambers, Thomas Christiano, Ruther Claassen, Chiara Destri, John Dunn, David Estlund, Maria Paola Ferretti, Miranda Fricker, Gerald Gaus, Chandran Kukathas, Jose Marti, Ana Matan, David Miller, Martin O'Neill, Fabienne Peter, Jonathan Quong, Kai Spiekermann, Steven Wall, Jonathan White, Andrew Williams, Jonathan Wolff and Lea Ypi. I have undoubtedly forgotten many others, for which I apologize.

Julija Perhat, Ena Dunatov and Maša Dunatov have helped proofread and format the first draft of the manuscript, although most of the work fell on Mia Biturajac, a great philosopher and a virtuous friend who provided countless valuable comments and suggestions, and with whom I have undertaken many great adventures.

While there is a lot of new material here, a few chapters draw from some of my previously published papers. The arguments presented there have been substantively modified and thoroughly rewritten to fit this publication.

Chapter 6 is roughly based on my paper "Plural Voting and Mill's Account of Democratic Legitimacy," published in *Croatian Journal of Philosophy* 16/1 (2016.): 91–106.

Chapter 8 is based on my paper "Antipaternalizam i višestruko pravo glasa u Millovoj političkoj filozofiji [Antipaternalism and Plural Voting Proposal in Mill's Political Thought]," published in *Političke perspektive* 7/1–2 (2017a): 43–60.

Introduction

Mill's moral and political philosophy is a vast and thoroughly discussed area of philosophical inquiry. Recent interpretations of Mill have shed new light on his works interpreting it through the lens of epistemic democracy. My book continues in this direction, characterizes Mill as an epistemic democrat and investigates how this classification can help us preserve consistency in Mill's political thought.

In this book I focus on his theory of democracy, addressing it primarily through his arguments presented in *Considerations on Representative Government* (1977a), as well as his other prominent works. Although Mill himself often characterized his view as democratic (Mill 1981a), his profound focus on unequally distributed political competence and his support for various mechanisms used to filter the public will (e.g., plural voting proposal) urged many philosophers to regard him as a non-democratic and elitist thinker, thus ignoring some of his more democratic ideas and proposals. Comparably, focusing on his arguments for (virtually) universal suffrage and citizens' participation in collective decision-authorization procedures, as well as on the protective function of political participation, some have endorsed Mill as a democratic and egalitarian thinker, somewhat neglecting his preoccupation with political competence. Combining the two allegedly conflicting principles (competence and education) became a difficult task and some have even acknowledged that Mill's thinking develops "along two quite different and inconsistent lines" (Anschutz 1969, 32). Finally, authors such as Dennis Thompson defend consistency in Mill's political thought by arguing that conflicting principles actually constrain one another and that, following Mill, political institutions should be designed to realize both values simultaneously (Thompson 1976, 10–11).

This book follows in Thompson's footsteps but goes deeper to the very foundations of Mill's moral and political thought. For Mill, both principles (competence and participation) are only instrumentally valuable and serve the same overall purpose—to produce "the greatest amount of beneficial consequences, immediate and prospective" (Mill 1861, 54). The best form of government takes this final end as a regulatory criterion and balances between the two principles seeking to scale them in a way that promotes optimal results. We evaluate various forms of government (and various decision-making and decision-authorization procedures) by focusing on their ability to produce optimal political results, understood as both their direct (laws, policies and decisions) and indirect (society's public culture) political outcomes.

Furthermore, the standard of correctness is defined independently of any form of government (or decision-making procedure). The results are good or bad, efficient or inefficient and just or unjust regardless of the purely procedural qualities that some form of government may exhibit. This view takes a form of epistemic instrumentalism, a position that evaluates various forms of government based on their ability to produce outcomes of considerable substantive (procedure-independent) quality. Assessing Mill's work in this manner, by reading him as an epistemic instrumentalist and an epistemic democrat, gives us a unique and an underexplored perspective that can be used to bring unity to his political thought.

The central aim of the research is to investigate the theoretical and practical implications of its main hypothesis (i.e., the idea that Mill can be seen as an early epistemic democrat) for the interpretation of the unity of Mill's thought, as well as for the resolution of the tension between political and epistemic values in contemporary debates. This reading casts a new light on many well-discussed ideas in Mill's political thought (e.g., plural voting proposal, antipaternalism, division of epistemic and political labor, political education) and might change how we perceive Mill's input on these and many other issues, as well as offer guidelines for a proper balancing between epistemic and political values in political philosophy.

Although the research in Mill's political thought might seem to deal with issues relevant only for the history of western philosophy, this book offers a few innovative contributions to the contemporary debate on epistemic democracy. *First*, it demonstrates that authors defending epistemic democracy should not abhor mechanisms filtering the public will. If we want to cultivate and improve democracy's epistemic qualities, we should embrace mechanisms that tend to protect it from vehemence and imprudence. *Second*, it invites us to reconsider various mechanisms that shape the appropriate division of epistemic and political labor. While many Mill's proposals cannot be implemented in contemporary politics, some can be modified and shaped to fit liberal views in the twenty-first century. Furthermore, even when Mill's own proposals differ greatly from the widely accepted practices, the arguments he uses to support these controversial proposals remain valuable and can often be used to motivate epistemic improvement of our democratic practices. *Third*, the book's final chapter introduces innovative considerations that can help us reconcile individual freedom and the democratic decision-making process. Namely, focusing on epistemic justification of democracy (but also on epistemic justification of liberal rights) can help us determine the proper scope of both democratic decisions and laws protecting individual rights.

RESEARCH BACKGROUND

This book presents John Stuart Mill as an epistemic democrat and investigates how this reading helps us achieve consistency in his political thought. Furthermore, it provides insights regarding the proper application of his proposals to the contemporary debate on epistemic democracy. Two minor clarifications and two important considerations have to be briefly addressed before we can proceed forth. I start by introducing the two clarifications since they are needed to properly understand arguments presented in this book.

The first clarification addresses the distinction between the quality of government and its legitimacy-generating potential. In accounts that locate the source of political legitimacy in democratic approval, public reason or the consent of the governed (Locke 1990, Nozick 1974, Estlund 2008, Simmons 2001, Rawls 2005, Gaus 2011, Pettit 2012), this distinction is strongly maintained. A form of government can be legitimate without being the best one there is (according to some procedure-independent standard). This means that a form of government can produce worse results than some other viable form of government but can nonetheless be considered legitimate. Similarly, the best form of government (according to some procedure-independent standard) can still be illegitimate, provided that some (reasonable) citizens cannot (or do not, or should not[1]) endorse it as a proper source of legitimate claims. David Estlund (2008, 7), for example, argues that epistocracy (the rule of the wise) can sometimes be considered as the best form of government, but it can still lack political legitimacy because not all reasonable (or qualified) citizens can endorse it as such.[2] However, accounts that locate the source of political legitimacy in beneficial consequences (Bentham 1843c, Mill 1977a, Wellman 1996, Binmore 2000) tend to disregard this distinction. A government's legitimacy depends on its ability to produce beneficial consequences, i.e., to ensure the happiness (and, in Mill's case, self-development) of its citizens. Of course, whether or not the citizens consent to the authority and legitimacy of the government still plays an important role. When citizens are governed by the laws created using the procedures they cannot endorse, their self-development will be seriously undermined. Such decision-authorization procedure will thus fail to produce the best consequences.[3] Mill insists that laws and political decisions should be authorized by a procedure that "can be understood and accepted by the general conscience and understanding. [The decision-authorization procedure should] not necessarily be repugnant to any one's sentiment of justice" (Mill 1861, 177).

However, citizens' consent is not the source of political legitimacy—beneficial consequences are. For Mill and other utilitarian authors, there is no relevant distinction (and no gap) between the quality of government and its legitimacy (Peter 2017). The best form of government, i.e., one that "is attended with the greatest amount of beneficial consequences, immediate and prospective" (Mill 1861, 54), is by this virtue also the legitimate form of government. Mill mostly writes on the quality of government, and this project follows in his terminology and style. However, when issues regarding political legitimacy appear within this book, they are normally (unless otherwise noted) regarded from Mill's standpoint, thus disregarding the distinction between the quality of government and its legitimacy.

The second clarification regards the distinction between decision-making and decision-authorization procedures. While most authors use only the former term, I believe stressing the difference between the two can be of utmost importance. Namely, while the 'decision-making' regards how political decisions are actually made, the 'decision-authorization' focuses on how decisions receive their political authority and legitimacy. Or, in Millian terms, while the former addresses only a technical process of making political decisions (typically conducted by the executive branch of the government), the latter regards where the real sovereignty resides (for Mill, in the legislative, or representative, branch of government). Democracy, typically understood as "the actual collective authorization of laws and policies by the people subject to them" (Estlund 2008, 38), does not imply that all citizens necessarily participate as equals in the decision-making process. Decisions authorized by a democratic procedure can be (and often are) made directly by a small group of people or even by an individual. This means that, within a democratic system, political and technical experts can make laws and public policies. However, the authority of these laws and policies will not come directly from the expertise of those who have made them, but from the fact that these experts were authorized by democratically elected political representatives (in the parliament) (Cerovac 2017b, 168, see also Festenstein 2009). Mill thus argues that "while it is essential to the representative government that the practical supremacy in the state should reside in the representatives of the people, it is an open question what actual functions, what precise part in the machinery of government, shall be directly and personally discharged by the representative body" (Mill 1861, 88–89).[4] The differentiation between decision-making and decision-authorization procedures helps us account for this.

Furthermore, two important considerations need to be addressed. First, what is epistemic democracy, and what do we imply when we characterize someone as an epistemic democrat? Second, some authors have already described Mill as an epistemic democrat (reference). How does the approach adopted in this book differ from their earlier contributions?

Epistemic Democracy

The intense discussion on epistemic democracy has been going on for over thirty years and many positions have been established. Some of these positions differ normatively (or theoretically) from one another, while some share the same normative assumptions and disagree only on details regarding its political implementation. However, in order to fit the description of epistemic democracy, a position has to endorse two fundamental claims. It has to affirm that:

1. We evaluate the quality of government (or the quality of a decision-authorization procedure), as well as its ability to produce legitimate political decisions, at least in part by evaluating its epistemic qualities.
2. Democracy is a form of government (or a decision-authorization procedure) that realizes this epistemic quality (and maybe some other, non-epistemic qualities) to a significant degree, enough to be considered the best form of government and to have legitimacy-generating potential.

One can reject the first claim and still argue for a democratic government. In fact, many scholars argue that democracy has legitimacy-generating potential without appealing to any epistemic quality it might have. For example, some argue that epistemic qualities do not reside within the political process (Arendt 1967, Schmitt 2007), while others endorse that democracy (or some other procedure) might have some epistemic value but emphasize that this has nothing to do with political legitimacy (Christiano 2008, Rawls 2005). These scholars affirm that democracy has some relevant moral qualities (e.g., it is fair and treats all citizens as equals, giving them equal political influence in the decision-authorization process), and maintain that (because of these qualities) democracy has legitimacy-generating potential and represents the best form of government. They can be considered democrats, but not epistemic democrats.

Similarly, one can endorse the first claim but reject the second. Some scholars thus believe that a decision-authorization procedure has to have considerable epistemic qualities, but simultaneously claim that democracy fails to meet these high standards (Plato 2000, Brennan 2016). Namely, political knowledge is unequally distributed within political community and some citizens (the majority) often act and vote irrationally, thus opting for bad, incorrect or harmful policies. These scholars end up endorsing some form of epistocracy[5] or "the rule of the knowledgeable," a form of government where a small group of experts authorize all relevant political decisions. While they focus on procedure's (or government's) epistemic qualities, they clearly cannot be considered democrats.

Epistemic democrats thus claim that democracy represents the best form of government and has legitimacy-generating potential due to its epistemic qualities (but not necessarily only due to its epistemic qualities). They disagree considerably when asked what these epistemic qualities entail. Some locate the procedure's epistemic value in its purely procedural qualities and virtues, e.g., its tendency to treat all citizens as equal epistemic agents, to promote responsiveness to arguments and to create space for the critical discourse (Peter 2011). Decision-authorization procedure can thus have legitimacy-generating potential regardless of the (procedure-independent) quality of political outcomes it produces. However, most scholars locate the procedure's epistemic value in its procedure-independent qualities, e.g., its tendency to create political outcomes that are correct, true or just according to some procedure-independent standard (Cohen 1986, Misak 2000, Marti 2006, Estlund 2008, Talisse 2009, Prijić-Samaržija 2018, Mladenović 2019, Cerovac 2020). While these scholars might disagree on many issues,[6] they will all hold that democracy's epistemic value comes from its tendency to improve the quality of political outcomes. John Stuart Mill, with his consequentialist (utilitarian) moral background, seems to fit this categorization. Following Mill, we evaluate the epistemic quality of various decision-authorization procedures by assessing the quality of their outcomes.

Background: Mill as an Epistemic Democrat

With the recent emergence of epistemic democracy (Cohen 1986, Estlund 2008), some new aspects of Mill's political thought come to light. Authors such as Estlund (2003) and Peter (2017) emphasize Mill's demand for the (procedure-independent) quality of political decisions. David Estlund (2003, 57) indicates that although Mill does not explicitly state that producing correct, efficient or just political decisions is the goal of good government, "it is hard to understand his argument in any other way." Similarly, Fabienne Peter (2017) argues that Mill presents "a view of the instrumental value of (deliberative) democracy" when he claims that "despotism is a legitimate mode of government in dealing with barbarians, provided that the end be their improvement" (Mill 1977d, 224). However, their engagement with Mill's political philosophy is sporadic and nonsystemic, thus missing the opportunity to present its unified reading through the lens of epistemic democracy.

Unlike the previous authors, some tend to put greater focus on Mill's free market of ideas and thus characterizes him as an epistemic liberal. Helene

Landemore, for example, writes that "Mill is probably more of an epistemic liberal—acknowledging the epistemic properties of a free exchange of ideas among the people outside the formal structures of government—than an epistemic democrat per se" (Landemore 2017, 76). Adam James Tebble argues in a similar fashion that, although Hume and Mill cannot "be considered as epistemic liberals in an unambiguous sense in which we see Popper and Hayek can," in contrast to Hume, "Mill's connection to the epistemic approach is more obvious" (Tebble 2016, 4). Finally, Melissa Schwartzberg follows this line of thought and argues that "rather than arguing that democratic decision-making will lead to wise decisions, Mill affirmed that a set of institutions protective of the individual liberty of inquiry and exchange would promote the discovery of truth" (Schwartzberg 2015, 197). However, like the previous authors, they also touch upon Mill's political thought only briefly and show no interest to fully elaborate this interpretation.

Gustavo Hessmann Dalaqua (2019) is the first to both characterize Mill as an epistemic democrat and to present a comprehensive and extensive overview of Mill's political thought. His *Representative Democracy, Conflict and Consensus in J. S. Mill* (2019) is a valuable read for all interested in these issues and gives a useful insight into Mill's political epistemology and a persuasive answer to Nadia Urbinati (2014) and other critics of the epistemic approach. Dalaqua's contribution, however, does not try to situate Mill's position within the contemporary discussion on epistemic democracy. Similarly, while it emphasizes the epistemic value of both conflict and consensus, it seems to completely neglect Mill's thoughts on unequal distribution of political competence and his epistemic justification of various filtering mechanisms (e.g., plural voting proposal, open ballot, division of political and epistemic labor) used to increase the quality of political decisions in the face of such inequalities in knowledge and competence.

There are many topics in Mill's political thought where this interpretation can be explored and applied. Mill's plural-voting proposal (1977a, 1977b) and the suggested division of political and epistemic labor (1977a) point towards an epistemic instrumental justification of democracy. He assesses the quality of the government by evaluating both its educational features (Anderson 1991, Baccarini 1993, Baccarini 2013, Brink 2013), i.e., its ability to improve the moral and intellectual capacities of the citizens, and its epistemic features (Baccarini 2013, Estlund 2003, Arneson 2003), i.e., its ability to track the truth and to produce correct political decisions. A unifying criterion behind these two features are beneficial consequences: both serve as best means to produce the desired outcome—the highest level of utility "grounded on the permanent interests of man as a progressive being" (Mill 1997d, 224, also emphasized in Peter 2011 and Claeys 2013).

Mill and the Three Tenets of Epistemic Justification

David Estlund (2008) introduces, and Ivan Cerovac (2020) further elaborates a useful scheme we can use to differentiate between various epistemic approaches. It builds upon three tenets typically related to the epistemic account. While a position can reject all three tenets and still be considered a form of epistemic democracy (e.g., Peter 2011), this scheme helps us systemize and differentiate between various accounts of epistemic democracy. The truth tenet states that political decisions can be right or wrong (correct or incorrect), and we can evaluate them as such regardless of the procedure that produced them. In fact, we can assess the epistemic value of political procedures by addressing their ability to produce correct, efficient or just outcomes. The knowledge tenet asserts that some people (usually a small group of experts) are more likely to produce correct political decisions than others. Their decision-making competences exceed those of an average citizen to a significant degree. Finally, the authority tenet maintains that those who are better in making political decisions (i.e., experts) should have greater political influence than those who lack these decision-making capacities (or have them to a lesser degree). Greater political knowledge thus implies greater political influence (Estlund 2008, 30–33 and Cerovac 2020, 9–10). Systemizing various accounts and positions following this scheme goes far beyond the scope of this book, and a helpful overview can be found in Cerovac (2020). However, it will be useful to set Mill's position within this scheme and to analyze which of the three tenets Mill endorses.

First, Mill embraces the truth tenet. He clearly states that we assess the quality of government by evaluating the quality of its results. These results, generally understood as "beneficial consequences, immediate and prospective" (Mill 1861, 54), are evaluated independently of the procedure that had produced them. In fact, the same decision-authorization procedure can yield different results when applied to political communities on a different level of social and political development. We evaluate forms of government, but also institutional mechanisms and practices (e.g., political representation, citizens' participation, division of epistemic and political labor, as well as filtering mechanisms like open ballot and plural vote), by assessing the quality of results they produce. This is clearly an instrumentalist approach and I provide support for this interpretation is the second chapter, where I indicate beneficial consequences as the cornerstone for two criteria of good government, in the third chapter, where I discuss instrumental epistemic value Mill ascribes to public deliberation and political conflict, and in the fourth chapter, where I address Mill's instrumental justification of democracy.

Second, Mill embraces the knowledge tenet. He believes that political knowledge is unequally distributed within political community, with some citizens knowing better than others what should be done. He indicates that citizens differ both in knowledge and intelligence on the one hand and in virtue on the other, and argues that their "capacity for the management of the joint interests" is unequally distributed (Mill 1861, 173). This is true for technical expertise, where some citizens have acquired (by education and practice) highly specialized knowledge in some field, but also for moral expertise, where some citizens have acquired (again by education and practice) superior moral and political knowledge. I discuss and demonstrate this primarily in the second chapter, where I analyze the organization of citizens' unequally distributed competences as one of the criteria of good government and in the sixth chapter where I discuss Mill's plural voting proposal. Furthermore, Mill's endorsement of the knowledge tenet is also found in the fifth and the seventh chapter, where some filtering mechanisms (e.g., local government, partisanship) are defended (in part) due to their ability to promote education and the transfer of knowledge from those who know better what should be done.

Third, Mill endorses the authority tenet. He believes that, although (virtually) all citizens should have a voice in the common concerns and thus exercise some political influence in the formal political sphere, not all citizens should have equal political influence. Those who know what should be done better than others should also have "a claim to a superior weight" in the collective decision-authorization procedures, and the institutions of the country should recognize that "the opinion, the judgment, of the higher moral or intellectual being, is worth more than that of an inferior" (Mill 1861, 172). He adds that "opinions, and even wishes" of those more qualified are "entitled to a greater amount of consideration" (Mill 1861, 173–174). I support this interpretation in the sixth chapter where I discuss his plural voting proposal, but also in the fifth chapter, where I analyze Mill's epistemic justification for other filtering mechanisms. However, although Mill clearly endorses the authority tenet, this does not lead him towards some form of epistocracy (rule of the wise), where those who know best have all the political influence while others have none. The third chapter explains why he puts strong constraints on the authority tenet, arguing that democratic political participation can have significant epistemic value. The best form of government has to find a way to harvest this epistemic value of diverse perspectives and combine it with the epistemic value of privileging competence over incompetence. These considerations simultaneously ground and limit Mill's adherence to the authority tenet.

Mill thus endorses all three tenets typically related to the epistemic account. His account remains democratic since he affirms the idea that actual collective authorization of laws and policies should be done by the people subject to them. However, the justification for the democratic authorization of laws and policies is instrumental and epistemic—democracy is the procedure with the highest tendency to produce correct, efficient, or just political outcomes.

METHODOLOGY

There are a few approaches one can use to assess and engage with the work of important authors from the past. Adrian Blau (2019, 4) usefully distinguishes between historical and philosophical approach. Using historical analysis, one focuses on putting the relevant texts in the appropriate historical contexts, and thus tries to determine what the authors had in mind and what kind of social and political change they were arguing for. This approach aims to describe and explain authors' ideas and to find out what motivated the authors to embrace or develop that (and not some other) set of political ideas. Using philosophical analysis, one tries to put the relevant texts in the appropriate textual contexts, evaluate the consistency and correctness of the employed ideas and the consequences of their political application. This approach entails critical evaluation of authors' ideas as well as suggestions on how the authors' positions can be strengthened or improved. Blau usefully emphasizes that the two approaches should not be considered in opposition. Instead, one should "be open to all available tools to understand the text" and use both approaches "as allies, not as alternatives" (Blau 2019, 3, 12).

Setting philosophical works written and published 150 years ago in the context of contemporary debates, as well as weighting even the most advanced ideas from that period against the current state of the art, might not seem either fair nor particularly useful.[7] In fact, doing so would be like "riding forth to do battle with a set of disused windmills, or solemnly and expertly flailing thin air" (Dunn 1969, ix–x). Scholars focusing on historical analysis argue that we should instead try to "restore the windmill to its original condition, to show how, creakingly but unmistakably, the sails used to turn (Dunn 1969, x, see also Ball 2004, 27). While I agree that we should try to determine what the authors had in mind, I do not believe that this exhausts their potential contribution. Namely, classical authors provide us with new insights only when we, from time to time, reinterpret them from alternative perspectives (Ball 1995). Interpretations are always theory laden (Blau 2017) and reading them in different time periods often brings focus on different aspects of the work.

Mill's work addressed and discussed within this book was written and published over a long period of time, from early 1830s to early 1870s. Furthermore, Mill produced works of various levels of generality, from comprehensive books and long essays addressing rather abstract ideas and principles to newspaper articles and parliamentary debates focusing on applied and narrow political and social issues. The book tries to preserve consistency in Mill's political thought by accounting for two types of textual context misreadings contemporary authors often commit while interpreting Mill's work. The first, mostly discussed in chapters on plural voting proposal, regards mistakes when relevant pieces of Mill's argument are overlooked, or their importance is underappreciated. These mistakes happen when authors focus exclusively on the historical context and disregard relevant passages in the text, even when they are just a sentence or two apart from the segments they focused upon. The second, mostly discussed in the final chapter, regards mistakes when two or more relevant texts are not properly linked. These mistakes happen when we read Mill's works (e.g., *On Liberty* and *Utilitarianism*) without realizing that the central argument in one is grounded in the ideas presented and defended in the other.[8]

This book combines historical analysis and philosophical analysis. However, it's central aim is not to provide a comprehensive overview or the final interpretation of Mill's political thought. Instead, it uses the wider framework of epistemic justification of government as an intermediary between Mill's theoretical utilitarian background and his more practical political ideas and views on political institutions and mechanisms. Furthermore, since epistemic democracy represents one of the contemporary theories of democracy,[9] the book tries to interpret Mill's work through a theory which was not present in his time. Again, the point is not to attribute Mill with ideas or proposals he himself did not have, but to demonstrate how reading Mill as an early epistemic democrat can help us bring coherence and unity in his political thought.

PLAN OF THE BOOK

This book has three parts. In the first part (first and second chapters) I discuss and elaborate on the two basic criteria Mill uses to evaluate different forms of government (or different decision-authorization procedures). Furthermore, I analyze Mill's argument for the epistemic value of political disagreement, which establishes Mill as an epistemic liberal but also represents a foundation for his future characterization as an epistemic democrat. In the second part (third, fourth, fifth and sixth chapters) I fully develop the epistemic interpretation of Mill's political thought, arguing that Mill values democracy for its instrumental epistemic qualities, but also addressing epistemic arguments for various mechanisms he introduces to filter the public will, thus protecting decision-authorization and decision-making procedures from incompetence, vehemence and negligence. Finally, in the third part of the book (seventh chapter) I address the alleged problem of paternalism and indicate how the epistemic interpretation can help us preserve consistency in Mill's political thought.

In the *first* chapter I address Mill's two principles (or criteria) of good government (education and competence) and discuss their prominent role in his moral and political thought. The chapter indicates why these two principles are so important and how the state can facilitate and promote them within formal and informal settings. Understanding what these principles entail will be of great importance later, since Mill's epistemic justification of democracy, as well as the justification of various filtering mechanisms, rests on these two principles.

The epistemic value of political conflict is discussed in the *second* chapter. Mill is characterized as an adherent of deliberative agonism, a position that sees political conflict and disagreement as a permanent state of politics. Mill is then portrayed as an epistemic (agonist) democrat who considers political conflict instrumentally valuable since it promotes the two principles of good government: it helps improve citizens intellectual and moral capacities, and it helps citizens evaluate their opinions and beliefs, discard those not supported by good reasons and arguments, and create new ideas and new solutions to existing problems. Political institutions should thus both stimulate and contain political conflict to keep it epistemically fertile.

The central argument of this book is presented in the third chapter, where I analyze Mill's epistemic argument for democracy. I characterize Mill as an epistemic instrumentalist and demonstrate that Mill uses the instrumental reading of the two principles of good government to argue against the despotic rule and in favor of a representative democracy. Furthermore, I emphasize that the two principles do not support any form of democratic government and provide the epistemic reading of major dangers of a democratic rule (e.g., the tyranny of the majority, the relative incompetence of the average voter). Since we need a decision-authorization procedure that will meet the two principles and reliably produce correct, efficient and just political outcomes, as well as a procedure that will be able to utilize the epistemic value of political conflict, we should prefer deliberative over aggregative democracy. Furthermore, we need a list of institutional mechanisms that can help filter the public will and promote the procedure-independent epistemic quality of decision-authorization procedures (and political outcomes).

Having established that a well-functioning democracy needs a list of filtering mechanisms to properly discharge its moral and epistemic role, I analyze some of these mechanisms in the *fourth* chapter. Having in mind the potential dangers of majority rule (class legislation and low level of political intellect, both significantly decreasing democracy's ability to properly realize the two principles of good government), Mill endorses an indirect (representative) over a direct democracy. His reasons for this are instrumental and epistemic:

separating (both spatially and temporally) talking from doing in the political process will increase the epistemic value of the procedures used to make and authorize decisions, thus increasing the quality of political outcomes. This chapter also addresses some of the many formal filters Mill uses to filter the public will (and to improve its epistemic contribution), including public balloting, advocacy as a model of political representation, division of labor between the representative body (the parliament) and expert bodies (legislative commissions and executive government), as well as the limited autonomy and authority of the local government. However, this chapter does not address two additional filtering mechanisms: Mill's plural voting proposal and his views on partisanship. Namely, these two mechanisms are often contested, and some scholars tend to disregard them altogether in order to preserve the consistency of Mill's project. I believe they represent a very important aspect of Mill's political thought, and I analyze Mill's epistemic justification of these mechanisms in the next two chapters.

In the *fifth* chapter I focus on plural voting proposal and argue that this inegalitarian voting mechanism fits nicely within the epistemic interpretation of Mill's political thought. Following his account of voting as a privilege (and not as an unconditional right), I characterize Mill as an egalitarian with regard to negative liberties (those directly affecting only the individual in question, like freedom of movement, freedom of religion, and freedom of speech) but inegalitarian with regards to positive liberties (those inherent to a participatory democratic process). Finally, I argue that Mill proposes plural voting as a permanent (and not only temporary) measure, and that the key reason for this is to increase the instrumental epistemic value of democratic procedures.

The *sixth* chapter emphasizes that many scholars have misinterpreted Mill's views on partisanship. I characterize political parties and partisan associations as one of the mechanisms Mill uses to filter the public will, indicating how they can improve the instrumental epistemic quality of a democratic process by promoting and structuring public deliberation and filtering the content that enters the public sphere, but also by introducing competence in democratic deliberation by connecting citizens, experts and political representatives who share the same worldviews. Mill also indicates that partisan associations can help strengthen the underrepresented classes, as well as to create a deliberative link between civil society and the state.

A famous inconsistency objection is addressed in the final, *seventh* chapter of this book. Many scholars consider Mill's epistemic defense of various filtering mechanisms as paternalistic—he filters the popular will and limits collective sovereignty to improve the quality of political decisions affecting the same political community. I defend Mill's filtering mechanisms (and particularly his plural voting proposal) against these objections and argue that they can be defended on non-paternalist grounds. Building upon Mill's moralized conception of voting (and exercising political power over others), I argue that, following Mill's account, we have a duty to use epistemically the best decision-making (and decision-authorization) procedure when we make or authorize political decisions that affect other citizens. We can thus legitimately limit collective sovereignty in order to protect the minority from incorrect or unjust political decisions.

NOTES

1. This formulation depends on a type of consent (actual, hypothetical, normative) that is required from the governed. For additional information see Peter (2017).

2. Estlund thus writes that experts or knowers "might simply be a more accurate source of knowledge about what should be done than any democratic procedure could ever be" (Estlund 2008, 7). He proceeds to argue that the question is not which procedure represents the best epistemic device available, but which procedure can be recognized by all qualified citizens as a procedure with adequate epistemic value.

3. Of course, there are some exceptions. When barbarous nations are in question, where citizens' level of development is so low that their own self-development cannot be achieved, lack of consent can sometimes be disregarded. In such cases, better results will be achieved by a benevolent despot than by a popular government (Mill 1977a, 402–403, 418–420, 562–578).

4. Furthermore, Mill writes that "the powers which [representative government] leaves in hands not directly accountable to the people, can only be considered as precautions which the ruling power is *willing* should be taken against its own errors" (Mill 1861, 88, emphasis added). In other words, various expert bodies and commissions receive their authority not from their own expertise, but from the democratic government which has mandated them to perform some political tasks and duties.

5. The term is introduced by David Estlund (2003), although he clearly rejects this position.

6. One point of disagreement might be whether epistemic qualities are enough to give democracy legitimacy-generating potential. While some will follow this line of thought (Misak 2000, Talisse 2009), sometimes arguing for strong division of epistemic and political labor and thus combining democracy with a moderate form of expertism (Prijić-Samaržija 2018), others will argue that democracy needs its moral qualities (along with its epistemic qualities) to have legitimacy-generating potential (Marti 2006, Estlund 2008, Mladenović 2019, Cerovac 2020). While Mill clearly sides with the former group, a more detailed assessment of his position will be provided in the fourth chapter.

7. Dunn, for example, indicates that there is "little purpose in recording hits on a target that has no existence outside our own minds" (Dunn 1969, x). When we deal with historical thinkers using philosophical approach, we shape their theories using meanings, ideas and concepts that are simply not there. Finally, we end up with a distorted and misleading interpretation, and our critique of such interpretations becomes

useless. For additional information regarding this approach, as well as for its shortcomings, see Ball (1995).

8. Of course, as Blau (2019, 12) points out, we can establish relation between the two by doing historical research and discovering that *Utilitarianism* was written before (but published after) *On Liberty*. This information is not part of the main text, and we get it through historical research. However, we are making a textual context mistake if we fail to acknowledge this relation.

9. Although there is some disagreement, most scholars agree that the contemporary debate on epistemic democracy starts with Joshua Cohen's (1986) famous paper "An Epistemic Conception of Democracy."

Chapter 1

Two Criteria: Education and Competence

Mill's political philosophy, even if we focus only on his thoughts on democracy and representative government, encompasses many relevant but also highly contested and debated topics. Additionally, since his publications and other works span a period of over forty years, providing a systematic overview becomes a demanding task. Dennis Thompson interprets and organizes Mill's thoughts by introducing two fundamental principles—the principle of participation and the principle of competence—and emphasizing that both principles have an educational and protective function (Thompson 1976, 13–90). This is a valuable approach, and with minor difficulties it can be used to portray Mill as an epistemic democrat. However, I find it useful to take a step back and start from Mill's two criteria of good government, the same foundation that Thompson uses for his approach.[1] This enables me to give a more unified overview without losing important aspects of Mill's political thought. Furthermore, it opens the door to a simple but comprehensive characterization of Mill as a democratic instrumentalist and epistemic democrat.

The chapter's innovative contribution can be summarized in two main points. First, it invites us to reexamine Thompson's (1976) organization of Mill's political thought and to consider a simpler approach, one focusing on Mill's two criteria of good government. Second, it lays foundation for the proper understanding of Mill's division of political labor, emphasizing the important difference between moral and technical knowledge and addressing Mill's thoughts on their unequal distribution within the population.

This chapter follows Mill's two criteria of good government (education and competence) and analyses their prominent role in his political thought. The first part of the chapter addresses citizens' education and discusses how the state can facilitate and promote it within formal and informal settings. While even despotic rule can promote formal education, informal education (which represents citizens' self-improvement) can only take place within deliberative, participative and democratic institutions. This does not mean, of course, that a democratic government should neglect formal education, since it is a prerequisite for the self-improvement of citizens, but also for well-functioning of democracy itself. The second part tackles Mill's thought on competence and expertise. It introduces the difference between technical (or instrumental) and moral knowledge, elaborates the roles Mill assigns to the two kinds of experts, and briefly explores Mill's thought regarding the relationship between competence, knowledge, and expertise on the one hand, and political authority and legitimacy on the other.

MILL ON EDUCATION

The development of the intellectual and moral capacities of citizens is one of the two central aims every political community should strive to achieve. It is not surprising that education, broadly understood as a process by which the capacities of citizens are developed and improved, plays a significant role in Mill's political thought. Mill's focus on education was substantial and widely recognized during his lifetime. Alan Ryan indicates that in mid-Victorian England Mill was considered an "educational institution": while Mill himself was appointed Lord Rector to the University of St Andrews, his books on logic and economy were taught at the University of Oxford, the University of London, and many other institutions of higher learning, while his colleagues in Parliament sometimes called him "finishing governess" to ridicule his obsession with education (Ryan 2011, 653–654). This part of the chapter addresses three important issues. First, it analyzes the reasons for Mill's almost fanatical preoccupation with education and asks how Mill's focus on education fits into his wider utilitarian theoretical framework. Having in mind that not all forms of education are the same, the second part addresses Mill's thoughts on education in the narrow sense, understood as a guided process that takes place in a formal setting (schools and universities). Although the analysis of the content of formal schooling might be relevant from the point of view of the philosophy of education, such inquiry goes beyond the scope of this book. I focus instead on political and epistemic aspects of education in a narrower sense—its role as a proper measure of citizens' political influence (plural voting proposal), and the role of the state in promoting formal education and in securing adequate access to education for all citizens. The third part addresses Mill's thoughts on education in a broad sense, understood as a set of all influences that affect the formation of a person's character. Again, I focus on the political and epistemic aspects of such (informal) education, including the mechanisms through which democratic and participative government can facilitate citizens' improvement and self-improvement.

The Role of Education in Mill's Moral Philosophy

Mill's moral philosophy is characterized by his principle of utility, a principle that grounds morality and directs all practical reasoning. Thus, he states that "actions are right in proportion as they tend to promote happiness, wrong as they tend to promote the reverse of happiness" (Mill 1985a, 210, see also Brown 1973). This is a typical utilitarian approach, where happiness is understood as "pleasure, and the absence of pain" (Mill 1985a, 210) and considered to be the only thing of value in itself. Mill seems to advocate a hedonic conception of utilitarianism, similar to Bentham's (1907) position, in which the only intrinsically valuable thing is the subjective feeling of happiness and all other things are instrumentally valuable provided that they contribute to the feeling of happiness. However, although nobler pursuits can be defended by claiming that they produce more pleasure, Mill quickly recognized that they can (and must) be put on a more secure footing (Brink 2018). He therefore ranks activities and pursuits not (only) by the quantity of pleasure they produce, but also (and primarily) by the quality of pleasure associated with them. Mill believes that a competent judge, one who is familiar with the pleasures of various activities, can qualitatively assess and rank these pleasures. If competent judges place one pleasure "so far above the other that they prefer it, even though knowing it to be attended with a greater amount of discontent and would not resign it for any quantity of the other pleasure which their nature is capable of, we are justified in ascribing to the preferred enjoyment a superiority in quality" (Mill 1985a, 211). This differentiation between higher and lower pleasures represents a clear departure from Bentham's quantitative utilitarianism, and some wonder whether Mill's account can even be considered a form of hedonic utilitarianism.[2] Mill associates higher pleasures with "the manner of existence which employs [individual's] higher faculties" (Mill 1985a, 211), thus arguing that some activities, roles, relations and pursuits (those requiring the employment of our higher faculties) have a higher tendency to contribute to our well-being than other activities (those do not require such employment of the higher faculties).

Since utilitarian moral philosophy typically aims to maximize valuable end states (in Mill's case, higher pleasures), education can be a valuable tool we can use to promote human well-being. Indeed, by developing the intellectual and moral capacities of citizens, we enable them to experience and appreciate higher pleasures. Mill reminds us of this when he expresses his appreciation of life "such as human beings with highly developed faculties can care to have" (Mill 1974, 952). Education can be valuable for two reasons. First, it enables citizens to better understand and predict the consequences of their actions, thus promoting prudent behavior and teaches citizens how to perform complex actions that require the exercise of their higher faculties. Second, it enables citizens to identify and pursue goals associated with higher pleasures. Furthermore, it enables them to choose not only those pursuits that ensure their own happiness but also the happiness of others around them (Ryan 2011, 659). Education enables citizens to identify and select valuable aims, as well as to devise the best means to pursue them. These two roles are beautifully illustrated by Mill's differentiation between moral art and moral science. Namely, "the art proposes to itself an end to be attained, defines the end, and hands it over to the science, [while] the science receives it, considers it as a phenomenon or effect to be studied, and having investigated its causes and conditions, sends it back to art with a theorem of the combinations of circumstances by which it could be produced" (Mill 1974, 944, see also Donner 2007, 259).[3]

While virtually everyone endorses the prudential value of education, Mill focuses more on its moral role. It enables citizens to form virtuous characters those preferring higher pleasures and endorsing pursuits that require the exercise of higher faculties. As Wendy Donner insightfully concludes, education promotes happiness by equipping people with relevant intellectual and moral capacities needed to "appreciate the more valuable kinds of satisfactions" (Donner 2007, 255).

But what is the epistemic (and political) value of education? How does it help citizens create correct, just, and efficient laws and policies? Mill's distinction between moral science and moral art can be linked to Christiano's distinction between technical and moral knowledge. While the former regards practical skills and information that can help us determine how to perform some action or to reach certain political aim (e.g., how to build a bridge or heal an injured person), the latter refers to our ability to competently decide which political aims are valuable and which political ideas and values we should pursue (e.g., should we aim for full employment or fiscal stability, should we fund sports or culture) (Christiano 2012). Education, then, can be valuable for epistemic democracy for two reasons. First, it helps citizens acquire technical knowledge and enables them to make more effective policies and political decisions. Combined with the division of labor between epistemic and political labor, it helps citizens to find more competent decision-makers (skilled administrators and legislators, see Mill 1977a, 433–434) who enable them to create better and more efficient means (laws, policies and decisions) to achieve desired aims. Second, it helps citizens to acquire moral knowledge and enables them to select better (more correct, more just) political aims. Combined with the institutions and mechanisms of representative democracy, it helps citizens to find more competent political representatives (members of the Parliament) and thus enables them to specify more valuable political aims the society should strive for.[4]

The two kinds of knowledge (technical and moral) can be acquired using two different forms of education. While the state encourages and oversees both forms of education, Mill is skeptical regarding its more active engagement. These issues are discussed in the following two sections.

Formal Education and the State

Mill understands education in a narrower sense as "the culture which each generation purposely gives to its successors" (Mill 1984a, 261, see also Donner 2007, 261). It takes place in a formal setting and is conducted by institutions whose primary goal is to disseminate knowledge and improve the skills and competences of their beneficiaries. Although formal education helps to develop the intellectual and moral capacities of citizens, it is not (usually) a form of self-development for citizens, as the process takes place under the authority of others. However, acquiring some (minimal) level of education is a prerequisite for citizens' autonomous self-development, as well as for their financial independence. Interestingly, Mill formulates this idea (at least in terms of childhood education) as a mandatory functioning, not a mandatory capability. In other words, the state should not only secure that all children have fair access to education, but it should also secure that all children receive some (at least minimal) level of education.[5] He considers it "almost a self-evident axiom, that the State should require and compel the education, up to a certain standard, of every human being who is born its citizen" (Mill 1859a, 188–189). Mill provides two arguments to support his claim that all citizens should receive some (minimal) level of education. However, I believe that an additional (third) argument can be found.

First, citizens who have not received even a minimum level of education are usually in a very unfavorable position in the labor market. Since they are not qualified to perform even some simple jobs, they often cannot enjoy financial independence and end up relying on other people's help or charity. Mill argues that "it is one of the most sacred duties of the parents, after summoning a human being into the world, to give to that being an education fitting him to perform his part well in life towards others and towards himself" (Mill 1859a, 189). Failing to properly discharge this duty represents "a moral crime, both against the unfortunate offspring and against society" (Mill 1859a, 189). A child is thus harmed because, by not receiving even the most basic education, he is precluded (or at least seriously disadvantaged) from finding meaningful employment and enjoying financial independence, and others are harmed by having to provide for that child's future financial dependence. While some[6] might argue that parents should have the liberty to decide whether to provide education for their children, Mill (1859a, 191) considers this appeal "misplaced." Namely, it is used to conceal a particular duty of parents to their children.

Second, while Mill praises intellectual diversity and approves citizens' self-development because it fosters autonomy and individuality, thus creating citizens with different characters and personalities, he nonetheless believes that a certain amount of education represents a necessary requirement for citizens' self-development. As Donner (2007, 261) insightfully emphasizes, "development of human capacities requires that the groundwork be laid in childhood education".[7] While there are many different forms of education that children may receive (and this diversity in formal education is a great thing), some minimum level of competence should be achieved by all citizens. That is, everyone should be brought above a certain threshold where one is able to reflect and formulate a conception of one's own good, one's own primary values and purposes and the best way to live in accordance with them. This conception includes, among other things, one's ambitions, life goals, and commitments to others. Furthermore, citizens above this threshold are able to understand that other people's freedom limits their own, as well as to consider how to pursue aims that ensure both their own happiness and the happiness of others.[8] When children are denied basic education, they are harmed because they are deprived not only of the opportunity for future self-development, but also of the chance to lead fully autonomous lives. While it might be argued that children can develop their capacities later in life, so the lack of minimal education does not necessarily impair their faculties (West 1965), it is still true that not receiving minimal education creates serious disadvantages and makes self-development far more difficult, thus harming the deprived person.

In addition to the two earlier arguments, I believe there is a *third* (epistemic) argument that further supports Mill's claim. Democratic deliberation is epistemically valuable because (among other things) it introduces various perspectives and opinions into public debate, exposes them to different kinds of criticism, and helps us endorse true beliefs and reject false beliefs. Mill believes that this form of government surpasses all others in epistemic quality (and in the correctness and efficiency of political decisions). However, it relies on the participation of (at least minimally competent) autonomous citizens. If we are to enjoy the epistemic qualities of democracy, we must ensure that all children receive at least a minimal education, i.e., become autonomous citizens who can contribute (with their diverse perspectives and opinions) to the democratic political process.[9]

As we can see from the previous paragraphs, Mill was adamant that all citizens should (as children) receive some minimum education. Education should be compulsory by law. But how should this basic level of education be provided? Mill is concerned that leaving compulsory education under the direct management of the state will promote uniformity and discourage autonomy and diversity. This process has a tendency to shape "people to be exactly like one another," to encourage character traits and personalities that please "the predominant power in the government," thus establishing "a despotism over the mind leading by natural tendency to one over the body" (Mill 1859a, 190, see also West 1965 and Anderson 1990). The state should not monopolize the provision of education. Instead, it should allow different private and public, religious and secular, charter and magnet schools to promote and implement different curricula and different teaching methods. Citizens should be allowed to choose the type of education that is appropriate for their children, but in the end all children will have to pass a standardized test issued by the state. Such a system will protect diversity and innovation, allowing for epistemically fertile political agonism.

While it might seem that, with regard to formal education, Mill does not ascribe a particularly important role to the state, this could not be further from the truth. First of all, while the content of curricula may vary from school to school, the state should monitor the educational process and intervene when some institutions depart from their original purpose (Mill 1984c, see also Ryan 2011). Mill is aware that parents often lack the appropriate knowledge to determine what is the best education for their children.[10] However, allowing parents a choice between different private and public schools introduces diversity and innovation to the educational process. He believes there is a way to resolve this dilemma: The state should define a certain minimum level of general knowledge that all children of a certain age should have. This general knowledge contains only objective facts and instrumental skills (i.e., it is value-free, and various religious and secular schools can provide it to their students) and is usually tested once a year by state examinations (Mill 1977d, 308, see also West 1965). The state can thus supervise the educational process and evaluate how the various schools are fulfilling their purpose—a school whose students regularly fail state examinations is clearly not up to the task and parents are discouraged from sending their children to such schools. Secondly, the state makes education compulsory by introducing the system of examinations mentioned above. If a child does not meet the minimum standard, the parents are taxed, and the money is invested in the child's education. Parents are thus encouraged to enroll their children in decent schools, that is, schools whose students usually or always pass the examinations. Mill believes that the state has a duty to compel universal education, and it discharges this duty by supervising educational institutions and ensuring that parents fulfill their duty to their children (by taxing parents whose children fail to meet the minimum standard). If parents are unable to provide for their children's education, and when (due to poverty or some other reasons) they cannot be taxed, the state should cover the cost of children's education (Mill 1965a). Third, the state can (and sometimes should) establish schools and other educational institutions that act as role models guiding the educational process by their example. These state schools should be "one among many competing experiments, carried on for the purpose of example and stimulus, to keep the others up to a certain standard of excellence" (Mill 1859a, 191), and should never aspire to replace or eliminate private schools. As we can see from the above, the state has a prominent role in the educational process. This role is somewhat similar to its role in local government: while the state establishes the content of the basic knowledge that all children (of a certain age) should have and has the final say in all educational matters (i.e., centralization of information and authority), private schools are left to implement various educational practices (i.e., deconcentration of execution) (see Ryan 1974, 206–207; 2011, 662; and Kurer 1989, 290).

Informal Education and the State

While Mill writes and touches upon several issues related to formal education (or education in the narrow sense), most of his political thought actually addresses informal education (or education in the broader sense) that takes place outside of schools and universities. He writes that "whatever helps to shape the human being, to make the individual what he is, or hinder him from being what he is not—is part of his education" (Mill 1984d, 217). As Stefan Collini famously argues, "we might, conversely, say that for Mill everything can be education" (Collini 1984, xlviii). Thompson (1976) and Donner (2007) usefully emphasize that, unlike Jeremy Bentham and James Mill, who take human nature as fixed and static, and seek a form of government that can best protect the interests of individuals with predetermined capacities and characters, Mill believes that human nature allows for improvement and therefore seeks a form of government that can, on the one hand, educate citizens and develop their capacities and, on the other, protect and promote their interests.[11]

Informal education takes place in various settings, including the formal and informal political sphere (participation in decision-authorization processes at the local and national level, as well as in partisan associations and other organizations, and in public rallies and the media), the personal sphere (relations with family members and friends), and the economic sphere (participation in the workplace). Participation in these settings can help citizens improve their intellectual and moral capacities (i.e., participation has an educational function, see Thompson 1976, 28–53) and is a form of citizens' self-development since it places the educational process under the authority of the agent himself (Donner 2007, 256). Informal education enables citizens to improve their higher capacities and to be in charge of this improvement.[12] Furthermore, while education in the narrow sense can impart useful skills and knowledge and thus lay the foundations for the future self-development of citizens, some capacities and virtues of character cannot be taught but must be practiced to be properly acquired. His famous statement that "the mental and moral, like the muscular powers, are improved only by being used" (Mill 1859a, 105) opens the floor for the argument about the importance of a broad education. Furthermore, Mill writes that "instruction is only one of the desiderata of mental improvement; another, almost as indispensable, is a vigorous exercise of the active energies; labor, contrivance, judgment, self-control: and the natural stimulus to these is the difficulties of life" (Mill 1965b, 934, see also West 1965), and is quick to add that it is important to cultivate "those endowments not merely in a select few, but in all."

However, the influence that different forms of participation have on citizens' capacities depends heavily on the qualities of the setting in which participation takes place. Mill evaluates political arrangements, social institutions, and economic systems, as well as particular laws, policies, and measures, by taking into account their effect on the development of citizens' capacities. Despotic rule and unqualified universal suffrage are thus, just as patriarchal hierarchy and slave-driven economy, criticized (in part) because they "exercise a bad influence on the voter' mind"(Mill 1977a, 478). There are two main arguments Mill uses to support his claim that political, social and economic institutions should be designed to promote education in the broad sense.

First, Mill believes that broad education can help citizens improve their higher capacities, thus enabling them to appreciate higher pleasures. Since Mill believes that happiness can only be attained through the habitual practice of intellectual and moral virtues (see Donner 2007), he perceives informal education as an important instrument in our pursuit of utility maximization. Although there is some disagreement as to whether (for Mill) improving our intellectual and moral capacities is an end in itself (Nussbaum 2004, Brink 2013) or just means for reaching the desired end (pleasurable experiences) (Macleod 2016), we can nevertheless see why informal education is an important part of his moral and political thought. This argument seems to have strong paternalist tendencies (Arneson 1980 and 1982), as it promotes the education (in a broad sense) of any particular citizen with the intention (and in order) to improve that particular citizen's well-being and happiness.

Second, while Mill is aware that political, social, and economic institutions have a strong influence on the development of citizens' capacities, he also emphasizes that citizens' capacities affect the functioning of these institutions. He reminds us that "government consists of acts done by human beings; and if the agents . . . are mere masses of ignorance, stupidity, and baleful prejudice, every operation of government will go wrong: while, in proportion as the men rise above this standard, so will the government improve in quality"

(Mill 1861, 29). Indeed, he believes that capacities and character traits developed through informal education contribute more to well-functioning of these institutions than capacities developed in schools or universities. Education in the broader sense is thus important for another (non-paternalist) reason—it is a crucial instrument for the proper functioning of political, social and economic institutions.[13] Mill argues that an active character, typically developed through democratic participation, is best not only for the individual in question, but for the whole society (Thompson 1976, 30). By improving the moral and intellectual capacities of citizens (through broad education), we improve institutions ability to authorize and make correct, efficient, and just decisions.

What influence do political, social, and economic institutions have on citizens? While Mill assesses and evaluates the broad education provided in various institutions, we should focus on the most important instances, including his thoughts on the educational function of democratic government (including local government), the workplace, and the family.

Mill strongly emphasizes the educational role of government. In fact, he explicitly states that its principal element is "the improvement of the people themselves."[14] This is consistent with Mill's first criterion for good government and the idea that we should evaluate various regimes by measuring their tendency to "foster in the members of the community the various desirable qualities, moral and intellectual" (Mill 1861, 30). Of course, he proceeds to argue that democratic government, characterized by participation of (virtually) all citizens in the decision-authorization process, promotes active character, improves citizens' political knowledge, and deepens their understanding of the general interest better than any alternative form of government (Mill 1977a, see also Thompson 1976). If citizens recognize that there is no higher power (e.g., a despotic ruler) to constrain their will and acknowledge that some part of political influence is vested in each of them, they will be motivated to participate in the political process and to change laws and policies that they believe are wrong or unjust. Democratic institutions thus promote active character as they encourage citizens to organize and change the world around them rather than passively endorsing the current state of affairs. Furthermore, Mill believes that participation improves citizens' political knowledge. While local participation can be fruitful in this regard, as it allows a large number of citizens to hold one of the numerous public offices at the local level, Mill holds that citizens who are not assigned any particular public duty can also benefit greatly from the democratic system. They will be better informed about political procedures, parties, and candidates, and their views will probably be more sophisticated (Mill 1977a, see also Milbrath 1981). Finally, by making decision that affect other people, citizens (and their representatives) will have to participate in public deliberation, defend their views, and voice their appeals by referring to the general interest. This does not mean, however, that every form of democratic government can fulfill this educational role. Simple majoritarian democracy, which can further deteriorate into a tyranny of the majority, will fail both to promote deeper understanding of the general interest and to improve citizens' political knowledge. Similarly, aggregative democracy, in which citizens participate simply by voting for their representatives, who then vote in the Parliament to authorize laws and policies will fail to adequately improve citizens' knowledge or their intellectual and moral capacities. Parliamentary debates,[15] but also discussions in the informal political sphere (public forums, partisan associations, media) have a tremendous role in this educational endeavor. Finally, even deliberative democracy could lead us astray if appropriate mechanisms (e.g., open ballot, plural voting proposal, division of epistemic labor) are not put in place to filter the public will. Many modern and contemporary thinkers do not share Mill's optimism. For example, Joseph Schumpeter (2008, 262) and Jason Brennan (2016, 2) argue that participative democratic procedures "not only fail to educate or ennoble us, but also tend to stultify and corrupt us." Similarly, Cass Sunstein (2011, 41) and Robert Talisse (2009, 56–60) warn that democratic politics often leads to group polarization and crippled epistemology, which in turn leads to decline and degeneration of citizens' intellectual and moral capacities. These worries are too complex to be properly addressed here. Mill would probably agree with his critics and acknowledge (as he already does) that, without proper filtering mechanisms, democracy can lose its educational potential. Allowing citizens to participate in decision-authorization procedures is simply not enough: their participation must be adequately guided, and their political will properly filtered.[16] Additionally, some social and economic preconditions have to be met in order to fully utilize the educational value of political participation. For example, Mill warns that media must not be monopolized by one social group, as "means of communication in mass society can preclude public and critical debate once they start to propagate the ideas of only one group" (Dalaqua 2018a, 7, citing Mill 1977a, 446).

Another important area for citizens' wide education is the work environment. Because citizens spend a significant portion of their adult lives in the workplace, living in a democratic system is often not enough to properly stimulate the development of their intellectual and moral capacities. Although participation in democratic procedures has an important educational effect, it "fills only a small place in modern life and does not come near the daily habits or inmost sentiments" (Mill 1984b, 296). In fact, authoritarian and non-democratic practices characteristic of work environment in typical capitalist economies often undermine the educational benefits of democratic participation (Ellerman 2010). Mill believes that participatory democratic practices should be implemented beyond (formal and informal) political sphere, thus creating participatory work environment. He warns us that, if humanity is to continue to improve, we need "not that which can exist between a capitalist as chief and workpeople without a voice in the management, but the association of the laborers themselves on terms of equality, collectively owning the capital with which they carry on their operations and working under managers elected and removable by themselves" (Mill 1965a, 775). The workplace thus becomes a "school of the social sympathies and practical intelligence" (Mill 1965a, 792, see also Schweizer 1995), in which workers will be able not only to elect managers but also determine the general aims their company is to pursue. Furthermore, even when workers have no direct and formal influence (e.g., when managers and the members of the board of directors have been elected), they should be allowed and be encouraged to deliberate on both the economic and social aims, and the technical means to reach these aims. Such deliberation mimics the one taking place in the informal political sphere (public rallies and meetings, campaigns, media) and constitutes an important part of workers' wide (or informal) education. Mill goes beyond the role of traditional trade unions (which typically organize workers and represent them on the board of directors) and argues that to be able to exercise this form of control, workers need to own the company they work in.[17] This pushes Mill toward some form of liberal socialism or property-owning democracy in which the free market is combined with state-owned firms controlled by workers (in the former case) or privately owned firms controlled by workers (in the latter case), a system he will endorse (at least in part) because of its epistemic (educational and organizational) benefits.[18]

Finally, along with the political and economic sphere, much of our informal education takes place in the personal sphere, where we interact with family members and close friends. In fact, the first education citizens usually receive comes from their parents and close relatives, making the family a potent site for education in a broad sense (Donner 2007, 265). However, the typical mid-Victorian family was far from the environment that Mill would consider ideal for the development of intellectual and moral capacities in childhood. In addition to the huge inequalities in power and wealth, and unequal access to formal education, the idea of separate spheres (domestic-public dichotomy) kept women out of the public sphere and the domains of politics, paid work, law and commerce, and thus did not provide them with sufficient access to informal (broad) education.[19] Such family represents "a school of despotism, in which the virtues of despotism, but also its vices, are largely nourished" (Mill 1984b, 294–295). Children need to grow up in families characterized by sympathy and equality, rather than power and obedience. Family arranged in such manner will help to improve the capacities of both female and male children by teaching them to live together as equals. Mill thus assigns a very important educational role to the family, arguing that " moral training of mankind will never be adapted to the conditions of the life for which all other human progress is a preparation, until they practice in the family the same moral rule which is adapted to the normal constitution of human society" (Mill 1984b, 295).

While formal education represents a prerequisite for the development of citizens' capacities, Mill considers informal education through participation as a driving force for citizens' self-development. However, participation can only realize its educational role when it becomes part of citizens' daily lives (Thompson 1976, 43). Therefore, informal education takes place in various spheres, and all of them must be arranged in a way that facilitates the improvement of mankind. This, of course, does not mean that Mill advances any particular character type as the best for everyone. He believes that having different characters and personalities improves our epistemic practices, but still believes that some character traits (e.g., vigor and courage) and others (e.g., cruelty, malice, envy) should not be part of everyone's character (Mill 1977d, see also Miller 2005).

MILL ON COMPETENCE

The proper organization of citizens' existing competences represents one of Mill's two central aims we should strive to achieve. We evaluate various forms of government (in part) by their ability to organize these competences in the most fruitful way, one that creates the most long-term beneficial consequences. While Mill wholeheartedly embraces (almost) universal political participation and often calls upon its beneficial educational effects, he clearly rejects the egalitarian position which attributes equal level of competence and thus the same political influence, to all citizens. As indicated in earlier chapters, Mill endorses the knowledge tenet (Estlund 2008, 30–34, see also Cerovac 2020, 10–12) and holds that political knowledge is unequally distributed within population, with some citizens knowing better than others what should be done, and some citizens being more competent than others to make correct, efficient or just political decisions. This part of the chapter analyses the epistemic role of competence in Mill's political thought.

Mill differentiates between two types of knowledge (or competence): instrumental (technical) and moral. The former regards the ability to discover or devise the best means to achieve a desired end, or to determine the most appropriate ends to fulfil one's long-term interests. Citizens who have received some special education or training (e.g., physicians, engineers, or lawyers) have this type of knowledge in their respected fields and may be considered more competent than those who have not received such education or training. The latter relates to the ability to select the appropriate valuable aims that we (individually or collectively) should pursue. It is more difficult to determine which citizens have superior moral expertise, yet Mill believes that those with more virtuous characters and those capable of recognizing the general interest fall into this category (Mill 1977a, 1985a, see also Thompson 1976 and Christiano 2012). This part of the chapter analyses the role of competence in Mill's political thought, the divide between technical and moral competence, and its application to different (executive and legislative) branches of representative government.

Technical (Instrumental) Knowledge

Due to the specialized nature of technical knowledge, for any particular field most citizens lack the professional training, skills, and talents required for competent selection and implementation of the best means required for attaining the desired aims. This is why we visit a doctor when we are ill, consult a stockbroker when we are planning new investments, or ask an architect to draw up the design for our new house. Mill holds that the same principle applies in politics as we strive to make correct, efficient, or just laws, policies, and political decisions. While Mill argues in favor of representative government and believes that political decisions should be authorized by representatives of the people, he nonetheless holds that only specially trained and skilled people can make political decisions of adequate moral and epistemic quality. He warns us that " freedom cannot produce its best effects, and often breaks down altogether, unless means can be found of combining it with trained and skilled administration" (Mill 1861, 116, see also Warner 2001, 406). Technical knowledge thus plays an important role in Mill's theory of government.

Mill makes a rough distinction between two levels of administration: legal experts within legislative commission and top-level managers in the executive government (e.g., ministers and their closest advisers) on the one hand, and civil servants in the national, federal or local government on the other. This division, of course, does not address the hierarchy in public administration or the transfer of authority—it concerns only the skills and competences required for each level.

Thus, members of the first group should have a high level of both technical and moral knowledge. Those in legislative commission should be trained in legal studies and be able to construct laws and other legal devices of substantive moral and epistemic quality. This includes the ability to properly understand the moral and political aims set by the parliament, the ability to construct and formulate laws that help meet these aims, but also the ability to understand the long-term effects of such laws and their potential effect on other laws and policies, including those that regulate other policy areas[20] (Mill 1977a, 428–429). They should also be able to distance themselves from their personal interests and preferences when drafting legislation and focus only on the aims set by the representative body and our fundamental interest as progressive beings. Similarly, Mill is aware that the minister in the executive government often cannot have all the relevant technical and professional knowledge. He should be "a good politician, and a man of merit," and the knowledge he should possess regards " general interests of the country" (Mill 1861, 252). However, while Mill argues that each minister should be accompanied by a small group of advisers to help him with technical issues, he still seems to imply that some level of technical knowledge and practical intelligence is required (Mill 1977a, 428–432). Civil servants engaged at a higher policy-making level (ministers and advisers) should, in addition to probity and concern for the public interest, demonstrate practical intelligence and have the knowledge in the relevant field (Ryan 1972, 60–62 and 2011, 656). As we can see, Mill asks a lot from members of the legislative commission and functionaries at the higher policy-making level: they should have both moral and technical competences (although not necessarily at the same level) and be among the greatest and most virtuous citizens of the country.

Members of the second group (i.e., civil servants at lower levels, clerks) should display technical knowledge in the appropriate (often narrow) area of expertise. Their main task is to follow orders from their superiors and to use their specialized technical knowledge to implement policies (Mill 1977a, 428–432). The need for technical training and skills is even more obvious at this level. Mill considers this self-evident and does not bother to provide additional justification for this claim.[21] However, he warns that employment in public administration is often used as "a social measure for poor but well-connected young men" (Ryan 2011, 655), thus replacing competence for aristocratic connections (Mill 1977a, 529–531). This seriously reduces the quality of policy implementation, but also undermines the public approval that political and social institutions should ascribe to (formal) education. Having this in mind, Mill argues for tests to select the most competent bureaucrats, but also provides additional recommendations, including criteria for promotion and measures for keeping civil servants accountable for their work.

Moral Knowledge

While we can quite easily determine how to evaluate technical (instrumental) knowledge, the attribution and measurement of moral knowledge represents a far more demanding task. Namely, while standardized tests within institutions of formal education (e.g., schools and universities) as well as vocational or other state-administered examinations (e.g., bar exams or medical licensing exams) can help us decide who is a technical expert, there is no analogous test or system of exams that can help us determine who is a moral expert. Similarly, while we can track a person's professional record and publicly determine whether that person is a technical expert (e.g., a physician whose patients have all been successfully treated and fully recovered is clearly an expert, as is a stockbroker who consistently makes huge profits), it is far more difficult to determine a standard of moral expertise that all citizens could endorse. Progressives and conservatives will disagree about the appropriate aims the society should pursue, and they might even disagree about the character traits and virtues that make a good citizen. Mill is fully aware of this challenge and, although he often seems to endorse a more progressive worldview, argues that both have an important social role and that the conflict between these two worldviews generates the best political (and epistemic) outcomes (Mill 1977d and 1982c, see also Kinzer 1981). This implies that we often cannot establish a firm substantive criterion we can use to ascribe moral knowledge and competence. How then can we determine who are moral experts?

Mill provides an indirect solution. He emphasizes that moral knowledge is based (to a lesser extent) on empirical knowledge and (mostly) on an understanding of higher pleasures. Unlike technical knowledge in a particular field, which is often held only by a small group of citizens who have received specific education and training, Mill believes that moral knowledge is more or less widely distributed and not related to any specialized education or training. It is "available to any person of developed faculties" (Mill 1985a, see also Miller 2005). Since it is difficult to find a firm substantive criterion by which we can ascribe moral expertise, Mill suggests focusing on relevant social markers that can help us identify those who have decent empirical knowledge and a good understanding of higher (or intellectual) pleasures. One's (formal and informal) level of education, for example, tends to shape our knowledge of human nature and the world around us, and makes one acquainted with a variety of higher pleasures. Furthermore, the desire to learn, to acquire new skills and competences, and to perform more demanding and challenging tasks is closely related to our aspiration for self-improvement, which Mill considers an indicator of virtuous character traits. In doing so, he provides an indirect measurement mechanism: we can evaluate citizen's moral knowledge and expertise by evaluating the citizen's education (Mill 1977a, 474–480). Finally, as discussed in detail in other chapters, Mill even argues that the level of citizen's political influence should correspond to his level of moral expertise (as measured by his level of education).

As we can see, Mill holds that moral competence is more or less widely distributed within the population—while only members of a small group of citizens (i.e., those who have received the best education) can be characterized as the most competent, Mill believes that some level of moral competence can be found among all citizens who have received at least a minimal education. Does this imply that there are no moral experts, only more and less qualified citizens? While this may indeed be the case, Mill nevertheless believes that members of two groups stand out and play a social and political role of moral experts (Warner 2001). The first group are the opinion leaders, usually (but not necessarily) well-educated citizens who invest a lot of time and effort to be informed about public affairs and often play a special role in the informal political sphere. They participate in informal public deliberation, speak and discuss at citizens' assemblies, write newspaper columns and articles, and sometimes participate in the work of partisan associations and political foundations. In second place are members of the Parliament, citizens whose job it is to represent the opinions and perspectives of various social groups, to deliberate in the formal political sphere, and to employ their knowledge, skills, and experience to formulate the best set of political aims that serve the long-term public interest. While having superior education is not a prerequisite for this function, and Mill explicitly states that members of parliament, "when properly constituted, a fair sample of every grade of intellect among the people" (Mill 1861, 106), he nevertheless believes that they should have highly developed deliberative and critical capacities.

Competence and Political Authority

Mill's second criterion of good government reminds us that it is not enough to have virtuous citizens and skilled technical experts to reliably make correct, efficient, and just political decisions. While the moral and technical competences of citizens are of paramount importance, government has to acknowledge these competences and organize the political decision-making and decision-authorization processes, as well as the social and political roles of citizens, in ways that make the best use of citizens' existing competences. Political institutions, then, must organize citizens' moral and intellectual capacities "so as to operate with the greatest effect on public affairs" (Mill 1861, 33). This calls for a division of political and epistemic labor in which different branches of government draw on the knowledge and expertise of different kinds of experts.

Mill's arguments for representative democracy as a form of government that can organize and improve citizens' existing capacities better than any alternative, supported by a list of mechanisms he introduces to filter the public will and improve the epistemic quality of political outcomes, stand in the heart of this book, but are beyond the scope of this chapter. Instead, I want to focus on the discussion of the source of political authority in Mill's political thought. This question will be elaborated in other chapters, and here I focus only on the most immediate challenge. Many scholars have characterized Mill as a philosopher who defends a form of sophisticated non-democratic elitism (Burns 1957, Kendall and Carey 1968, Annan 1968, Cowling 1990), and contemporary interpretations (Baccarini 1993, Urbinati 2002, Donner 2007, Riley 2007) tend to reject this categorization. However, some scholars have recently started investigating the elitist implications of Mill's theory of government for twenty-first century democracy. For example, Jason Brennan argues that democracy has been tested for nearly two centuries and the results clearly turned out negative. While Mill was an optimist regarding democratic rule in his day, nowadays he would have to abandon his optimism and replace democracy with a form of epistocracy (Brennan 2016, 1–10). Similarly, Elvio Baccarini offers a "partly Millian proposal" and argues that, when the only competent people are the members of a restricted elite (e.g., climatologists regarding the climate policy, or infectious disease doctors in relation to vaccination policy), then we must attribute to them the legitimacy to rule (Baccarini 2021, 384–385). This approach tends to attribute political authority (and, more importantly, political legitimacy) on the basis of technical knowledge and expertise. When technical knowledge is relevant to the quality of the final political decision, and when technical knowledge is unequally distributed, we should favor some form of moderate epistocracy (e.g., technocracy[22]).

While I can understand the appeal of this implication, I still think Mill's views suggest a more democratic system (e.g., scholocracy). The epistemic (instrumentalist) interpretation of Mill's political thought recognizes and emphasizes his focus on the quality of political outcomes in the long run, yet it does not call for technocracy or any other form of moderate epistocracy. We should embrace the decision-authorization procedure that has the highest chance of producing the most beneficial results (and the one that has the highest instrumental epistemic value), and Mill is adamant that democracy, properly shaped by plural voting, open balloting and other filtering mechanisms, is such a procedure. Of course, technical experts in executive government should be allowed to propose laws and make public policies and political decisions without much interference from the representative assembly (Mill 1977a, 423–434). However, the executive government does not base its legitimacy in its expertise (although it is still very important to have a government composed of experts), but (primarily) in the fact that it was authorized to make political decisions by the Parliament. Supreme authority is vested in the representative and deliberative assembly, and the Parliament has legitimacy-generating potential (it can mandate the executive government to make public policies and political decisions) because it possesses instrumental moral and epistemic qualities that surpass the qualities of any other form of government. Mill "works toward balance" (Warner 2001, 410) between expertise and participation, but is aware that "a balanced constitution is impossible" and therefore considers it essential that "the practical supremacy in the state should reside in the representatives of the people" (Mill 1861, 88). In fact, he proceeds to explicitly deny that "bureaucratic oligarchy" is the best form of government for any civilized people, adding that even a skilled bureaucracy always tends to fall into incompetence and corruption of a "pedantocracy" (Mill 1977a, 437–440 and 1977d, 305–310, see also Riley 2007, 221–222). This can only be avoided if technical experts in executive government are subjected to popular control.

Technical expertise is not the foundation on which Mill makes the transition from the knowledge tenet to the authority tenet. A technocratic government will fail for several reasons: it will fail to produce decisions of optimal (or best available) epistemic quality, but it will also not be able to properly educate citizens and encourage them to develop their capacities through participation. Moral expertise seems a more suited candidate to bridge the gap between the two tenets, but again Mill takes an indirect route. Namely, he does not think that only moral experts should participate in the decision-authorization processes. Mill merely argues that those with greater moral knowledge should have greater political influence in the authorization process. However, the main reason for this unequal distribution of political influence is not merit or justice, but the (instrumental) epistemic quality of such an inegalitarian democratic decision-authorization procedure. Therefore, expertise (technical or moral) does not automatically imply political authority. In order to make this demanding step and bridge the gap between knowledge and authority tenet, Mill provides an extensive epistemic (instrumental) argument for democracy characterized by various filtering mechanisms. This epistemic argument is the focus of this book.

NOTES

1. Thompson explicitly indicates that his interpretation of Mill's theory of democracy "follows the pattern suggested by his two criteria for the 'goodness of government'—how well a government uses the qualities that exist in a polity at a particular time, and how well a government contributes to the improvement of those qualities over time" (Thompson 1976, 175).

2. The question remains whether higher pleasures are subjective pleasures or objective pleasures. For example, David Brink (2013), Thomas Green (2003), and Martha Nussbaum (2004) favor the latter interpretation, arguing that by introducing

a differentiation between higher and lower pleasures, Mill abandons hedonism and introduces perfectionist elements into the utility principle. These authors argue that for Mill, activities that employ our higher faculties are not instrumentally valuable—they are not the best means of obtaining high-quality subjective pleasures. Instead, the exercise of these activities is intrinsically valuable. Unfortunately, this interesting and important discussion is beyond the scope of this book. See, e.g., Loizides (2013).

3. Another useful way to illustrate the two roles of education is to appeal to Rutger Claassen's (2018) differentiation between navigational and participational agency. On the one hand, we exercise navigational agency when we can freely and autonomously choose which actions we want to take, which social roles we want to have and which relations to engage in. On the other hand, we exercise participational agency when we perform actions, have social roles, and engage with others. While education fulfills its prudential role when it teaches us how to exercise our participational agency (e.g., how to play tennis, how to be a good parent or a good lawyer), it fulfills its moral role when it enables us to exercise navigational agency (e.g., to competently decide whether to spend our free time playing tennis, whether to become a parent and what career to pursue). The state should not promote (through compulsory education, or through coercive laws and policies) any particular exercise of participational agency—that would be a form of despotism and would impair both the development of the person in question and the improvement of mankind (1977d). Instead, the state should guarantee and foster education that promotes navigational agency, making citizens able to competently decide for themselves how they want to improve their capacities. This will have epistemic benefits by making "people unlike one another" (Mill 1977d, 274) and thus harnessing the epistemic value of diversity and political agonism.

4. Furthermore, it enables citizens to develop "a sense of citizenship" and "active character," traits Mill considers essential for the proper functioning of the democratic society (Pedersen 1982).

5. For more information of the difference between capabilities and functioning see Sen (1992), Nussbaum (2000) and Claassen (2018).

6. Nowadays only a few philosophers defend this claim. Kukathas (1997, 70), for example, writes that the state should tolerate practices such as "group or community customs of child-rearing which restrict the opportunities of the child to prepare for the life outside the original community." Similar ideas as defended (although in a less explicit form) by Galston (1989) and Poulter (1999). For further discussion on these issues see Kukathas (2003) and Barry (2001).

7. There are some similarities between this approach to education and Mill's opinions on "barbarous nations." Although Mill addresses education in a wide sense when he writes about barbarian peoples, he claims that educational effects of democratic government cannot be properly established in nations that have not yet reached a certain level of social and political development. While democracy can help already developed nations to further improve (and self-improve), the same does not stand for nations below a certain level of development. When applied to an individual level, Mill again believes that liberty can have an educational effect and help individuals improve (and self-improve) their capacities. However, to be able to utilize liberty in

such a productive way, citizens need to have their competences already developed to a certain standard. See Mill (1977a, 562–578), Applbaum (2007) and Ten (2012). Also, see this theses' chapter on the epistemic value of democracy.

8. This vaguely corresponds to Rawls' two moral powers: rationality and reasonableness. However, unlike Rawls (2001, 18–19), who takes it as a starting point that citizens have these two moral powers above some minimal threshold, Mill argues that they are developed through (formal and informal) education.

9. The idea that every citizen should be able to contribute to the democratic decision-authorization process does not imply that political influence should be equally distributed. See the chapter on the plural voting proposal for additional information.

10. He indicates that parents do not have a natural right to determine the content of education their children will receive. Namely, parents are often ignorant, and they should not be allowed to pass that ignorance to their children. He thus writes that "the uncultivated cannot be competent judges of cultivation" (Mill 1965b, 947, see also Ryan 2011, 663).

11. Mill criticizes Bentham's approach by arguing that he completely neglects (informal) education and the government's ability to change (and improve) citizens under its jurisdiction. Bentham thinks that the government fulfills its role when it successfully "deters citizens from actually committing the crime." This can be achieved, for example, by introducing heavy punishments (Draconian laws). However, Mill believes that the government's primary goal should be to "render people incapable of desiring a crime," i.e., to help them understand why some actions are wrong and illegal and to develop their moral understanding (Mill 1985b, 9).

12. This does not imply that self-development occurs spontaneously and does not require teaches and mentors. Mill emphasizes that "it is a poor education that associates ignorance with ignorance" and adds that "the utility of the instruction greatly depends on its bringing inferior minds into contact with superior" (Mill 1861, 293). However, unlike schools or universities, the educational process is informal and guided by citizens themselves. For additional information see Thompson (1976, 79–80) and Kurer (1989, 298).

13. The whole argument cannot be given here. See the chapter on the epistemic justification of democracy for more information regarding citizens' capacities and their effect on the quality of the government. See the chapter on paternalism and filtering mechanisms for clarification why this epistemic argument does not represent a form of paternalism.

14. Mill regards his educative argument to be more important than the protective argument (Thompson 1976, 28). In the discussion on benevolent despotism, Mill warns us that the worst despot is the one who successfully protects citizens' other interests and thus promotes passive characters and blocks citizens" self-development. Benevolent despot thus fails to promote citizens' most important interest, one for self-improvement. See Mill (1977a, 399–412).

15. Mill famously argues that "besides being an instrument of government, Parliament is a grand institution of national education, having for one of its valuable offices to create and correct that public opinion whose mandates it is required to obey" (Mill 1977c, 348).

16. While this casts an elitist shadow on Mill's political thought, it does not directly disqualify him as a democrat. Many accounts of epistemic democracy introduce some filtering mechanisms (e.g., political representation, division of epistemic labor) to improve the epistemic value of a decision-authorization procedure. However, this does not make such accounts elitist or non-democratic. For example, see Estlund (2008) and Cerovac (2020).

17. We can notice some similarities with Mill's argument against unqualified universal suffrage. Mill argues that citizens who have no income and pay no taxes should not be granted voting privileges. He offers a few reasons to support this claim. First, allowing such citizens to participate in decision-making on how to use the public funds, knowing that they gave no contribution all to the total amount of public money that is going to be spent, is unjust. Second, and more important, political contribution by citizens who are so passive and dependent on others that they do not want to find jobs and have an income of their own will is more likely to decrease than to increase the epistemic quality of the collective decision-authorization process. Third, and most relevant for our current debate, Mill believes that citizens "who pay no taxes, disposing by their votes of other people's money, have every motive to be lavish, and none to economize" (1861, 169). Therefore, to exercise a good influence on citizens' minds, political participation has to take place in an environment that stimulates citizens to carefully think and deliberate, and not to spend money recklessly. Similarly, political participation at the workplace can have beneficial and educational role only in the environment that stimulates the workers to seriously consider how the funds of the company will be spent. Worker ownership over (at least part of) the company is thus needed for the full educational effect of workplace participation.

18. More information on liberal socialism and property-owning democracy can be found in Meade (1964) and Rawls (2001), as well as in O'Neill (2012) and Taylor (forthcoming). Many will remain skeptical regarding the organizational epistemic benefits of liberal socialism or property-owning democracy. They usually argue that the capitalist enterprise, characterized by the free market as a solution to society's knowledge problem, is more efficient (Hayek 2012a, 2012b, see also Tebble 2016). On the other hand, some scholars disagree and even point advocates of workplace democracy towards solutions such as institutional changes in incentives (Schwartz 2012). This interesting discussion, however, goes beyond the scope of this book.

19. For more information on mid-Victorian family see Hoppen (2000).

20. Mill warns us that the representative body often tends to overstep its role by trying to directly affect legislation, e.g., by changing the law made by the legislative commission or by endorsing only particular clauses of the law sent for authorization, and not the entire law. Such practices can greatly decrease the epistemic quality of the law in question, but also the quality of other laws and policies, those whose scope, application or enforcement substantively changes when a new law is introduced. (Mill 1977a, 428–430).

21. To be more precise, Mill thinks that everyone can agree that some people are better at discovering and devising means to reach the desired ends, and that receiving special education and training greatly improves one's ability to contribute to

the means-discovering and means-devising process. For additional information see Thompson (1976, 55–56).

22. Elitism is a broad term and generally encompasses the idea of society being led or governed by an elite. Epistemic elitism, one Mill is sometimes accused of, defines elite as a group of people who know better than others what should be done. Epistemic elitism usually takes one of the following two forms. Epistocracy, the rule of a small group of citizens surpassing others with regard to moral knowledge, entails the idea that most citizens should not participate in the political process since they are incompetent to determine the proper aims and values the society is to pursue. Authors focusing on the inegalitarian character of Mill's plural voting proposal typically blame him for this type of elitism. Technocracy, the rule of a small group of citizens surpassing others with regard to technical knowledge, implies that most citizens should not participate in the political process since they are incompetent to contribute to the quality of laws and policies. Authors focusing on Mill's division of political and epistemic labor, and in particular on his thoughts on the division between representative and executive (or administrative) government, accuse Mill of this type of elitism. For additional information on various forms of epistemic elitism see Cerovac (2017c, 238–239 and 2020, 116–127).

Chapter 2

The Epistemic Value of Political Conflict

Mill holds that individuals do not acquire justified, correct or just beliefs in isolation from other members of society. Other people are an important tool in our search for truth. But how do other people help us in this endeavor? And how can political institutions assist us in our search for truth? This chapter introduces the idea that political conflict can be epistemically valuable, and then proceeds to argue that political institutions should be constructed with the capacity to shape and moderate political conflict, enabling it to properly realize its epistemic values.

This chapter characterizes Mill as an epistemic liberal and focuses on his instrumental (epistemic) justification of individual rights and liberties, particularly his justification of freedom of expression. Its innovative contribution regards three important ideas that will be of great significance for characterizing Mill as an epistemic democrat. First, the chapter demonstrates that political conflict plays an important epistemic role in Mill's political thought. Second, the chapter investigates how political institutions and mechanisms can moderate political conflict. Third, it sets the stage for future chapters by inquiring what kind of qualities do political institutions need to have in order to stimulate and moderate political conflict.

The chapter is divided in two parts. In the first part I present a brief overview of the discussion on the epistemic value of collective deliberation, indicating the difference between deliberative holism, a position arguing that public deliberation is epistemically (and politically) valuable because it leads to a consensus on substantive reasons for or against some political decision, and deliberative agonism, a position that sees political conflict and disagreement as a permanent state of politics, but nonetheless ascribes it considerable epistemic value. Mill is than portrayed as an epistemic (agonist) democrat, and this interpretation is supported by analyzing some of the key arguments in his famous essay *On Liberty*. In the second part I discuss two important epistemic roles political conflict plays in Mill's political thought. It enables citizens to form better justified opinions and to create new ideas and solutions to existing problems. Additionally, it helps citizens improve their moral and intellectual capacities by forcing them to constantly reevaluate their opinions and values. Finally, since political conflict has such an important epistemic role in Mill's political thought, I follow Dalaqua (2018a) and argue that Mill shapes political institutions to simultaneously stimulate and contain political conflict, thus making it epistemically fertile.

MILL ON POLITICAL AGONISM

Holism and Agonism

What is the desired and epistemically valuable end of rational deliberation? Philosophers defending various versions of epistemic democracy disagree on this evaluative standard. While most agree that deliberative procedure that embodies some relevant epistemic virtues should, at least in the majority of cases, produce decisions of considerable epistemic quality,[1] the disagreement persists when we focus on the recognition of these outcomes by citizens participating in democratic deliberation.

Deliberative holism is characterized by the aspiration that well-ordered deliberation will, ideally, end in consensus on the final political outcome. Although not many believe that deliberation will inevitably lead to consensus on political decisions and the substantive reasons supporting these decisions, there is a strong hope that well-ordered deliberation among rational citizens will enable them to remove epistemically flawed reasons and arguments. The only reasons left will be those that can endure the critical scrutiny of other rational citizens. The preferable result will be a set of reasons (and laws and policies based upon and justified by these reasons) that all rational (or, for some authors, reasonable) citizens can endorse (Cohen 1986, 1997, Habermas 1996, Dryzek 2000, Chambers 2003). Some might go even further by stressing that the persistence of conflict in democratic deliberation signifies that there is something wrong with the reasons used in the process of justification.[2] Therefore, the persistence of conflict in democratic deliberation implies that some error must be present in the procedure, and the final decision thus cannot have proper epistemic value. If everything is correct, however, rational deliberation will end in consensus.

Deliberative agonism, on the other hand, sees conflict as a permanent condition of democratic politics. While both positions will agree that some conflict is a precondition for democratic deliberation, holism claims that this conflict should be overcome through well-ordered deliberation, while agonism sees deliberation as a permanent process that does not end in consensus. This does not, however, imply that nothing has changed from the one stage to another (Walzer 1999, Mouffe 2009). Reasons can still be discarded as epistemically flawed, initial perspectives changed, and new positions constructed. The persistence of conflict is, thus, not a sign that deliberation lacks its epistemic value (Dalaqua 2018b).

What about Mill's own account of deliberative democracy? Some see his approach to democratic politics as a quest for homogeneity and unity (Cowling 1990). In fact, they seem to ground this claim in the epistemic reading of Mill's position. Critical and well-ordered deliberation will yield consensus and homogeneity among rational citizens (Cowling 1990, 34), and this will indicate that the decisions we have reached have substantive epistemic quality. Most philosophers, however, endorse a different interpretation. Skorupski (2006, 71), for example, emphasizes that Mill thought of conflict of interests and ideas as a permanent condition of politics, while Urbinati (2002, 82) underlines Mill's approach to agonism as one of the virtues of his political thought. However, scholars favoring the agonistic interpretation of Mill's philosophy typically neglect the epistemic component of his political project, with Landemore (2017) and Dalaqua (2018a, 2018b) as notable exceptions.

This part of the chapter argues in favor of an epistemic agonistic interpretation. I reject both epistemic holistic reading and non-epistemic agonistic reading, arguing instead that Mill valued permanent political conflict for epistemic reasons, i.e., because he found it instrumentally valuable for producing correct or just political decisions. This reading can be supported both in Mill's writing on liberty and on democracy.

Epistemic Value of Agonism in *On Liberty*

Mill provides a comprehensive defense of freedom of expression, and by extension of all basic individual liberties (Mill 1977d, 227, 260), in his famous essay *On Liberty*. He discusses censorship as a practice that tries to promote truth and morality by suppressing false and immoral claims and enlists four reasons why such practice fails its original aim. First, Mill (1977d, 228–243) argues that the censored opinion might be true. No censoring body can rule out this possibility without assuming its own infallibility. Since human beings are not infallible, the only way to properly assess the truth of any opinion is to subject it to critical evaluation from multiple perspectives, and to allow those who hold it to provide reasons and arguments for such opinion. Furthermore, considering the fallibility of any censoring body, this exchange of reasons and arguments should be done in the public sphere,[3] where all competing reasons and evidence can be exchanged and evaluated. Censorship should be avoided because we risk censoring a correct opinion. Second, even if the censored opinion is partially false, it might contain a part of the truth (Mill 1977d, 252–257). Interestingly, Mill believes this is the most common case—both the opinion that is considered correct and the opinion that is considered incorrect contain a part of the truth, and we should compare reasons supporting each of them, as well as potential advantages and disadvantages of each opinion, instead of censoring one of them. Opposed opinions can improve and supplement each other, and the best way to do this is through free public deliberation. Mill's second reason against censorship foreshadows his account on the epistemic value of agonism discussed in this part of the chapter. We create new, epistemically more justified positions through the conflict of opposing beliefs. Third, Mill (1977d, 229, 244–246) argues that, even if completely incorrect, the censored opinion might prevent correct opinions from becoming dogma. While the opinion we hold might be true, we need to be aware of the reasons and arguments supporting it, and we must be able to defend it from criticism, in order to call it knowledge (Mill 1977d, 244, see also Ten 1980, 126–128). We cannot develop our intellectual capacities necessary for obtaining new true beliefs without public deliberation in which our existing opinions (even those that are true) are questioned and criticized, and we are required to defend them. Having people who disagree with us, even when we are correct, is epistemically valuable since it enables us to develop our epistemic capacities. Fourth,[4] having unchallenged opinions will not only hinder our intellectual and moral development, thus preventing us from acquiring new correct opinions, but will also affect the correct opinions we already have. Mill (1977d, 247, 257) argues that, as a dogma, an unchallenged opinion will lose its meaning. To understand that some opinion is correct is to understand the reasons and arguments that support it. When we lack insight into the justification of an opinion we hold to be true, our comprehension of the opinion in question is flawed.

As we can see, Mill defends individuals' freedom of expression, yet here he makes little mention of the interests of the individuals whose opinions are being censored. Appealing to censored individual's own interests would be a simple liberal move, yet it seems that Mill introduces an epistemic argument in his justification of freedom of expression. His arguments have less to do with *intrinsically* valuable liberal rights and more with the interest of the group in its search for truth (Landemore 2017, 80, emphasis added). Of course, this does not imply that Mill disregards the positive impact freedom of expression has on one's self-development and one's permanent interests as a progressive being. However, being a sophisticated utilitarian, Mill was aware that grounding freedom of expression exclusively in the private interests of an individual might not be enough. Namely, freedom of expression might then be reduced or even denied by the appeal to utility calculus, with private interests of the majority to censor an opinion outweighing the individual's private interest to hold and express such an opinion. Mill (1859a, 33) thus indicates that "were an opinion a personal possession of no value except to the owner; if to be obstructed in the enjoyment of it were simply a private injury, it would make some difference whether the injury was inflicted only on a few persons or on many." While freedom of expression is an important precondition for upholding the private interests of individuals (e.g., interest for self-improvement and the improvement of one's intellectual and moral capacities), these interests are *instrumentally* valuable since they contribute to the improvement of mankind (Baccarini 1993, 36, 41). This is why Mill (1859a, 33) writes that "the peculiar evil of silencing the expression of an opinion is that is robbing the human race: posterity as well as the existing generation; those who dissent from the opinion, still more than those who hold it. If the opinion is right, they are deprived of the opportunity of exchanging error for truth: it wrong, they lose what is almost as great a benefit, the clearer perception and livelier impression of truth, produced by its collision with error." We can thus see that Mill's main argument for freedom of expression is both instrumental and epistemic, and is founded in consequentialist moral philosophy: the best means for acquiring true and justified beliefs (which are needed to make political decisions that will produce the best possible consequences) are grounded in anti-censorship policies. Our collective search for truth will benefit far more from freedom of expression than from censorship of opinions that the majority considers false.

Though Mill defends freedom of expression, it is clear that this freedom can have its epistemic value only in the conditions of diversity of opinions. In a society of like-minded individuals, where everyone shares the same opinion on some issue, freedom of expression would not have a particular epistemic value. There would be no alternative opinion that might be true, but also there would be no possibility of improving our existing opinion by reviewing reasons for and against our (and for and against alternative) opinion. Finally, our opinion would inevitably become dogma since it would not be questioned and challenged by alternative views. This is why Mill argues that "if opponents of all important truths do not exist, it is indispensable to imagine them and supply them with the strongest arguments which the most skillful devil's advocate can conjure up" (Mill 1859a, 68, see also Baccarini 2013). We can see that, for Mill, freedom of expression has epistemic value because it enables and facilitates free exchange of conflicting ideas and opinions. Diversity is important, but to properly realize its epistemic value we need conflicting opinions, those challenging each other's justification (reasons, arguments and evidence supporting the conflicting opinion). The epistemic value thus rests in the conflict itself—political agonism is (instrumentally) epistemically valuable. Its epistemic value lies in its ability to enhance the epistemic quality of political discussion (Mill 1977a), and it does so in two ways. First, it helps the political community to assess the reasons and arguments for various conflicting opinions, enabling it to form ideas and beliefs that are better justified and more accurate. This is based on the first and the second argument against censorship in *On Liberty*, where Mill demonstrates how freedom of expression can help us (the individuals and the political community) have better justified and more correct beliefs. Second, it helps participants develop their epistemic capacities, thus indirectly increasing the quality of political discussion. This consideration is based upon Mill's third and fourth argument against censorship, where he stresses the negative impact dogmas have on citizens' intellectual and moral capacities. Conflict thus has instrumental epistemic value since it "weeds out inaccurate information, expands the knowledge of politicians and helps make more reasonable, wiser decisions" (Dalaqua 2018a, 17). Diversity of opinions is a precondition for political conflict, yet by itself it does not help us improve the epistemic quality of our beliefs. Different opinions have to be weighted against each other, arguments supporting them have to be scrutinized and evaluated, and in political arena this can only take place when opinions are in conflict.

Before proceeding forth, let us elaborate further on these two epistemic advantages that political conflict introduces in a public debate. These will prove to be valuable for our later argument regarding the epistemic value of partisanship.

MILL ON THE EPISTEMIC VALUE OF POLITICAL CONFLICT

The Constructive Role of Political Conflict

Are citizens' preferences and opinions fixed raw data a decision-making procedure has to account for before making a social choice? Can a decision-making procedure change citizens' preferences and opinions? And if it can, should it do so? In what conditions should this transformation take place to be justified?

Mill does not believe that every citizen has a pre-given and unchangeable set of political preferences. If that were the case, there would be little reason for political deliberation: we could use aggregative mechanisms like voting and simple majority rule to make laws and policies. These procedures would be fair (Dahl 1989) but could also help us maximize collective utility (Arrow 1963) and even make decisions of considerable epistemic quality (Condorcet 1994). In particular, Kenneth Arrow's social choice theory might appear as a solid candidate for many utilitarian philosophers. The utilitarian philosophy of Jeremy Bentham, for example, advises us to compare alternative social states in terms of their consequences on the individual utility and select the social state that maximizes the individual utility (Arrow 1963, 22–23, see also Peter 2011, 15–16). Mill's approach is evidently different: while beneficial consequences are still the criteria against which we compare all forms of government, there is a clear skepticism regarding our individual competences to know what the good consequences are and how to obtain them, as well as skepticism toward the idea that the best social choice represents a simple aggregation of individual preferences. As rational beings, we can modify and correct our political opinions and preferences when faced with new evidence or better reasons and arguments. Collective deliberation helps us increase accuracy and correctness of political decisions by forcing us to review and, if needed, change our preferences in light of better reasons. Furthermore, the political conflict does not have to end with one set of preferences or opinions winning over the other—it can construct new opinions, new perspectives and new solutions.[5]

Political conflict helps us acquire more accurate and better justified beliefs, but also to make better laws, policies and political decisions. However, there is an additional, less direct but no less important, epistemic function of political agonism. When Mill indicates that "the antagonism of influences . . . is the only real security for continued progress" (1861, 42) and the guiding principle of "the spirit of improvement" (1977d), he is not referring only to the quality of decisions a procedure produces. Mill is convinced that political conflict within liberal democracies enables us to construct new perspectives, and he proceeds to claim that these newly constructed perspectives often have significant epistemic advantage over those originally conflicted (Ypi and White 2016, 62). This is based upon Mill's second argument against censorship, where he indicates that often neither the belief held by the majority nor the censored belief contain the whole truth. The whole truth is seen as "a question of reconciling and combining the opposites" and is made by "the rough process of a struggle between combatants fighting under hostile banners" (Mill 1859a, 86, see also Dalaqua 2018a, 17). This struggle has to be public and should be reflected both in formal (e.g., the Parliament) and informal (e.g., the media, public debates, campaigns) political sphere to have this constructive power. The creation of new phrases and the transformation of existing ones can, for example, represent a fruitful method for remedying hermeneutical epistemic injustice (Fricker 2007), and can only take place in societies characterized by the freedom of expression and association.

The Educative Role of Political Conflict

Political conflict, as demonstrated so far, can have epistemic value in a direct way—it can help us ground our public decisions in better reasons and arguments, as well as construct new perspectives that can help us grasp the truth better. In addition, conflict can be instrumentally valuable in a different way—it can help citizens and political representatives develop their intellectual and moral capacities, thus improving their ability to produce correct and just decisions.[6] Even more so, the development of these capacities is impossible in conditions that lack political conflict.

Mill holds that political conflict can have a beneficial effect on the development of reason in both citizens and their representatives. This idea is based upon the third and the fourth argument against censorship, where Mill discusses the negative effect of dogmatic beliefs on citizens' moral and intellectual capacities. Political deliberation with citizens who disagree with us can be a way of discovering some important truths about ourselves[7] and determining which opinions are genuinely our own (Mill 1977d). Agonistic debate can thus be seen as a precondition for the autonomous development of our individuality (Claeys 2013, see also Lukes 2006). As Dalaqua (2018b) clearly indicates, Mill was aware that socioeconomic conditions we live in influence the way we assess the world around us. Our religion, family, social class and many other influences (Rawls calls these disagreement-producing conditions burdens of judgment, see Rawls 2001, 35–37 and 2005, 55–58) shape our perspective and the guiding principles that direct our political behavior. We can become aware of these influences, or more precisely, become aware of how exactly they affect and manipulate our behavior, only when we can take a step back from our perspective. Political conflict is valuable because public deliberation with citizens holding opposing views and preferences enables us to access different perspectives, to see the best reasons and arguments that support an opinion we do not share, but also to understand values and background assumptions these reasons and arguments lie upon. Finally, assessing these values and assumptions helps us to better understand our own perspective and to evaluate how socioeconomic conditions affect our own worldview. In the end, we are able to withdraw from our initial perspective and formulate free and autonomous opinions. Political conflict that fuels well-structured public deliberation thus enables us to become free and autonomous individuals and more virtuous epistemic agents. Citizens who are able to form their opinions this way are much harder to manipulate, and their deeper insight into the sources of political conflict can enable them to cultivate non-dogmatic stances, to better articulate key political problems and to endorse a decision-making procedure that can resolve these problems in an epistemically optimal way.

The epistemic value of political conflict assumes its full potential when applied to political representatives, whose main task is to participate in parliamentary discussions and deliberate on various laws and policies. Unlike ordinary citizens, who can sometimes avoid political conflict by deliberating only with like-minded people within deliberative enclaves (Sunstein 2011), political representatives have to deliberate with people who hold opposite opinions and preferences, and often argue from perspectives very different from their own (Dalaqua 2018a). This, of course, does not imply that ordinary citizens are unable to receive full epistemic benefits of political agonism—they read (or write in) newspapers, analyze parliamentary debates, organize or participate in public rallies and deliberate with other citizens, all this within informal political sphere. However, coming from different backgrounds and representing views of different social groups, political representatives address the best objections that can target their own views. These objections usually come from highly motivated and competent citizens (other political representatives in the Parliament) who are often able to indicate problems in others' views but can also take constructive criticism and change their initial beliefs in light of better reasons and arguments. This is precisely the reason why Mill rejects imperative mandates and pledges (1977a, 1977b)—political representatives should be free to utilize the epistemic value of conflict and the transformative function of public deliberation, thus changing their opinions and preferences. Deliberation among political representatives thus takes place within formal political sphere, which Mill (quite optimistically) considers to be a better epistemic environment than informal political sphere. However, we should not forget that Mill regards parliamentary debates as they should (and can) be, and not as they are.

Political Institutions and the Epistemic Value of Political Conflict

Mill's account of political representations is discussed in detail in the next chapter of this book. However, it will be useful to emphasize two key points and bring them in relation with Mill's argument on the epistemic value of agonism, thus foreshadowing the central theme discussed in the next few chapters. Namely, having established that political agonism can be epistemically fertile, it remains to be seen through which political institutions can this epistemic value be realized.

First, Mill argues in favor of a system of proportional representation, one that is able to reflect opinions, views and perspectives from all relevant minorities in a democratic society. Ideally, "every minority in the constituency should be represented by a minority in a representative body" (Mill 1859b, 33). He is interested in representation of opinions shared by relevant social groups, and not in representation of their interests. Mill thus indicates that "what is needed is a representation, not of men's differences of interest, but of the differences in their intellectual points of view" (Mill 1977c, 358). He proceeds to elaborate that having lawyers or shipowners in the Parliament is (epistemically) valuable not because of particular class interests they can promote or defend in the deliberative assembly, but because of the professional skills and competences they introduce into public deliberation. Rejecting secret ballot can thus be seen as a filtering mechanism aiming to discourage private and sectarian interests from affecting the voter's mind during the election process. Proportional representation is epistemically valuable since it ensures that all opinions in the political community (any many of these will be conflicting and incompatible) will be expressed and discussed in the Parliament. Proportional representation enables and injects political conflict in the formal political sphere. However, Mill is aware that the epistemic value of conflict is lost if one social group, having the majority in a deliberative assembly, can make decisions without having to provide reasons and arguments in support of their views. In order to protect the persistence of conflicting views and avoid the danger of class legislation (but not only for these reasons), Mill introduces another filtering mechanism—plural voting proposal. Following this idea, political influence is distributed unequally, with better educated citizens and those engaged in more demanding occupations having greater political input (more than one vote). This is why Mill argues that "opinions and wishes of poorest and rudest classes may be very useful as *one influence among others* . . . on Legislature" (Mill 1859b, 42, emphasis added), but is worried that, due to the sheer number of such citizens, their influence will become so dominant that it would preclude any deliberation between conflicting views in the Parliament. Political representation, as we have seen, has an important role since it introduces epistemically valuable conflict in the deliberation within formal political sphere.

Second, Mill considers agonist deliberation within representative institutions as epistemically more valuable than agonist deliberation characteristic of direct democracy. Arguments for this claim presented in the following chapters can be summarized along two lines. Political representation sets public deliberation (in the formal political sphere) within an assembly that contains "the elite of the nation" (Mill 1977c, 362). Representatives are recognized by citizens as "the most distinguished man on their own side," who embody epistemic and moral virtues relevant for upholding a high epistemic quality of collective deliberation.[8] Furthermore, representation sets members of parliament in epistemically favorable conditions (which cannot be guaranteed for all citizens)—they have more time to think on any particular issue, to consult the experts and to deliberate with others. Additional filtering mechanisms are introduced at this stage, including Mill's rejection of pledges and campaign promises, as well as the division between deliberative and executive bodies of government.

As we have seen, representation is important for political conflict for two reasons: it fuels the conflict by introducing all relevant political opinions and views in the public debate, and it shapes it by keeping it within favorable epistemic conditions, filtering the public will through various mechanism of indirect democracy. The epistemic value of political conflict has a strong impact on the moral and intellectual development of mankind (Robson 1968), yet its beneficial effect on political decision-making processes cannot be fully realized outside democratic representative institutions characterized by a set of mechanisms filtering the public will.

This chapter served a simple purpose—it demonstrates that, for Mill, political agonism has important epistemic value. Democratic societies should not try to reduce the existing level of political conflict. In fact, they should stimulate and encourage it. However, in order to have its epistemic function, political conflict should be contained within democratic and liberal institutions and should be properly shaped and moderated by appropriate political organizations.

NOTES

1. Alternative view is presented by Fabienne Peter (2011), who holds that outcomes of a deliberative procedure cannot be evaluated independently of the procedure that had produced them. Some problems with this approach are highlighted by Marti (2006), Cerovac (2016a) and Prijić-Samaržija (2018). Peter later transformed her view and now holds that a decision-making procedure should be evaluated both by its purely procedural qualities and by its ability to procedure outcomes of a high procedure-independent quality.

2. Nadia Urbinati (2014) points in this direction when she analyses the implications of some forms of epistemic democracy (those that set truth as the central aim of democratic politics). She is, however, very skeptical regarding the epistemic conception of democracy and believes that democracy "didn't emerge as a standard for achieving correct decisions—that was never the point." She proceeds to claim that democracy primarily stands "in the name of the basic condition of political equality, liberty, equal rights, representation, power sharing, and the capacity to come through with real consent" (Knight et al 2016, 147).

3. Notice, however, that this does not imply that the decision-making process should necessarily take place in the public sphere. While everyone should have an equal right to voice his opinion and to support it with the reasons and arguments he finds appropriate, this does not imply that everyone's opinion is of equal importance for political decision-making process, nor that everyone should have equal political

influence. For a more detailed view of this distinction see the chapter on plural voting proposal.

4. Some (Kumar 2006, 72, Yenor 2015, 29) argue that there is little difference between Mill's third and fourth argument against censorship. I agree that the arguments are closely connected, even to the extent that it might seem that both affirm the same idea. However, they address two different undesirable consequences of censorship: while one refers to the epistemic damage a true belief suffers when it becomes a dogma, the other addresses unwanted epistemic effect censorship has on citizens' moral and intellectual capacities.

5. An excellent example how political conflict can be productive and construct new perspectives, solutions and institutions is the struggle between the King on the one side and aristocrats and landlords on the other in the seventeenth century England. This political struggle founded first elements of free government since the landlords wanted both recognition of their civil liberties and a political institution that could protect these newly recognized rights and liberties (i.e., the Parliament). Thus, the conflict between different groups gave birth to representative institutions that regulate this conflict (Dalaqua 2018b).

6. This does not imply that correct and just decisions are the only political aim for Mill. Individual's self-development can be a good thing in itself, so the development of citizens' intellectual and moral capacities can be valuable both intrinsically (since it is a component of citizens' self-development) and instrumentally (since it serves as good means for producing even better political decisions). This part of the chapter claims merely that political conflict is instrumentally and epistemically valuable because it fosters the development of citizens moral and epistemic capabilities. Whether these capabilities have instrumental or intrinsic value is not discussed in this chapter. This question is briefly addressed in the first chapter.

7. David Estlund (2008) discusses this aspect of public deliberation when he evaluates pure deliberative proceduralism. Deliberating with citizens who hold conflicting opinions can help us re-evaluate our own opinions and preferences. Furthermore, inquiring into the reasons why we hold some opinion can enable us to recognize some hidden influences that might endanger our autonomy. However, he emphasizes that the former position usually falls into some form of epistemic proceduralism and characterizes Mill as one of the forefathers of this new position.

8. There are two confusing (and seemingly incompatible) attributes Mill ascribes to the Parliament. First is the elitist qualification: Mill considers Parliament as an institution containing "the elite of the nation" (Mill 1977c, 362) in a form of "some of the most distinguished man in the country." This clearly sets political representatives apart from the citizens—members of the Parliament are better (both in moral and epistemic sense) than regular citizens. Second is the democratic qualification: Mill sees Parliament as "a fair sample of every grade of intellect among the people," rather than as "a selection of greatest political minds in the country" (Mill 1861, 106). This claim, on the other hand, seems to imply that political representatives are no more qualified to rule that the average citizens. Both claims are important for Mill's political thought, and their incompatibility is only apparent. The first (elitist) claim refers to the difference between representatives and citizens. Members of the Parliament

are here indeed qualified as more competent, but not due to some particular expert knowledge, but due to their epistemic and moral virtues. They are considered "more competent in the *general affairs of life*" (Mill 1859b, 25, emphasis added). The second (democratic) claim refers to the difference between political representatives and experts in the executive government, the latter often called "individuals specially trained to govern and legislate" (Mill 1861, 106). Mill is here referring to the technical and not to the moral knowledge. For a detailed distinction between these two forms of knowledge see Christiano (2008) and Prijić-Samaržija (2011). Mill claims that representatives hold (or should hold) greater moral knowledge than their constituencies, and ministers and executive government officials hold (or should hold) greater technical knowledge than political representatives.

Chapter 3

Democracy and the Quality of Political Outcomes

Democracy is nowadays, without much contestation, widely regarded as the best form of government. Despite recent doubts, mostly focused on the appropriate role of experts in democratic decision-making processes and the harmful effects of populist politics and fake news on collective will-formation (Brennan 2016), democracy remains the dominant decision-authorization procedure with no serious competition in sight. Even single-party regimes like North Korea and China, theocratic republics like Iran and illiberal countries like Hungary declaratively endorse the idea of popular sovereignty and rarely miss the chance to emphasize their devotion to democratic ideals. Social and political circumstances in which we are in significantly differ from those in the nineteenth century, when democracy was just one of the competing decision-authorization procedures and when many serious scholars argued against political inclusion and democratic participation of many large social groups. Along with other progressive thinkers of his time, Mill dedicated much of his work to argue in favor of the expansion of suffrage, as well as to demonstrate that (properly institutionalized) democracy represents the best form of government.

But what makes democracy the best form of government? What qualities make democratic government superior to alternatives, like the rule by a benevolent despot or a small council of experts? Answers to these questions are of paramount importance because, by determining the criteria that make democracy the best form of government, we are also specifying which form democratic procedures should take and how they should be institutionalized. Additionally, answering why democracy is desirable will also answer which form of democracy is desirable.

John Stuart Mill provides one of the most acknowledged arguments for (representative) democratic government (Wolff 2006, 93). Starting from his consequentialist moral background, Mill argues that the best form of government is one that produces the best long-term consequences. Furthermore, taking into account his sophisticated utilitarian ideas, Mill recognizes best consequences as the greatest possible (moral and intellectual) improvement of mankind, which he considers "the permanent interest of man as a progressive being" (Mill 1977d, 224). Finally, he concludes that (provided a certain level of development has been reached) democratic government is better suited to produce such beneficial consequences than any other form of government. This chapter sets Mill's account in the wider explanatory framework of political legitimacy developed by Thomas Christiano and characterizes it as a form of political (democratic) instrumentalism. This classification recognizes Mill's focus on results and outcomes of political decision-making and decision-authorization processes (political decisions and the beneficial effect they have on the development of citizens) as the sole criteria for the evaluation of their legitimacy-generating potential. The chapter also reassesses Mill's two more explicit criteria of good government and analyses how democracy meets them.

This chapter plays a central role in the book and introduces the main argument for reading Mill as an early epistemic democrat. Its innovative contribution regards the reassessment of Mill's arguments against despotism and for democracy through the lens of epistemic justification of government. The chapter demonstrates that Mill characterizes representative deliberative democracy as the best form of government primarily due to its instrumental epistemic qualities.

The chapter proceeds as follows. The *first* part introduces a useful distinction between two opposite approaches to political justification: instrumentalism and proceduralism (Christiano 2004). Mill's account of good government is then characterized as a form of democratic instrumentalism. Following Richard Arneson (2003), this part of the chapter also addresses the difference between two forms of (democratic) instrumentalism, one focused on the correctness standard and the other on the best results standard. Taking into consideration his sophisticated utilitarian background, Mill is identified as a representative of the latter form of instrumentalism. Finally, this part establishes the relation between epistemic democracy and Mill's instrumentalism. The *second* part of the chapter analyses Mill's two criteria of good government: its ability to efficiently organize existing moral and intellectual capacities of citizens under its jurisdiction, and its ability to adequately improve them. Mill holds that no form of despotism is able to meet these criteria. When applied to developed nations and compared with alternative forms of government (e.g., despotism), well-functioning democracy meets the two criteria of good government better than any other competing form of government. The *third* part discusses why Mill believes some forms of democracy can meet these criteria. Building upon the chapter on epistemic value of agonism, democracy realizes its high epistemic value not through mere aggregation of preferences, but through exchange of opinions, ideas and arguments in public deliberation. The chapter then proceeds to compare the mid-Victorian electoral system, sometimes referred to as the Originating system (Colomer 2007), with Thomas Hare's electoral reform praised and endorsed by Mill. Furthermore, it addresses reasons Mill used to argue that the Originating system was unable to properly meet the two criteria of good government, as well as Mill's reasons for endorsing Hare's proposal. His arguments for various filtering mechanisms of collective will (plural voting, secret ballot, partisanship) are not discussed here but represent the central theme of subsequent chapters.

THE BEST FORM OF GOVERNMENT?

How can we compare and evaluate different forms of government? The traditional approach is to enlist a set of relevant qualities and virtues and then assess which form of government best meets the relevant criteria (Swift 2006). Contemporary political philosophy divides these virtues depending on whether they are the virtues of a decision-authorization process or of the final outcome produced by this process (Christiano 2004, also Cerovac 2016b). The relevant criteria can thus focus on the quality of political outcomes (i.e., whether they are good or bad, just or unjust) or on the processes by which these outcomes are produced (i.e., by a procedure that is fair or unfair, inclusive or exclusive). To properly understand Mill's account of good government, as well as to emphasize its epistemic elements and to compare it with contemporary forms of epistemic democracy, we first have to clarify the above-mentioned criteria and set Mill's view in this explanatory framework.

Proceduralism and Instrumentalism

Thomas Christiano (2004) usefully introduces a distinction between monistic and non-monistic accounts of political legitimacy. Although the debate on political legitimacy cannot simply be reduced to the debate on the quality of government,[1] it can give us valuable insights and help us map conflicting positions. Monistic positions take only one form of qualities (either qualities regarding the procedure itself, or qualities related to its outcomes) into account when evaluating the decision-authorization procedure in question. Conversely, non-monistic positions assess both the qualities of the procedure itself and the qualities of the outcomes it produces when they evaluate its legitimacy-generating potential. Two monistic accounts represent the two poles in the discussion.[2]

Pure proceduralism focuses only on purely procedural qualities of a decision-authorization procedure (or government) when assessing its legitimacy-generating potential. These intrinsic qualities are defined and determined regardless of the procedure's ability to produce a valuable goal or an outcome. Decision-authorization procedure (or a form of government) thus has legitimacy-generating potential because it embodies some important moral (or epistemic) qualities, and not because it has a tendency to produce results of some moral (or epistemic) value. Procedural fairness, understood as giving every citizen equal political influence or equal chance to participate in the decision-authorization process, is one of the common qualities pure proceduralists adhere to when assessing the procedure's legitimacy-generating potential (Peter 2011, Cerovac 2016b). A political decision is then considered legitimate if (and only if) it is authorized by a fair procedure, even if the decision in question is substantively incorrect, unjust or inefficient, and even if the fair procedure has an overall tendency to produce decisions of poor moral and epistemic value. Positions developed by Hannah Arendt (1967), Robert Dahl (1989), Gerald Gaus (1996), Iris Marion Young (2000) and Fabienne Peter (2011) are notable examples of pure proceduralism.

Instrumentalism, on the other hand, focuses only on procedure-independent qualities of a decision-authorization procedure (or a form of government) when assessing its legitimacy-generating potential. These instrumental qualities reflect the procedure's ability to reach a desired aim or outcome—a decision-authorization procedure has legitimacy-generating potential because of its ability to authorize with considerable procedure-independent (moral or epistemic) quality. Procedure's (or government's) ability to generate outcomes that are true or just, or its ability to maximize total happiness or produce some other desired consequence[3], are some examples of such instrumental quality (Peter 2011, Cerovac 2016b). A collective decision will thus be considered legitimate if (and only if) it was produced or authorized by a procedure (or a form of government) that has high tendency to authorize correct or just decisions (or to maximize total utility in general) and performs this task better than any other competing procedure (or form of government). Decision-authorization procedure can thus have legitimacy-generating potential while still lacking some purely procedural qualities (such as procedural fairness or inclusiveness). Positions developed by Philippe Van Parijs (1996), Richard Arneson (2003) and Steven Wall (2007), as well as by Cheryl Misak (2000), Robert Talisse (2009) and Snježana Prijić-Samaržija (2018), are some examples of political instrumentalism.

Pure proceduralism and instrumentalism are monistic positions: they establish political legitimacy by appealing either to purely procedural or to procedure-independent qualities. By contrast, non-monistic positions appeal to both types of qualities, arguing that a decision-authorization procedure (or a form of government) acquires its legitimacy-generating potential by having both purely procedural and instrumental qualities. David Estlund's (1997, 2008) rational epistemic proceduralism represents an excellent example of a non-monistic position, one that focuses on both the fairness of the procedure and the procedure-independent quality of the outcomes it procedures. Positions developed by Joshua Cohen (1986), Jose Marti (2006), Fabienne Peter (2016, 2019) and Ivan Cerovac (2020) are other relevant examples of non-monistic accounts of political legitimacy[4].

John Stuart Mill as a Political Instrumentalist

Traditional utilitarian approach, first formulated by Jeremy Bentham (1907, see also Binmore 2000), invites us to value actions as right or wrong (obligatory or prohibited) depending on their consequences or their ability to promote utility. No action is intrinsically right or wrong—only end states have intrinsic moral value, and actions can have only instrumental moral value. They are right or wrong depending on their performance as an instrument used to produce the desired (intrinsically valuable) end state (Timmons 2013, 111–113). Utilitarians employ a similar approach in political philosophy: a decisions-authorization procedure (or a form of government) is thus evaluated by assessing its ability to be a good instrument for producing (intrinsically valuable) political outcomes. Since utilitarians provide a necessarily moralized conception of legitimacy (Peter 2017) and link government's (or procedure's) legitimacy-generating potential to its ability to improve the happiness of the citizens, this approach is both maximizing and scalar.[5] It is maximizing since only the form of government that is best at this task can have legitimacy-generating potential. It is scalar since it establishes that legitimacy comes in degrees, and some forms of government can have greater legitimacy-generating potential than others (depending on their ability to produce beneficial consequences). A utilitarian account of political legitimacy thus clearly takes an instrumentalist form: a form of government is evaluated not according to its intrinsic (purely procedural) properties, but by its instrumental ability to produce valuable end states. John Stuart Mill's predecessors, including Jeremy Bentham (1907) and James Mill (1992, see also Hamburger 1965, 1999), have already steered utilitarianism in a democratic direction, arguing that a representative democratic government improves citizens' happiness and well-being better than any other form of government. However, as emphasized by Urbinati (2000) and others, they believed the mechanisms of aggregative democracy will produce the best consequences since they produce political outcomes that are in the interest of the majority. As demonstrated later in this chapter, John Stuart Mill rejects this conclusion and argues in favor of deliberative procedures.

Mill seems to embrace the utilitarian approach when he asserts that the best form of government is the one that produces the best results. His position is monistic since only the consequences of a particular form of government (i.e., its ability to produce decisions and other political outcomes that improve the well-being of citizens and develop their moral and intellectual capacities) are taken into account when assessing its quality and its legitimacy-generating potential (Sandel 2010, 56, Peter 2017). Taking into consideration Mill's utilitarian account characterized by the differentiation between higher-quality and lower-quality pleasures, the best form of government is the one that produces maximal aggregate long-term utility (Cerovac 2020, 132). Mill (1861, 54, emphasis added) thus writes that "the ideally best form of government is . . . the one which . . . is attended with *the greatest amount of beneficial consequences*, immediate and prospective."

To better understand what Mill considers "beneficial consequences" we have to focus on his two criteria of good government, which specify his position more clearly and differentiate it from somewhat similar positions adopted by Jeremy Bentham and James Mill. He indicates that the best form of government is the one that best achieves the following two goals: (i) improves the virtue and intelligence of the people under its jurisdiction, and (ii) organizes the existing virtues and good qualities of the people in a way that promotes the long-term common good.[6] These criteria represent a cornerstone of Mill's political thought and appear, more or less modified, throughout his philosophical work. Mill indicates that "one criterion of the goodness of a government [is] the degree in which it tends to increase the sum of good qualities in the governed, collectively and individually; since, besides that their well-being is the sole object of government, their good qualities supply the moving force which works the machinery," while the other "[is] the quality of machinery itself; that is, the degree in which it is adapted to take advantage of the amount of good qualities which may at any time exist, and make them instrumental to the right purposes" (Mill 1861, 30–31). A form of government can thus be evaluated depending on "a degree in which it promotes the general mental advancement of the community, including . . . advancement in intellect, in virtue, and in practical activity and efficiency; and partly of the degree of perfection with which it organizes the moral, intellectual and active worth already existing, so as to operate with the greatest effect of public affairs" (Mill 1861, 33). Both criteria, however, seem to be grounded in a single unifying (and foundational) criterion—beneficial consequences (Peter 2017).

Mill clearly uses a procedure-independent criterion to evaluate the quality of end states. Political outcomes are good or bad regardless of the procedure (or a form of government) used to produce them. Two examples confirm this interpretation.[7] *First*, when Mill writes on the instrumental quality of government, he indicates that government's ability to produce the best results depends on the people it is exercised upon. He emphasizes that whether a form of government is suitable for a group of citizens depends upon "the degree in which they possess certain special requirements" (Mill 1861, 70). Tyranny will be the best form of government for barbarian tribes, since it will best improve their intellectual and moral qualities (e.g., teach them to obey the laws), as well as organize them in a manner they, because of the lack of discipline, would otherwise be unable to do themselves. Democracy is preferred to tyranny, but only when discussing developed societies where certain preconditions have already been met.[8] This emphasizes the instrumental approach used by Mill: what form of government is legitimate depends on the type of society it is applied upon. Different forms of government will yield different results in different societies. *Second*, when Mill uses an epistemic argument to argue against despotic monarchy, he indicates that (for developed nations), even if there was be a wise benevolent despot, such ruler would be unable to detect and promote the common good, as well as particular interests of different individuals, as efficiently as a representative (democratic) government does. A political decision is thus good or bad regardless of the procedure that has produced it; its quality is evaluated in the light of its consequences (Cerovac 2020, 132).

The Two Forms of Instrumentalism

In his sophisticated defense of (pure) instrumentalism, Richard Arneson (2003, 123) differentiates between two conceptions of instrumentalism. While both conceptions follow the basic instrumentalist form of reasoning (where a decision-making procedure is evaluated exclusively following the quality of the results it produces), they differ on what is considered a desirable result or a desirable political outcome. The first conception, grounded in the correctness standard, asserts that a decision-making procedure has legitimacy-generating potential only when it produces (morally and epistemically) the best possible laws and policies. This conception represents a form of narrow instrumentalist justification, where the desired results are correct, efficient or just political decisions. The second conception, grounded in the best results standard, holds that a decision-making procedure has legitimacy-generating potential only when (in the long run) it produces (morally and epistemically) the best possible end states. Unlike the former, this conception takes a form of wide instrumentalist justification, and the desired results are not merely correct or just laws and policies, but the most just and efficient social, economic and political states.

Arneson (2003, 123–124, see also Bester 2010, 35) invites us to consider two decision-making procedures (or two forms of government): autocracy and democracy. He invites us to imagine the autocracy has higher tendency to produce just, correct or efficient political decisions than democracy. Following the correctness standard, autocracy would be preferred over democracy. However, Arneson invites us to imagine that, along with its comparatively lower tendency to produce correct decisions, democracy has a much higher tendency to "render citizens more virtuous," and thus leads to better outcomes in the long run. Following the best results standard, democracy would be preferred over autocracy. Although Arneson makes no mention of Mill in this paper, Mill's position seems to follow the standard of best results and clearly endorses wide instrumentalist justification (Bester 2010).

Bester's interpretation points into this direction. When Mill indicates that one of the two criteria of good government regards government's ability to improve intellectual and moral capacities of citizens (Mill 1977a, 390), he does not consider this valuable only because such improvement will tend to increase the quality of democratic political decisions. Although this can be (and often is) the case, Mill finds the improvement of citizens' capacities valuable and desirable regardless of the impact it can have on the quality of political decisions. While this interpretation has its merits, it tends to neglect Mill's arguments on the necessary relation between just and correct decisions and the good results over the extended period of time. To better understand this relation, we have to address his arguments for the two criteria of government.

As argued earlier, Mill (1861, 17) claims that government is only the means of reaching the desired end—to "promote the interests of any given society," or more precisely, to promote "nothing less than the whole of the interests of the humanity."[9] He proceeds to argue that, although all societies share the same common interest, their particular and temporary interests (and thus the specific tasks of good government) will depend on the societies' current level of development. Good government depends on some causes and conditions, the most important among them (and "the one which transcends all others") bring "the qualities of the human beings composing the society over which the government is exercised" (Mill 1861, 28). He proceeds to support this claim by arguing that "government consists of acts done by human beings; and if the agents, or those who choose the agents, . . . are mere masses of ignorance, stupidity and baleful prejudice, every operation of government will go wrong: while, in proportion as the men rise above this standard, so will the government improve in quality; up to the point of excellence . . . where the officers of the government, themselves persons of superior intellect and virtue, are *surrounded by the atmosphere of a virtuous and enlightened public opinion*" (Mill 1861, 29–30, emphasis added). Therefore, improving citizens' moral and intellectual capacities can be one of the government's long-term goals (as Bester argues), but when Mill discusses the two criteria of good government this plays a different role—it is a precondition of (but also the result of) good government.[10]

Mill and (Epistemic) Democracy

Mill has thus far been characterized as a proponent of political instrumentalism, a position which evaluates decision-authorization procedures (and forms of government) exclusively on their ability to produce desired outcomes. Furthermore, he was characterized as a wide political instrumentalist, one focusing not only on the substantive quality of political decisions, but on the overall quality of (direct and indirect) results of some form of government. Having correct, just or efficient political decisions is important, but it is also not the only important result. However, if we characterize Mill as an instrumentalist accepting the good results standard (instead of the correctness standard), can we still portray him as an epistemic democrat? Epistemic democracy usually focuses on the quality of direct political outputs (laws, policies and decisions) and not on the overall consequences of some decision-authorization procedure. David Estlund (1997, 173–180, see also Arneson 2003, 123), for example, focuses on the procedure-independent epistemic value of political decisions ('qualified' correctness standard[11]) when he assesses epistemic quality of decision-authorization procedures and establishes the standard account of epistemic democracy. Can epistemic democracy be compatible with wide political instrumentalism?

Contemporary epistemic democrats can address the epistemic value of decision-authorization procedures in more than one way: they can take a purely procedural approach and argue that such procedures are valuable because they embody some epistemic virtues (Peter 2011), or they can pursue some form of an instrumental approach and argue that such procedures have high tendency to produce epistemically valuable results. While the former approach has nothing in common with political instrumentalism, the latter has to be taken into careful consideration. We should thus narrow the discussion and ask whether the standard account of epistemic democracy (Estlund 2008, Cerovac 2020) or the pragmatist account of epistemic democracy (Misak 2000, Talisse 2009), both of which use the correctness standard and address procedure's epistemic value from the standpoint of narrow political instrumentalism, can be compatible with wide political instrumentalism and the use of the best results standard. I believe not only that it can be compatible, but also that Arneson's (2003) distinction might be misguiding. Namely, it seems to suggest that there is a sharp division between procedures that produce political decisions that are correct, just or efficient (according to some procedure-independent standard) on the one side, and the procedures that produce the best results in the long run on the other. Consider McCloskey's

(1965) famous thought experiment: in a small town torn apart by racial tension, a white woman was raped, and the crowd is convinced that the perpetrator is a black man. Civil unrest with disastrous consequences is about to ensue if the man is not prosecuted and sentenced. Should the judge (or the sheriff) prosecute and sentence the man despite having strong evidence indicating he is not guilty? Or should she free that man, aware of the disastrous civil unrest that will surely follow? When applied to Arneson's distinction, it seems that the correctness standard would instruct her to use the procedure that frees the man (produces correct or right outcome), while the best results standard would instruct her to use the procedure that sentences the man, thus preventing even worse consequences. However, some moral theories, like utilitarianism, will not be able to perceive this difference. As McCloskey indicates, for a utilitarian judge (or sheriff) freeing the man would be the wrong act, since the standard by which we assess whether the decision to let him go was correct or right is the best results in the long run.[12] Similarly, when utilitarians assess laws, policies and political decisions, they establish their correctness (i.e., whether such laws are correct, efficient or just) based on the effect these have on the overall utility in the long run. Arneson's distinction between narrow and wide political instrumentalism might not be suited for utilitarian justification, where the two standards are correlated—correctness always depends on the best overall results in the long run.

The same can be said for Mill's own account of political justification. He writes that there is a plurality of (often conflicting) principles of justice, yet when these principles conflict, "from the confusions there is no other mode of extrication than the utilitarian" (Mill 1985a, 245). Laws, policies and political decisions are considered right or wrong (correct or incorrect) depending on their long-term consequences and their impact on citizens' well-being. Consider, for example, Mill's thoughts on expanding the suffrage to citizens who have not received any education. He rejects this proposal and, though he finds exclusion of any citizen from suffrage highly undesirable and thinks that (at least minimal) education should be made available to all citizens as soon as possible, he argues that, until such preconditions can be met, uneducated citizens should not receive voting privileges.[13] Mill thus writes that "it is a personal injustice to withhold from anyone, *unless for the prevention of greater evils*, the privilege of having his voice reckoned in the disposal of affairs in which he has the same interest as other people" (Mill 1861, 166, emphasis added). He is afraid that enfranchisement of uneducated citizens might reduce the quality of political decisions and thus produce terrible political results and harm other citizens. Therefore, Mill's political instrumentalism can be understood as both narrow and wide. There is a clear and unifying procedure-independent standard of correctness we can use to evaluate political decisions and decision-authorization procedures, and no decision (or procedure) can be evaluated independently of this standard.

WHY NOT DESPOTISM?

This part of the chapter, with title mirroring Estlund's (2003) famous article "Why not Epistocracy," analyses Mill's arguments against the rule of an individual, regardless of how wise and benevolent the individual might be. Mill defines benevolent despotism as "a government in which there is no positive oppression by the officers of the state, but in which all the collective interests of the people are managed for them, and in which their minds are formed by, and consenting to, this abdication of their own energies" (Mill 1861, 48–49). A benevolent despot is thus a liberal ruler who prefers to let citizens decide for themselves how they want to run their individual lives. However, when political issues have to be regulated, the benevolent despot does not invite citizens to participate in the decision-making process but instead personally takes care of the entire process, leaving citizens to focus only on the issues within their private (individual) sphere. Contemporary epistemic democrats typically reject this form of despotism by arguing that it would not be able to meet the liberal principle of legitimacy (Rawls 2001, 41, see also Freeman 2003, 37 and Michelman 2003, 395) because of invidious comparisons. Namely, due to the lack of qualified agreement on who should be the benevolent despot, we cannot publicly agree on any particular ruler (Estlund 1997). Unlike contemporary scholars, Mill is more concerned with the harmful effects the rule of a benevolent despot would have both on the quality of political outcomes and the capacities of citizens. Following the scheme indicated earlier, Mill targets the instrumental epistemic value of despotism and argues that it fails to produce satisfactory political results.

Some might wonder what we can learn analyzing Mill's argument against despotism—while this was indeed an important discussion in the nineteenth century, its possible contribution to contemporary political debates is (at best) dubious. While I agree that the traditional challenge of despotism is nowadays mostly irrelevant, I believe a lot can be gained by studying Mill's arguments on this issue. Namely, even though we cannot simply apply his arguments and solutions to contemporary liberal societies, by analyzing them we can gain a deeper understanding of Mill's political thought. This can in turn enable us to address contemporary problems from a Millian standpoint.

Can Despotism Ever Be Justified?

As indicated earlier in this chapter, Mill (1977a, 390–391) argues that the best form of government is the one that (i) *organizes* the existing virtues and good qualities of the people in a way that promotes the common good in the long run better than any other form of government, and the one that (ii) *improves* the same virtues and qualities of the people under its jurisdiction better than any feasible alternative. Government's ability to achieve these two goals is contingent and depends on many external considerations, including the society's current level of (moral and intellectual) development, as well as its existing legal system, history and tradition (Mill 1977a: 392–398). He thus writes that the quality of any kind of government is "a question of time, place and circumstance" (Mill 1981a, 177). No particular form of government can be universally applied and considered to be the best—the quality of government's results will depend on the kind of society it functions in.

Mill thus believes that, under certain circumstances and in some societies, despotism can be the best form of government. There are instances where the two criteria will be best achieved not by a democratic government but by a rule of a benevolent despot. Namely, democratic institutions and procedures will be able to organize and improve citizens' existing capacities only after some level of development has already been reached. Before such conditions are met, despotic government can have a prominent role in the organization and the development of citizens' capacities. A benevolent despot's duty is to prepare the society for democratic government—to rise it to the level where democratic institutions and procedures can exercise their beneficial influence on citizens' minds. In other words, Millian benevolent despot has a self-extinguishing role (Chiu and Taylor 2011). Its mission is to uplift the society to the level of competence and civic morality where it will no longer be needed.

There are several virtues barbaric societies have to acquire before they are ready for democratic government. Obedience and patient industry are taught in the *first stage*, and Mill goes so far as to even justify personal slavery in the early stages of social development, but only when such slavery is exercised as a means to encourage these virtues.[14] Members of such barbaric societies are regarded as children, and Mill finds paternalist approach to be fully appropriate in this stage of social advancement (Mill 1977a, 394–395, see also Mill 1977d). Acquiring these two virtues is, of course, not enough to prepare people for democracy—Mill acknowledges that slaves will never be transformed into self-governing people unless they acquire additional virtues (Chiu and Taylor 2011, 1241). Obedience and patient industry serve primarily as prerequisites for the acquisition of other virtues. In the *second stage*, the benevolent despot promotes the development of new virtues, such as intelligence, prudence and self-control (Mill 1965a, 281). Though the citizens are not yet ready to exercise coercive power over others, they are encouraged to develop self-regarding responsibilities and to exercise control over their own lives. They are not allowed to rule others, but (unlike slaves or children) are permitted and encouraged to rule themselves: to acquire property, to form bonds and contracts with other willing people, to trade goods and services and to decide how to lead their own lives. In this stage the benevolent despot maintains "a general superintendence over all the operations of society," yet "necessarily leaves and induces individuals to do much of themselves" (Mill 1861, 39–40). However, being able to take care of oneself is a precondition, and not a guarantee that one will be able to properly participate in democratic decision-authorization processes. Additional virtues thus have to be acquired. In the *third stage* the benevolent despot promotes the final two virtues: willingness to resist tyranny and the spirit of nationality (Mill 1977a, 419–422, see also Chiu and Taylor 2011, 1243). People should be able to obey the laws but also understand the concept of the rule of law, thus being able to resist or criticize political authority when it does not abide by their rule. Similarly, citizens are taught to look beyond their narrow personal, local and sectarian interests and to focus on the common interests of the society in general. Benevolent despot can promote these virtues by calling citizens (or their representatives) to form advisory boards, where they can get a better understanding of the rule of law as well as of the common interest. However, once citizens have acquired these virtues and sufficiently developed their moral and intellectual capacities, despotic rule ceases to promote and starts to hinder their further improvement.[15]

Despotism and Modern Liberal Societies

It is no secret that Mill firmly opposed all forms of despotism in modern societies, considering it as a direct opposite to liberty (Urbinati 2007, 67). Mill clearly warns that "a good despotism is an altogether false ideal, which practically (except as a means to some temporary purpose) becomes the most senseless and dangerous of chimeras" (Mill 1861, 53). His two arguments follow the familiar scheme and indicate why a despotic ruler, even when he is wise and benevolent, cannot properly meet the two criteria of good government. Furthermore, these arguments enable us to clearly see instrumentalist and epistemic elements in Mill's political thought.

First, Mill believes that despotism (in modern societies) fails to adequately organize the existing virtues and good qualities of the people in a way that promotes the long-term common good. A despot would have to be "not merely a good monarch, but an all-seeing one" (Mill 1861, 45). Such ruler would have to be informed correctly and in detail on various branches of public administration (Mill finds this omniscience very implausible) or at least be able to select a small group of trustworthy experts he can rely on (this meta-omniscience, perfect knowledge of the knowers, is also implausible) (Landemore 2017, 78). Despot would have to be so informed, insightful and observant as to be "superhuman" (Stevenson 2016, 402). Even if one person could hold all this knowledge, Mill is convinced that the task is so demanding that none of the few competent persons would consent to undertake it, unless only temporarily and to prevent some great evil (Mill 1977a, 400). However, there is an additional difficulty. Relevant political knowledge used in decision-making and decision-authorization processes is not integrated and cannot be held by an individual. Instead, it is widely dispersed among the population in small, often inconsistent parts. As indicated in the previous chapter, various (and often conflicting) opinions and perspectives that citizens have can produce epistemically fertile agonism, thus enabling us to acquire more robust and justified beliefs, but also to construct new opinions and new perspectives, including better solutions to existing political problems (Mill 1977d). No individual, no matter how wise or benevolent, can perform this task.[16] A benevolent despot fails to be a good instrument for reaching the epistemically valuable goal: to properly harness and organize existing knowledge and competences in the society and to reliably produce good political outcomes. We need to find alternative terms of political association (but also a decision-authorization procedure) that will allow us to harness this widely dispersed knowledge and use it to make good political decisions.

Second, Mill indicates that despotic government (in modern societies) fails to improve the existing moral and intellectual capacities of its citizens. A rule by a "man of superhuman mental activity managing the entire affairs" (Mill 1861, 46) would lead to a society of mentally passive people. Citizens would still take care of their personal affairs,[17] but without thinking and acting on public good. They would stay constrained within "a certain narrow range of ideas" without any real chance to further develop their intelligence. Even those rare citizens who decide to focus their attention on politics (e.g., political scientists under a despotic regime) would acquire only theoretical (or dilettante) knowledge, thus failing to improve their practical skills. Furthermore, citizens' moral capacities would be harmed as well since people under despotic rule would not be able to develop affiliation towards other citizens nor to form a meaningful relation toward their country. Mill considers these negative effects "inherent necessities of a despotic government" (Mill 1861, 49)—they are not simply unwanted side effects that might or might not occur but characterize any form of government where an individual or a small group of people authorize all political decisions (Thompson 1976). Despotism necessarily exercises a harmful effect on citizens' minds and, once a society has reached certain level of development, impedes any future improvement, both of citizens moral and intellectual capacities and of the society in general.

Despotism thus fails to be the appropriate form of government for modern societies. Following Mill's instrumentalist account, after a certain level of social development has been reached, despotism simply fails to be the proper means for producing the best consequences. It represents an epistemically inferior decision-authorization procedure since it cannot adequately organize the existing knowledge and knowledge-producing capacities widely dispersed within a modern society, thus failing to take into account all relevant perspectives and consequently being unable to produce political outcomes (laws, policies and decisions) of adequate substantive quality. Similarly, it again represents an epistemically inferior procedure of public education since it is ineffective in improving citizens moral and epistemic virtues.

Democracy—A Successful Alternative

Mill endorses democracy just as wholeheartedly as he rejects despotic government. He indicates that "the ideally best form of government is . . . the one which is attended with the greatest amount of beneficial consequences," and readily adds that "a completely popular government is the only polity which can make out any claim of this character" (Mill 1861, 54). Namely, when applied to developed nations and compared with alternative forms of government (e.g., despotism), democracy meets the two criteria of good government better than any other competing form of government.

First, unlike despotism, democracy can efficiently organize citizens' existing competences and make use of the relevant knowledge widely dispersed within society.[18] Democracy thus enables us to make correct, efficient and just decisions, and here it outperforms all other forms of government. It performs this demanding task in two ways. First, it organizes decision-authorization procedures in a way that encourages and enables citizens to actively participate in the process by which they protect and promote their interests. Mill indicates that "rights and interests of every or any person are only secure from being disregarded, when the person interested is himself able, and habitually disposed, to stand up for them" (Mill 1861, 54, see also Thompson 1976, 14–27). No one is more motivated (and thus able) to protect one's interests better than the very person whose interests are in question (Anschutz 1969, 57).[19] To be correct, an efficient or just political decision has to take into consideration the interests of all individuals, yet "the interest of the excluded is always in danger of being overlooked" (Mill 1861, 56). Well-functioning democracy can produce outcomes of sufficient epistemic quality because it enables all citizens to participate in the decision-authorization process, thus ensuring that instead of promoting the interest of an individual or a small group (or even the majority), political decisions aim toward the public interest. Second, democracy enables perspectives of various individuals and social groups to enter into collective deliberation, thus expanding the pool of relevant knowledge and enabling fertile epistemic agonism to take place (Dalaqua 2018b). Mill warns us that, even when interests of excluded citizens are taken into account, "when looked at, [they are] seen with very different eyes from those of the persons whom they directly concern" (Mill 1861, 56, see also Baccarini 1993, 50). He notices that, having no workers' representatives, the Parliament rarely or never "looks at any question with the eyes of a working man," and proceeds to claim that an epistemically valuable perspective is thus lost. Only a completely popular government[20] can adequately assess all relevant perspectives and intellectual points of view and thus properly harness the epistemic value of diversity (Kelly 2006).

Second, again unlike despotism, democracy (in modern societies) allows and encourages citizens to think and act on public issues, thus fostering the improvement of their intellectual and moral capacities. Mill indicates that "the possession and the exercise of political, and among others of electoral, rights, is one of the chief instruments both of moral and intellectual training for the popular mind" (Mill 1859b, 22). He considers this improvement valuable both in relation to its tendency to increase the quality of political outcomes and independently of its direct political effects.[21] However, Mill's political thought focuses primarily on the former, i.e., on beneficial effects that one's moral and intellectual improvement has on the well-being of society. He thus asks, "which of two common types of character, *for the general good of humanity*, it is most desirable should predominate—the active, or the passive type?" (Mill 1861, 59, emphasis added). As we can see, Mill's argument for democracy does not take a paternalist turn—the improvement of one's capacities is not argued for the sake of that individual's well-being (though Mill believes such improvement, in general, also contributes to one's well-being), but because of the beneficial effects such improvement will have on the well-being of others, or on humanity as a whole. His argument concerning the improvement of citizens' intellectual and moral capacities, and consequently his justification of democracy, thus takes a form similar to political (and not perfectionist) republicanism (see Weithman 2004). Democracy allows "the maximum of the invigorating effect of freedom upon the character" to be obtained (Mill 1861, 66) and does so by motivating and encouraging citizens to think and act on public matters. He uses the example of the practice of dicastery (a judicial body of about five hundred members, which administered justice by a majority vote) and ecclesia (a popular assembly of approximately six thousand members, which had final say on legislation and could call magistrates to account) and argues that these practices "raised the intellectual standard of an average Athenian citizen far beyond anything of which there is yet an example in any mass of men, ancient or modern" (Mill 1861, 67). Democracy acts as the "school of public spirit" (Mill 1977a, 412), improving citizens' competences and making them more apt for political participation, and thus increasing the quality of political results.

Despite being convinced that popular government meets the two criteria better than any feasible alternative, Mill is worried that democracy might deteriorate and become even worse than the rule of a (malevolent) despot. Therefore, simply having a popular government does not imply that the two criteria will automatically be met—Mill has to specify the process by which political decisions are authorized, determine the appropriate division of epistemic labor and indicate which mechanisms that filter the public (if any) should be in place.

DEMOCRACY, DELIBERATION AND REPRESENTATION

There are two important questions that have to be answered in this part of the chapter. First, how should political decisions be made and authorized? Different models of political authorization (e.g., voting, deliberation) will surely have different effects both on democracy's ability to efficiently organize the existing capacities in the society and its ability to improve them. Second, who should participate in the direct process of making and authorizing such decisions? The level of citizens' participation (whether the decisions are directly made or authorized by all citizens or by just a few representatives) will again surely affect democracy's ability to meet the two criteria of good government.

The Epistemic Value of Representation

Mill is well-known for his famous defense of representative government—after all, one of his most influential works in political philosophy is entitled *Considerations on Representative Government* (1977a). It comes as no surprise that Mill considers decision-making (and decision-authorization) processes within representative institutions epistemically more valuable than those taking place within institutions characteristic of direct democracy. Again, following his two principles of good government, arguments for this claim can be summarized along two lines.

First, political representation helps us organize citizens' existing moral and intellectual capacities in the optimal way. Unlike direct democracy, where citizens of all degrees of intellectual and moral capacity participate in decision-authorization procedures and directly exercise their political influence, political representation sets decision-authorization (in the formal political sphere) within an assembly that contains "the elite of the nation" (Mill 1977c, 362). Representatives are recognized by the citizens as "the most distinguished man on their own side," who embody epistemic and moral virtues relevant for upholding high epistemic quality of collective deliberation.[22] Furthermore, representation sets members of parliament in epistemically favorable conditions (which cannot be guaranteed for all citizens)—they have more time to think on any particular issue, to consult the experts, to find epistemic support within partisan associations and to deliberate with others. Representation is thus seen as the basic mechanism for filtering the public will (Barker 2015): when exercised properly, political representation will harness the epistemic value of diversity and include all relevant perspectives in the decision-authorization process while simultaneously filtering the epistemic vices (e.g., gullibility, dogmatism, prejudice, closed-mindedness and negligence[23]) that often characterize the intellectual character of most citizens. Of course, political representatives will still be fallible and vulnerable to epistemic vices, yet Mill holds that they will, on average, be more competent to participate in the formal collective deliberation and in the direct decision-authorization processes than average citizens. This does not imply that, for Mill, citizens should not participate in decision-making and decision-authorization processes between elections—it only implies that their influence should not be direct (like that of members of the Parliament), and should be exercised indirectly, through informal political sphere (e.g., through media or civil society organizations). Most of this book revolves around the very idea that political representation is epistemically valuable since it allows us to filter public will, thus improving the epistemic value of decision-authorization processes and the epistemic quality of resulting political outcomes. Mill's thoughts on representation and other, more specific filtering mechanisms (like plural voting and open ballot) are discussed in detail in the following chapters.

Second, political representation helps improve citizens' existing moral and intellectual capacities better than political alternatives linked to direct democracy. It achieves this goal in two ways. First, Mill seems to suggest that, while direct democracy might exceed in fostering the quantity of citizens' participation (since citizens are called to participate in decision-making processes on numerous public issues coming from all areas of government), it fails in advancing the quality of citizens' participation. Namely, Mill thinks that, in order for political participation to exercise the desired educative effect on citizens' minds, it has to be performed responsibly. He praises the discipline learned "from the occasional demand made upon the citizens to exercise, for a time and in their turn, some social function" (Mill 1861, 66) and argues that this exercise requires citizens to responsibly weigh the interests of others along with their own and to make decisions focusing on the common good (Warner 2001). However, Mill warns us that, when performing some social function, "responsibility is null when nobody knows who is responsible" (Mill 1977a, 520). When a large number of citizens is regularly called to make or authorize decisions, and when their responsibility is divided and thus seriously weakened, they will approach the matter at hand in a sloppy and negligent way, thus failing to properly engage their moral and intellectual capacities, and consequently fail to train them through this practice. Mill believes that citizens' participation is an important means for their moral and intellectual improvement, yet holds that wide participation is compatible with representative institutions. He turns to local (representative) government (discussed in the following chapter) as the chief instrument of public education (Mill 1977a, 535) and emphasizes that "in local bodies, many citizens have a chance of being elected, and many fill one or other of the numerous local executive offices" (Mill 1861, 276, see also Kurer 1989, 297). The improvement of citizens' capacities is thus best achieved through representative institutions at the local level. Second, Mill also holds that political representation can help citizens improve their capacities in an alternative way. By following the discussions in the Parliament citizens are introduced to some of the best arguments for and against various policy proposals—they can learn from representatives who share their values but are seen as the best among them, and who have many epistemic resources normally inaccessible to regular citizens at their disposal. The Parliament thus becomes the "grand institution of national education," creating and correcting the public opinion (Mill 1977c, 348, see also Selinger 2019, 188). More on the educative role of political representation in Mill's political thought can be found in one of the following chapters.

The Epistemic Value of Deliberation

John Stuart Mill is not the first utilitarian philosopher to use instrumentalist justification to defend popular government. Both James Mill and Jeremy Bentham argue that some form of democratic government, characterized by majority rule, would serve as the best means for identifying what is in the interest of the majority, and therefore which actions will produce the best consequences (or meet the interests of the largest number of people). General interest is thus equated with the best consequences, which can be achieved by following the interest of the majority (Urbinati 2000, 769). Though both Bentham (1843c) and James Mill (1992) favor representative democracy, they perceive political representatives as agents mirroring the exact interests of their constituencies—that was, after all, the central prerequisite for democracy's instrumental role as a mechanism for discovering what is in the interest of the majority. If political representatives started to act in favor of decisions that do not promote the direct interest of their constituencies, the final decisions (endorsed by the majority of representatives) would no longer be in the interest of the majority of citizens, and their results would have bad and undesirable consequences for the people.

Bentham and James Mill focus on the representation of interests, and not opinions and perspectives. They argue in favor of aggregative democracy and believe that the fair aggregation of citizens' interests can help us determine what is the most desirable political outcome, and by extension the outcome that produces the greatest overall utility. Of course, we cannot simply follow what produces the most utility in the moment, but must adhere to our long-term interest, taking into consideration that some policies, though they might increase the total happiness for a week or a month, lead to unavoidable economic declines and reduce our total long-term utility. Since not all citizens are able to properly do hedonic arithmetic, with some forgetting or poorly calculating the value of some of the seven features of felicific calculus (intensity, duration, certainty and uncertainty, propinquity and remoteness, fecundity, purity and extent),[24] Jeremy Bentham and James Mill think that only the interests of the more industrious citizens should be directly represented (Pratt 1955, Urbinati 2000). Disenfranchisement of some non-industrious social groups (e.g., women, workers, the poor) might in fact be instrumentally valuable because their members, lacking the ability to properly engage in utility calculus, might (by exercising their voting rights) reduce the overall quality of political outcomes. Of course, James Mill and Bentham emphasize that the well-being of the members of such groups is just as important as the well-being of more industrious citizens—they simply doubt in such citizens' capacity to know which policies are in their own best interest, and in the best interest of the society. Interests of such citizens should be indirectly promoted through the interests of those more industrious (Bentham 1843c, Urbinati 2000). Jonathan Riley interprets John Stuart Mill in a similar fashion, indicating that Mill "has in mind a democratic voting process in which individual preferences . . . are given equal positive scores or votes and their votes are added up to select an outcome that has the greatest sum total of votes" (Riley 2015, 328), thus discovering what laws and policies best improve the social welfare. Of course, Mill is far more inclusive than his predecessors, arguing that all citizens who meet some minimal preconditions should have a vote, yet Riley's interpretation seems to overemphasize the role aggregation plays in Mill's political thought. Although he grounds his arguments in the same utilitarian foundations as his father and Jeremy Bentham, John Stuart Mill strongly disagrees with their views and opposes aggregative democracy by offering a few important arguments.

First, aggregation of citizens' interests (or to be more precise, aggregation only of interests of more industrious citizens) does not represent the epistemically optimal way of organizing the citizens' existing moral and intellectual capacities. Mill does not think citizens' particular interests are something that should enter political decision-making and decision-authorization process. Unlike Bentham and James Mill, he is convinced that citizens' political input should not revolve around their specific individual or group interests[25]—a political process that simply aggregates citizens' preferences will produce political outcomes (laws, policies and decisions) of suboptimal quality. As we have seen earlier, Mill argues in favor of a system of proportional representation, one that is able to reflect opinions, views and perspectives of *all* relevant minorities in a democratic society. Ideally, "every minority in the constituency should be represented by a minority in a representative body" (Mill 1859b, 33). He is interested in representation of opinions shared by relevant social groups, and not in representation of their particular interests. Mill thus indicates that "what is needed is a representation, not of men's differences of interest, but of the differences in their intellectual points of view" (Mill 1977c, 358). He proceeds to elaborate that having lawyers or shipowners in the Parliament is (epistemically) valuable not because of particular class interests they can promote or defend in the deliberative assembly, but because of the professional skills and competences they introduce into public deliberation. Proportional representation is epistemically valuable since it ensures that all opinions in the political community (and many of these will be conflicting and incompatible) will be expressed and discussed in the Parliament. Proportional representation thus enables and injects political conflict in the formal political sphere. Of course, the model of representation favored by Bentham and James Mill also introduced political conflict in the formal political sphere, yet this was the conflict of interests, one that lacks transformative and creative power discussed in the previous chapter. Simple aggregation of preferences does not make the existing political conflict epistemically fertile, and even when it produces some form of compromise it does not foster transformation of one's own nor the understanding of others' preferences. Deliberation on existing opinions, on the other hand, introduces the epistemic value of political agonism, thus enabling citizens (and their representatives) to detect and abandon incorrect beliefs (or beliefs that lack proper justification), to recognize beliefs grounded in biases and prejudices, and sometimes to create completely new beliefs (Mill 1977d). This has a significant effect on decision-making and decision-authorization processes since it enables us to create better, more just and more efficient laws and policies.[26] Furthermore, it also contributes to the descriptive (perceived) legitimacy of political outcomes since all citizens can see that the coercive laws and policies were produced by appeal to what were, for the majority of their representatives, considered to be the best reasons and arguments. Finally, Mill believes that grounding political decisions in reasons and arguments instead of individual or group preferences enables decision-makers to construct progressive laws and policies, or to "shape their measures with some regard not solely to present exigencies, but to tendencies in progress" (Mill 1861, 105). However, Mill is aware that the epistemic value of conflict is lost if one social group, having the majority in a deliberative assembly, can make decisions by simple aggregation of votes, without having to provide reasons and arguments to support its views. In order to protect the persistence of conflicting views and avoid the danger of class legislation (but not only for these reasons), Mill introduces several filtering mechanisms (e.g., plural voting, rejection of secret ballot and pledges) discussed in the next chapter.

Second, public deliberation can improve citizens' existing moral and intellectual capacities far better than any aggregative procedure. While aggregative democracy is a form of popular government, and citizens thus have an incentive to participate in the collective decision-authorization procedures and to think about issues of public concern, its epistemic value fades in comparison with deliberative democracy. Here citizens (and their political representatives) are called not only to think about issues of public concern from their own perspective, but also to consider, listen and critically scrutinize the reasons and arguments offered by their political opponents, as well as to offer justification for their own views and opinions. As indicated in the previous chapter and addressed many times in Mill's (1977d) famous essay *On Liberty*, free and uncensored deliberation has several beneficial effects on citizens' minds: it helps citizens get rid of false opinions and views (i.e., those not supported by adequate reasons and evidence), helps them eliminate their own biases and prejudices, but also resist dogmatic beliefs and beliefs acquired in a habitual manner, without proper critical scrutiny. Finally, free deliberation enables the collision of opinions and sometimes, when each of them holds a portion of the whole truth, enables the creation of new epistemically valuable opinions and perspectives (Mill 1977d, see also Landemore 2017, 77–80, and Roberts 2004, 71–73). Mill thus firmly believes that collective decision-making and decision-authorization procedure characterized by public deliberation will meet the two criteria of good government far better than an alternative procedure based on aggregation of citizens' preferences.

As we have seen, representation is important for political conflict for two reasons: it fuels the conflict by introducing all relevant political opinions and views in the public debate, and it shapes it by keeping it within favorable epistemic conditions. The epistemic value of political conflict cannot be fully realized outside democratic representative institutions, characterized by a list of mechanisms filtering the public will. More on these mechanisms, including Mill's thoughts on open ballot, partisanship and plural voting, can be found in the following chapters of this book.

NOTES

1. Fabienne Peter (2017) acknowledges three accounts addressing the source of political legitimacy. First account considers consent of the governed as the primary source of political legitimacy—government can have legitimacy-generating potential only when all qualified subjects under its jurisdiction have consented (directly or indirectly) to its authority. Second account focuses on beneficial consequences and argues that, in order to have legitimacy-generating potential, government has to produce political outcomes (e.g., maximize total utility) better than the alternatives. Third account, sometimes understood as a variation of the consent account, regards public reason or democratic approval as the appropriate source of political legitimacy. Government has legitimacy-generating potential only when it makes political decisions in accordance with the constitution the essentials of which all qualified citizens can endorse. For advantages of each account, as well as their most important flaws, see Simmons (2001).

2. Another useful overview of the key positions in the debate on political legitimacy can be found in Destri (2017).

3. Richard Arneson (2003) introduces a useful distinction between two standards in instrumentalist argumentation: the correctness standard and the best results standard. This differentiation will be thoroughly addressed later in the chapter.

4. This diagram is based on Thomas Christiano's (2004, 266–268) overview of the two accounts of political legitimacy and appears in Cerovac (2016b).

5. This is built upon David Brink's (2018) interpretation. However, while Brink limits his view only on the concept of right action, I tentatively extend it to political legitimacy.

6. Dale Miller usefully characterizes these two criteria as "educative" and "effective" (Miller 2010, 171).

7. These examples are first presented by Fabienne Peter (2017) and later elaborated in Stevenson (2016) and Cerovac (2016b, 2020).

8. Mill believes that, in order to be suitable for a group of people, a form of government has to meet three criteria. It has to be such that the people it is applied upon (i) would be willing to receive it, (ii) would be willing and able to do what is necessary for its preservation, and (iii) would be willing and able to fulfil duties which it imposes on them (Mill 1977a, 413). Democratic government in barbaric nations would thus produce worse results than a form of "kingly government, free from the control (though perhaps strengthened by the support) of representative institutions" (Mill 1977a, 418).

9. The idea that all governments should strive towards this desired end (to promote the common interests of the humanity) opens the terrain for cosmopolitan interpretations of Mill's political thought. For more information on this account see Varouxakis (2008).

10. When Mill discusses moral and intellectual development of citizens' capacities as one of the criteria of good government, he seems to imply that, at least sometimes, improvement of human capacities can be means to some other end (e.g., justice). He thus asks, "of what efficacy are rules of procedure in securing *the ends of justice,*

if the moral condition of the people is such that the witnesses generally lie, and the judges and their subordinates take bribes?" (Mill 1861, 28, emphasis added). Having just or correct decisions here takes the role of a desired end, and moral and intellectual development of citizens' capacities is (along with rules of procedure) just a means for reaching the desired end.

11. Of course, Estlund (1997, 2008) presents a non-monistic position and explicitly rejects the "too epistemic" standard of correctness theory. Decision-authorization procedure does not receive legitimacy-generating potential because it has the highest tendency to produce correct outcomes (according to some procedure-independent standard), but because it represents the procedure all qualified citizens could endorse, i.e., the procedure whose epistemic qualities can be recognized and affirmed by all qualified citizens. However, when he assesses the quality of a decision-authorization procedure, Estlund seems to focus on its direct results (laws, policies and decisions), and not on the long-term outcomes that such procedure could produce in a society.

12. This, of course, does not answer how would Mill resolve McCloskey's dilemma. It only indicates that, for Mill, the correctness of any political decision ultimately depends on the quality of its results.

13. Of course, this does not imply that Mill wanted to consolidate such situation of inequality. Disenfranchisement of uneducated citizens was only a temporary measure, one that should be combined with publicly funded education and civic participation available to all citizens (Mackie 2012, 298).

14. Mill also indicates that "a people of savages should be taught obedience, but not in such a manner as to convert them into a people of slaves" (Mill 1861, 40–41). This would preclude the development of some of their capacities (intelligence, self-control, prudence) and make such people "unfit for the step next beyond."

15. Many scholars have focused on Mill's thoughts regarding the role of benevolent despot in the colonial era. This book does not advance in that direction. For more information on this topic see Sullivan (1983), Kurfirst (1996), Holmes (2007), Urbinati (2007) and Bell (2010), and for some contemporary applications and criticisms see Lustig and Benvenisti (2014).

16. This has a form similar to society's knowledge problem (Hayek 2012a, 2012b), where the knowledge is dispersed throughout the political community, but is also subjective in nature and held individually and tacitly, making it impossible for any individual to have all the relevant knowledge. Though there are some similarities, Mill clearly holds that collective deliberation and collective decision-authorization procedures can help us alleviate this problem. In fact, he believes that public deliberation can help us not only to select the best solution from the predefined set of solutions, but also to construct new solutions and new perspectives. For a detailed analysis of Hayek's approach see Tebble (2016), and for additional information on Mill see Cerovac (2018).

17. Even this might be brought in question: while a bad despot, once all his needs and desires have been met, might sometimes let people focus on their own affairs, a good despot will act with paternalist tendencies and try to help citizens manage their own affairs, thus infringing their liberties even more (Mill 1977a, 410).

18. This by no means implies that knowledge is dispersed equally among all citizens. Mill believes some individuals (and even some social groups, like the educated) can know what should be done better than others and should thus have greater political influence in decision-authorization procedures (plural voting proposal). Nonetheless, Mill is adamant in claiming that even those who know less still have some useful knowledge and their input in collective deliberation is epistemically valuable, so they should have some (albeit smaller) political influence in decision-authorization procedures. For more information see Mill (1977a, 473–474), and for some interpretations see Estlund (2003) and Cerovac (2020). Also, plural voting proposal is discussed in detail in the following chapters of this book.

19. For an alternative reading, see Thompson (1976, 19). However, this is not a very important distinction since Thompson agrees that, according to Mill, government and society usually do not know better than the individual what is in his interest. Thompson just emphasizes that Mill acknowledges individual's fallibility with regard to his own interests.

20. Some exceptions are allowed, including the disenfranchisement of uneducated citizens, but only temporarily and only to prevent greater evils.

21. There is an interesting debate on whether, for Mill, the improvement of citizen's character is intrinsically or instrumentally valuable. One might argue that the improvement of individuals' moral and intellectual capacities is never intrinsically valuable. Namely, even when individual improvement is examined independently of its effects on the quality of political decisions, it still seems it does not represent the final end in Mill's utilitarian moral theory. The development of our capacities is instrumentally valuable since it represents a valuable means for acquiring happiness, characterized as sensation or experience of higher pleasures (Macleod 2016). Of course, the more our intellectual and moral capacities are developed, the more will we be able to experience and enjoy higher pleasures. This interpretation builds upon Mill claim that "happiness is the sole end of human action," uttered on several occasions in *Utilitarianism* (Mill 1985a). Alternative interpretations build upon his essay *On Liberty* (Mill 1977d) and claim that, for Mill, the ultimate end are not sensations or experiences of higher pleasures, but instead human flourishing realized through development of one's character (Nussbaum 2004, Brink 2013). Though this is an interesting and important debate, it does not affect the central points of this book. It suffices to say that, for Mill, the improvement of human capacities was valuable not only because of its positive impact on the quality of political outcomes.

22. There are two confusing (and seemingly incompatible) attributes Mill ascribes to the Parliament. First it the elitist qualification: Mill considers Parliament as an institution containing "the elite of the nation" (Mill 1977c, 362) in a form of "some of the most distinguished man in the country." This clearly sets political representatives apart from the citizens—members of the Parliament are better (both in moral and epistemic sense) than regular citizens. Second is the democratic qualification: Mill sees Parliament as "a fair sample of every grade of intellect among the people," rather than as "a selection of greatest political minds in the country" (Mill 1977a, 433). This claim, on the other hand, seems to imply that political representatives are no more qualified to rule than the average citizens. Both claims are important for

Mill's political thought, and their incompatibility is only apparent. The first (elitist) claim refers to the difference between representatives and citizens. Members of the Parliament are here indeed qualified as more competent, but not due to some particular expert knowledge, but due to their epistemic and moral virtues. They are considered "more competent in the *general affairs of life*" (Mill 1977b, 324, emphasis added). The second (democratic) claim refers to the difference between political representatives and experts in the executive government, the latter often called "individuals specially trained to . . . govern and legislate" (Mill 1977a, 433). Mill is here referring to the technical and not to the moral knowledge. For a detailed distinction between these two forms of knowledge see Christiano (2008) and Prijić-Samaržija (2011). Mill claims that representatives hold (or should hold) greater moral knowledge than their constituencies, and ministers and executive government officials hold (or should hold) greater technical knowledge than political representatives.

23. For more information on vice epistemology see Cassam (2016) and Kidd, Battaly and Cassam (2020).

24. Bentham believes there are several variables that determine the degree or amount of pleasure that a specific action is likely to cause. Leaving any variable outside of our utility calculus might point us toward choosing a suboptimal action, one that does not maximize our total long-term well-being (Bentham 1907, see also Timmons 2013). For example, we may end up endorsing an action that might produce the utility of greatest intensity and duration but fail to realize that the probability that such action will result in this particular outcome is negligible, while some alternative action might be accompanied by the result that is far more probable and only a bit less intense and durable. Put in the context of early nineteenth-century England, Jeremy Bentham and James Mill feared that many workers would, given franchise, make this mistake in the utility calculus and vote for extremely egalitarian distributive laws and policies, thus temporarily increasing their level of well-being but simultaneously ruining the economy and producing the loss in total utility in the long run.

25. These specific individual or group interests are interests people have apart from "the permanent interest of man as a progressive being" (Mill 1977d, 224), one that characterizes and constitutes Mill's moral (utilitarian) philosophy.

26. Of course, Mill is aware that deliberation will not be able to solve every political conflict, and public deliberation will often have to be followed by some voting procedure (Mill 1977a, see also Holmes 1995). However, he is convinced that post-deliberation voting is (as a decision-making or decision-authorization mechanisms) epistemically far superior to pre-deliberation voting.

Chapter 4

Political Representation and Filtering Mechanisms

Previous chapters introduced beneficial consequences as a common goal and a regulative ideal against which different decision-making procedures and models of government are evaluated (Mill 1977a, 404). Since the consequences are considered substantively good or bad based on the effects they have on "actual, positive well-being of the living human creatures who compose the population" (Mill 1988c, 67), regardless of the procedure that had produced them, and since our evaluation of decision-making procedures is based on the results they produce (and not the other way around), I have characterized Mill as a political instrumentalist. Furthermore, since Mill measures the procedure's capacity to produce beneficial consequences through its capacity to foster and encourage citizens' moral and intellectual (self)-improvement and its capacity to produce efficient, correct or just decisions (Mill 1977a, 390–392), I have characterized him as an early epistemic instrumentalist. Finally, since Mill considers democracy to be the best form of government,[1] one that (when properly exercised) has the capacity to produce the most beneficial consequences, I have characterized his as an early epistemic democrat.[2]

Democracy can take many forms and there are numerous issues on which democrats disagree. Who should be allowed to participate in a collective decision-making or decision-authorization process? Should there be some formal filters that disqualify some people from political participation? Should political decisions be made directly by the people or should they be made by citizens' political representatives? If the latter is the case, should political representatives act as delegates (or trustees) or as advocates? How (in)dependent should they be? Should decisions be made using an aggregative mechanism or through public deliberation? Should citizens (regardless of whether they vote for their representatives or for a particular political decision) cast their votes in secrecy or under the scrutiny of public? Mill had a clear stance on all of these questions, and his reasoning was guided by a simple principle we have already discussed—beneficial consequences. He gives comprehensive instrumental and epistemic arguments for his stance on these and many other relevant issues, and this chapter traces and analyses Mill's arguments to re-affirm his characterization as an early epistemic democrat.

Innovative aspects of this chapter regard thorough analysis of Mill's filtering mechanisms and his argument for the epistemic value of indirectness. The chapter thus allows us to see how epistemic considerations shape Mill's view of a proper democratic procedure. Furthermore, it motivates us to consider other filtering mechanisms and democratic innovations (e.g., mini-publics), those more appropriate for contemporary political practice, which can help improve the epistemic qualities of a democratic decision-making process.

The chapter is divided in two parts. The *first* part introduces differentiation between direct and indirect democracy. Having in mind the dangers introduced by the majority rule (low political intellect and class legislation, both of which can endanger the quality of political decisions and the improvement of citizens' capacities), Mill opts for indirect forms of democratic government, those where *talking* is separated (both spatially and temporally) from *doing* (Urbinati 2000). Political representation plays an important role in this since it removes both the deliberative[3] and the executive function from citizens, transferring these functions, in accordance with the division of epistemic labor, to the parliament and the expert commissions of executive government. This does not imply that citizens are left with no political influence between the elections. They can still shape both the public deliberation and the creation of laws, policies and decisions. Yet, their influence is indirect and comes from the informal political sphere. The *second* part addresses some of the many formal filters for the creation of the public will and mechanisms for democratic self-control, including public balloting, advocacy as a model of political representation, division of labor between the parliament and expert commissions, as well as the limited autonomy of local government. Plural voting proposal, another formal filter and an important mechanism of democratic self-control, will not be discussed here yet will be extensively addressed in the next two chapters. Similarly, partisan associations, which can also help filter public will and shape democratic deliberation, are not discussed here. Their epistemic value and their role as a filtering mechanism are analyzed in one of the upcoming chapters.

THE EPISTEMIC VALUE OF INDIRECTNESS

Democracy, typically understood as "government of the people, by the people and for the people" (Lincoln 2000), usually entails the idea that all citizens participate in the collective decision-making process as equals. Direct democracy, where citizens directly participate in decision-making processes (including both deliberation and voting on the final decision), is thus often understood as a realization of citizens' autonomy and self-government. Political representation, which turns to be a necessity for modern societies (Constant 1993), is on the other hand often seen as a necessary evil, an instrument needed for organization of political life in modern states which extend over large territories and gather citizens of different cultural backgrounds (Pitkin 1967). It is "evil" since representation, especially its neo-Schumpeterian model,[4] promotes passive citizenry and divides people in two groups: those who are fit to rule (a small elite) and those who are not (the majority) (Ranciere 1998, see also Cerovac 2014). But although procedures and mechanisms that make collective decision-making less direct by introducing a (temporal or spatial) gap between deliberation, voting and political action are sometimes considered harmful (since they seem to weaken citizens' self-governance), they can have considerable epistemic value. They can help us remove dangers of low political intellect and class legislation that come along with democratic rule. Mill was aware of the epistemic advantages of indirect rule but shared some concerns regarding passivity of citizens and firmly rejected the Schumpeterian model of democracy. This part of the chapter discusses the epistemic value of indirectness in Mill's political thought by focusing on his arguments for proportional representation.[5]

The previous part of this chapter establishes the epistemic value of deliberative democracy in Mill's political thought. It reconstructs Mill's justification of two important claims: first, democracy is epistemically superior to alternative forms of government (e.g., despotism), and second, deliberative democracy is epistemically superior to aggregative democracy. But how does indirectness improve both the epistemic qualities of a democratic decision-making and decision-authorization process and the epistemic qualities of collective deliberation? How indirectness helps create better (more correct, efficient or just) policies and decisions, and how it helps improve the intellectual and moral qualities of citizens?

Direct democracy, particularly in ancient republics, was characterized by "direct and physical presence of citizens in the place where decisions were made" (Urbinati 2000, 762). All citizens were allowed to participate in the assembly by voting on proposals or speaking to the public. However, this does not imply that all (or even the majority of them) exercised these rights. Hansen (1993, 268, also Urbinati 2000, 762–763) distinguishes between three kinds of citizens in Athens. According to him, there are *passive* participants, who do not go to the assembly meetings and neither speak nor vote on matters of public interest. *Standing* participants participate in the meetings, listen what others have to say and vote on what they consider to be the best proposal, but never address the assembly with their own opinions and arguments. Then, there are *wholly active* participants who regularly address issues of public concern, argue in favor of or against existing proposals even and propose new ones to the assembly. When compared to modern democracies, passive citizens would correspond to those who abstain from voting in the elections, standing citizens would be those who exercise their right to vote, while wholly active citizens would be political representatives, those who participate in parliamentary debates. One of the key differences, however, lies in the role of standing participants, who in modern democracies no longer vote on every law, policy or political decision, but instead exercise this right every few years. While in ancient republics decision-making and decision-authorization processes were merged and are both conducted by a single political body, in modern democracies these processes are separated. Citizens no longer directly participate in the decision-making processes in the formal political sphere, but instead periodically participate in the authorization of laws, policies and decisions by voting in the elections. Mill holds that the indirectness thus introduced produces several epistemic advantages.

Indirectness Introduces Competence in Politics

Mill held that the quality of deliberation, but also the quality of laws, policies and political decisions, depend on the moral and intellectual capacities of those included in the deliberative decision-making and decision-authorization processes (Mill 1977a, 390–392). This, of course, does not imply that only the most competent should be included in the *decision-authorization* processes (e.g., that only the most competent should be allowed to vote in the elections). It merely states that, other things being equal, a group of citizens with better developed intellectual and moral capacities will be better suited to participate in the collective decision-authorization process, and the results of this process will have a tendency to be substantively better (or more correct and just) than the results of similar processes taking place in a group whose members' capacities are not as developed (Estlund 2003). Mill does claim, however, that only the most competent should be included in *decision-making* processes (e.g., that only the most competent should draft laws or policy proposals). In order to make correct, efficient and just political decisions, people engaged in these activities need to possess specialized technical knowledge attained through extensive training and education. Most citizens will lack this specialized knowledge and will thus be unfit to participate in the decision-making processes. Mill's (1977a, 520–533) division of labor between the parliament, which deliberates and approves legislation, and the professional Commission of Codification, which creates and proposes laws to the parliament, clearly indicates that the decision-making process should be done by a few competent citizens.

But if the citizens (through elections) indirectly participate in the decision-authorization process,[6] and the experts and professionals directly participate in the decision-making process, what is the proper role of the members of a parliament? Many have stressed that they participate in the direct authorization of laws and policies (Urbinati 2000, Barker 2015). Mill seems to claim the same when he indicates that "nothing but the restriction of the function of representative bodies within rational limits will enable the benefits of popular control to be enjoyed in conjunction with skilled administration and legislation." This can be achieved by "disjoining the office of control and criticism from the actual conduct of affairs, and devolving the former on the representatives of the Many, while securing for the latter the acquired knowledge and practiced intelligence of a specially trained and experienced Few" (Mill 1861, 106–107). The parliament should not try to directly participate in the decision-making process as it is unfit for this demanding role. However, there are reasons to believe that Mill did place indirect decision-making role on the representative body, as its role is not only to approve or decline legislation, but also to deliberate on laws and policies, giving the experts in decision-making commissions access to new perspectives, as well as new reasons and arguments (Cerovac 2016b). Mill indicates that the parliament should not directly "interfere with [such expert commissions], *except by unlimited latitude of suggestion and criticism*" (Mill 1861, 106, emphasis added). This is again emphasized when Mill (1861, 97, emphasis added) argues that "a numerous assembly is [not] fitted for the *direct* business of legislation [and administration]." Parliament therefore has a dual role: it directly participates in the decision-authorization process (by approving or declining legislation), but also indirectly participates in the decision-making process (by providing suggestions and criticism on legislation). While the former role is clearly more important and Mill emphasizes it more urgently, the latter role should not be neglected.[7]

Accordingly, the members of the parliament have a dual role as well. Their intellectual and moral capacities reflect on the quality of both the decision-authorization and the decision-making process. While proportionality enables all relevant perspectives and ideas to be included in the deliberative process,[8] representation ensures that these ideas are argued and defended by their most capable proponents. Mill (1861, 104) indicates that political representation enables every person to find "somebody who speaks his mind, as well or better than he could speak it himself." Therefore, representation structures and filters public deliberation by ensuring that only the most capable citizens (or those recognized as such and elected by the people) participate in public discussions in the formal political sphere.

Table 4.1 Political Participation

	Indirect participation	Direct participation
Decision-authorization process	Citizens *(by voting in the elections)*	Members of the parliament *(by voting in the parliament)*
Decision-making process	Members of the parliament *(by deliberating and providing suggestions and criticism)* Citizens *(by participating in the informal political sphere)*	Experts and professionals *(by drafting laws and policy proposals)*

Source: Author created.

Furthermore, it filters and improves formal decision-authorization process by enabling only the most capable citizens (or those recognized as such and elected by the people) to participate in approving or rejecting legislation by voting in the parliament. Though members of the parliament are not required to have extensive technical knowledge (which is, in turn, a requirement for executives and professionals in the administration), they are expected to have greater moral knowledge than average citizens (Mill 1977b, 324). In other words, they should be better suited to deliberate on various issues of public interest, to critically engage different perspectives of the public good, to offer good reasons and arguments in support of their own views, to negotiate and make compromises, but also to recognize better arguments and revise their own views in light of better reasons.

Following Mill's political thought, representative democracy does not improve the quality of political decisions by enabling experts and professionals to make these decisions instead of citizens who lack specialized and technical knowledge. This type of division of political and epistemic labor is compatible with direct democracy as well. For example, Rousseau (1977, see also Urbinati 2000) suggests a model of direct democracy where political action is performed by chosen magistrates. They are elected by the people as instruments for political action, and only they participate directly in the decision-making process. These decisions are, just like magistrates' autonomy, quite limited and technical in nature. Political reasoning and will-formation are, on the other hand, performed by the citizens themselves, without any representatives acting as a buffer between the executive government and the sovereign (i.e., the people). Citizens thus directly participate in the formal decision-authorization process, but also indirectly in the formal decision-making process, since they set political aims that particular decisions (made by elected magistrates) have to serve. Mill's model of representative democracy introduces competence in the direct decision-authorization process, as well as in the indirect decision-making process, both in the formal political sphere. Political representatives replace the role of citizens (and not experts and professionals) in approving the decisions made by the magistrates, as well as in setting the aims the society is to pursue.[8] Since representatives (on average) have better developed moral and intellectual competences that average citizens, they are able to improve both the quality of direct decision-authorization process and the quality of the indirect decision-making process.

Indirectness Enables Better (Re)Presentation of Relevant Ideas and Opinions

Direct democracy sets high demands both on citizens' competences and their resources. Even in ancient Athens most of the citizens were passive and did not participate in assembly meetings (Hansen 1999, Thorley 2005), and among those who did participate, only a few "masters of the art of rhetoric" (Urbinati 2000, 764) actually debated on issues of public interest. Most of the standing participants did not think that they are competent enough to speak to the assembly, limiting their influence to voting only. Furthermore, many of the citizens avoided assembly meetings due to financial reasons, so standing participation was (unsuccessfully) encouraged by paying a daily salary to citizens who participated in the meetings. These measures, in addition to being inefficient, are also inapplicable to modern democracies (Constant 1993). Trying to copy the ancient model to mid-Victorian England would introduce two serious threats: first, some groups (or classes) of citizens would lack the relevant skills to properly voice and argue in favor of their opinions, and second, some groups (or classes) of citizens would, due to the poor financial situation, be unable to participate in the assembly meetings. In both cases, an epistemically valuable perspective would be lost,[9] and public deliberation would be unable to profit from epistemically fertile political agonism.

Mill had this in mind when he proposed his account of indirect (representative) democracy and tried to account for these dangers by modifying his theory of representation. Some believe that Mill proposes a descriptive model of representation (Miller 1999), where 'assembly should reproduce the demographics of the nation' (Dalaqua 2018b, 114) and where the representative must be a member of a political group he represents. This model of representation, however, would be unable to alleviate the problem of poor representation of some classes and social groups. I follow an alternative interpretation. For Mill, being represented means having your voice in the representative assembly, not having your copy there (Dworkin 1988, Urbinati 2000). This means that a member of one class, gender or ethnic, cultural, social or religious minority group can represent electors from another class, gender or group in the parliament. Mill develops this idea first when he supports Hare's system and indicates that some minorities can be represented by members of parliament elected from other boroughs (Mill 1977b, 329–330). He later discusses optimal representation for laborers' opinions and perspectives concluding that members of wealthier classes might be better suited to represent the working class in the parliament (Mill 1977a, 401). Namely, members of one group can understand demands, interests and opinions of those belonging to another group, and can sometimes even represent and defend these opinions better in the deliberative assembly (Dalaqua 2018b, 114). Of course, this does not imply that representatives, especially those coming from a class different than the one of most of their constituencies, can instantly know what the demands, interests and opinions of the people they represent are. For Mill, democratic representation requires continuous interaction between representatives and their constituencies (Dalaqua 2018a, 6).

In his discussion with Austin (2015), Mill (1977c, 346) ends up agreeing with the conservative author[10] that statesmanship is an art and that only those who devote themselves to it can acquire necessary competences for proper rule. Austin (2015) notices that, while electors are a democratic body, the elected are mostly, in personal and social sense, aristocratic.[11] Mill (1977c) endorses this as both a descriptive and a normative claim—there is nothing wrong if members of the parliament have skills and competences (as well as the virtues of character) that exceed those of the people they represent. In fact, the previous part of this chapter explains how representation introduces competence in democratic politics. However, this part demonstrates how representation can also improve the way opinions and perspectives of some classes are presented and defended in the parliament.[12] Finally, it is important to emphasize that for Mill "aristocratic" does not refer to one's family background or financial status, but to one's skills and competences developed through (both formal and informal) education and training, which should be available to all citizens (Mill 1977d, 302, see also Barker 2015, 1150).

Indirectness Enables Better Interaction Between Experts and Citizens

In the earlier parts of this chapter, I hinted that, for Mill, members of the parliament participate not only in the decision-authorization process, but also indirectly shape laws, policies and political decisions. However, since they lack relevant technical knowledge, they have to be advised by the experts, either from non-governmental (partisan associations can be quite useful here, as indicated in one of the following chapters) organizations or from the government itself. Furthermore, as indicated earlier, Mill understood political decision-making as a bidirectional process. Political deliberation in the parliament establishes political principles and common interests which serve as basic guidelines for public administration which drafts laws, policies and decisions. These are then presented in the parliament and, unless they are approved, are returned to public administration for revision and improvement. The process of mutual coordination can go wrong in two ways. First, experts and professionals in public administration can misunderstand the political principles (or their comparative importance) that particular laws, policies and decisions should be based upon. Second, political representatives can misunderstand the reasons and arguments supporting the laws, policies and decisions drafted by public administration and sent to the parliament for approval. Thus, a particular law or policy can be based on a political principle that the parliament affirms, yet (due to lack of technical knowledge) members of the parliament are unable to see that.

Though these two dangers cannot be avoided, they can be remedied by continuous coordination between the parliament and the executive government. Mill (1861, 100) argued that this can be partially remedied "by allowing the Government to be represented in either House by persons in its confidence, having a right to speak, though not to vote." These professionals would be better suited than ministers or members of parliament to present and defend the law or policy in question, since they would know the full strength of their case and the best reasons by which to support it meaning that they would be "wholly capable of meeting unforeseen objections" (Mill 1977a, 429–430). The indirect character of representative democracy, with parliament consisting of a few hundred members,[13] enables this form of continuous coordination. Members of the parliament can discuss proposals of laws and policies among themselves, but also with the experts and professionals from public administration. Furthermore, when needed, they can acquire limited technical knowledge, as well as consultants and advisors who can help them understand the proposal in question and evaluate its merits. Mill reminds us that a minister in the executive government, just like any member of the parliament, 'may be a good politician, and a man of merit. . . . But his general capacity, and the knowledge he ought to possess of the general interests of the country, will not, unless by occasional accident, be accompanied by adequate, and what may be called professional, knowledge. . . . Professional advisers[14] must therefore be provided for him' (Mill 1861, 252–253). Though political representatives lack technical knowledge, they can (through the consultation process with relevant experts) acquire sufficient competences to understand the proposal in question and to competently deliberate on it. Since they can acquire these minimal technical competences, but also have good understanding of opinions, interests and perspectives of their constituencies, they can provide valuable feedback and give quality recommendations and suggestions to public administration and executive government. This is not an option in direct democracies, where all citizens directly participate in the decision-authorization process and indirectly in the decision-making process.

It is impossible to ensure that all citizens can properly understand the proposals in questions (since it is impossible to provide each and every citizen with minimal technical competences). Furthermore, since they might lack the proper understanding of the laws and policies in questions, citizens' feedback will be less useful and might even reduce the epistemic quality of thus revised laws and policies.[15]

In conclusion, Mill holds that, in order to produce epistemically the best laws, public policies and political decisions, we need continuous coordination between citizens (or their representatives), experts and professionals in public administration and executive government. Since the citizens lack relevant technical knowledge (but also the access to it), direct democracy precludes epistemically fertile coordination with experts and professionals. Indirect (representative) democracy, on the other hand, enables political representatives to acquire relevant competences (or advisors and consultants on technical matters), thus facilitating better coordination between citizens (i.e., their representatives) and the experts.

Indirectness Fosters the Educative Role of Democracy

Mill indicates on numerous occasions that a more popular basis of government is needed for two reasons: to help us create better laws and policies, and to help improve the moral and intellectual capacities of citizens. We develop and improve our capacities when we use them, and though private affairs might to a small degree improve them, it is in public affairs that we exercise and train our capacities the most. The political system has to be organized to foster participation and exercise the best possible influence on an individual's character (Mill 1977a, 406). Mill thus sees practical political activity of individual citizens as "one of the most efficient means of training the societal feeling and practical intelligence of the people" (Mill 1977e, 168–169). This would suggest that direct democracy, where citizens participate in both decision-authorization and decision-making processes in the formal political sphere, would be superior to indirect democracy, at least with regard to its educative role. Chris Barker (2015) seems to follow this conclusion but emphasizes that Mill still prefers indirectness due to its beneficial effect on the quality of political decisions. Barker (2015, 1162) writes that, for Mill, "direct political education is too dangerous for liberty" and continues to argue that "[Mill] degrades public participation by lacking trust in the wisdom of the people." Education through participation is in conflict with the quality of political decisions produced by the competent few, and though Mill still holds that education is important, he ends up favoring competence.

This interpretation has a lot of merit. It explains why Mill still holds that every citizen should, at least occasionally, be called to take an actual part in the government by the personal discharge of some function (Urbinati 2000, 78), yet still limits this function mostly to the local level, jury service and parish duties. Local politics is where citizens have the opportunity to become active and improve their capacities, as well as develop public spirit and intelligence. Mill thus indicates that the local government is the "chief instrument of public education" (Mill 1861, 275). However, political participation of most citizens is limited to the local level since this guarantees that ignorance and lack of virtue will not significantly infringe upon liberties of other citizens. This is how Mill reconciles the principles of participation and competence (Thompson 1976).

Although this interpretation explains why Mill, despite advocating the importance of direct participation in politics for public education of citizens favors indirect over direct democracy, I believe an additional argument can be made, one that appeals to education alone. Of course, this argument is an addition to the previous interpretation, not a replacement of it. When Mill discusses the educative effect of political participation, he emphasizes that it is not derived from autonomous action (Kurer 1989, 298). Simply allowing or even encouraging the citizens to participate in political decision-making processes, without any additional educative mechanisms that would enable them to learn and improve their capacities, would be "a poor education that associates ignorance with ignorance" (Mill 1861, 293). Instead, we need "the means of making ignorance aware of itself, and able to profit by knowledge" (Mill 1861, 280–281). When we desire a good school, we "do not eliminate the teacher."

Who, then, is the teacher? Mill is obviously not writing about technical knowledge, one that can be acquired at schools and universities, but about moral knowledge. While it is rather easy to identify institutions that acquire and disseminate technical knowledge, what kind of institution could acquire and disseminate moral knowledge? For Mill, this institution is the parliament (Urbinati 2002, 42–122, Selinger 2019, 188). During the parliamentary debates, citizens can learn about different reasons and arguments (many of which they were unaware of) supporting their own opinions, as well as other opinions conflicting with their own. Furthermore, this conflict and struggle between opposing perspectives can construct new ideas, beliefs and opinions that change how citizens reason and think about public issues (Cohen 2009). In his discussion with Austin (2015), Mill (2077c, 348) writes that the parliament, beside making laws, has another important function, and that is "maturing and enlightening the public opinion itself." Its role is not merely to approve laws and appoint decision-makers, but also to introduce, discuss and support new ideas that should, but at present cannot, be realized (e.g., suffrage for women). Parliament can thus mobilize new constituencies (Dalaqua 2018a) and influence debates in the informal political sphere. For these reasons Mill (1977c, 348, emphasis added) highlights that, "besides being an instrument of government, Parliament is *a grand institution of national education*, creating and correcting the public opinion whose mandates it is required to obey." This function can only be carried out by a representative body within the framework of indirect democracy. Without the parliament (or a similar representative assembly that gathers citizens with above-average moral capacities who simultaneously defend and represent conflicting ideas and perspectives), there would be no way to correct the public opinion.

This part of the chapter demonstrated four ways how indirectness can help improve both the epistemic quality of political decisions and the moral and epistemic capacities of citizens. Along with epistemically beneficial effects of the temporal and spatial gap between the moment of deliberation and the moment of decisions, indirectness introduces competence in democratic politics by ascribing greater political influence (in various moments of decision-making and decision-authorization process) to political representatives, who are (in Mill's view) more moral and intelligent. Furthermore, indirectness enables better insight into perspectives of underprivileged groups and classes, enables better interaction between citizens (or to be more precise, their representatives) and experts, and improves and facilitates the educative role of democracy. In the next part of the chapter, I analyze several filtering mechanisms Mill recommends in order to improve the epistemic qualities of a democratic decision-making and decision-authorization process.

MILL'S EPISTEMIC JUSTIFICATION OF FILTERING MECHANISMS

Mill, especially after his split with the Radical Party (Kinzer 1981) and the start of his intellectual relationship with George Grote (Murata 2017), can be considered a political reformist (Mill 1981a). Recognizing the dangers of a political, social and economic revolution, he advocated strong political reforms adjusted for non-ideal circumstances, yet "conceived with an eye to the further changes which might be expected hereafter" (Mill 1859b, 8). Therefore, in conditions where radical measures are impossible or might at the time produce more harm than good, Mill believes that "a half-measure should be so constructed as to recognize and to embody the principles which, if no hindrance existed, would form the best foundation of a complete measure" (Mill 1859b, 8). Following his idea, although many reforms, measures and institutional mechanisms Mill advocates are designed to address the conditions existing in mid-Victorian England (and cannot be applied in contemporary democracies), we can analyze and use them to get a better understanding of the principles which they embody and promote.

Much of Mill's political though focuses on creating, justifying and defending various institutional mechanisms that serve two important functions. *First*, they have to make the existing, mid-Victorian electoral system more democratic, ensuring proportional representation that would enable opinions and ideas of previously disenfranchised classes to be heard and discussed in the representative assembly. Furthermore, they have to shape political process and make it inclusive enough to adequately improve the intellectual and moral capacities of citizens. *Second*, they have to prevent functioning democracy from deteriorating into "false" democracy, one characterized by class legislation and tyranny of the majority. Additionally, they have to ensure that democratic decision-making and decision-authorization processes, which have transferred much political influence to uneducated citizens, produce correct, efficient and just outcomes. These two functions correspond to Thompson's (1976) account, which indicates that all Mill's reforms are based on principles of participation and competence, each of which has both an educative and a protective function. However, this depiction of Mill's criteria helps us put his proposals in the context of political, social and economic conditions Mill had in mind when he developed his arguments for democracy. Political reforms thus had two goals (corresponding to the two functions indicated earlier in the paragraph): to make political institutions both inclusive and direct enough, and exclusive and indirect enough, to promote and improve democracy's ability to produce correct, efficient and just outcomes. Mill was aware that a balance has to be found between too exclusive and too inclusive procedures, since moving in either direction would reduce the epistemic quality of political decisions and produce a negative influence on citizens' minds. Too exclusive procedures (e.g., benevolent despot, epistocracy) would be unable to harness the epistemic value of political agonism since the perspectives of some classes would be excluded from public deliberation. These procedures would also encourage widespread passiveness among citizens (Mill 1977a, 414–416), which has a negative effect both on the quality of political decisions and on the development of citizens' capacities. Too inclusive (and too direct) procedures (e.g., direct democracy, "false" democracy characterized by the tyranny of the majority) would be unable to harness the epistemic contribution of competent individuals and enjoy the beneficial effects of the division of labor. These procedures would also promote irresponsible political engagement, one that would contribute neither to the quality of political decisions nor to the development of citizens moral and intellectual capacities.

Institutional mechanisms and reforms that address the problems of mid-Victorian electoral system, sometimes referred to as Originating system (Colomer 2007, 265), by making it more proportional and inclusive are addressed in the first part of this chapter. This part focuses on a few formal filters used to keep democratic procedures from becoming too inclusive and too direct. Some formal (e.g., plural voting proposal) and some informal (e.g., partisanship) filters will not be discussed here but will instead by addressed in detail in subsequent chapters.

Open Ballot

For Mill, as well as for many philosophers before him, how ballot is performed can have a significant influence on voters' mind, as well as on the subsequent quality of political decisions. Should ballot be performed in secrecy, or should one's vote be cast under public scrutiny? What are the positive and the negative effects of publicity and secrecy? How should we organize collective decision-authorization procedure to promote both the quality of laws and policies and the development of citizens' capacities?

Jeremy Bentham (1843a, 1843b) and other philosophical radicals before Mill strongly supported and argued in favor of a secret ballot (Theuns 2017, 496, see also James 1981 and Hayward 2010). They thought secrecy could be of great help in minimizing direct political power of old aristocracy and protecting popular will from the effects of money and prestige (Barker 2015). Mill recognized the merit of these arguments and agreed that secrecy can be desirable when "the motives acting on the voter through the will of others are likely to mislead him while, if left to his own preferences, he would vote as he ought" (Mill 1859b, 37). However, he also recognized that secrecy can be undesirable when "the voter's own preferences are apt to lead him wrong, but the feeling of responsibility to others may keep him right" (Mill 1859b, 37). Whether the ballot should be public or secret depends, in the end, on political, social and economic conditions in which elections take place. In an "old aristocratic state," where citizens are dependent on a few wealthy individuals, the benefits of secrecy might outweigh its harms. However, in a "democratic social state," where citizens' votes are no longer an expression of coercion, secrecy is devoid of its benefits, but its harms are present as much as always (Mill 1977a, 493, 1977b, 333).

The argument for open ballot is built upon two important premises. First, Mill (1977a, 489) claims that citizen's vote is "strictly a matter of duty." Second, he demonstrates that open ballot will help us exercise this duty better than the secret ballot. Put together, these two considerations build a duty-based argument for the open ballot. Their justification is analyzed in the next two paragraphs.

Exercising voting rights, even in indirect democracy where we elect political representatives and do not vote on particular political decisions, is a form of exercise of power over others. As indicated in earlier chapters, Mill argues that this exercise of power should be conducted by using epistemically the best procedure available.[16] Indirect democracy, characterized by plural voting and other filtering mechanisms, sometimes referred to as scholocracy (Estlund 2003, 57), is seen as such decision-authorization procedure—one with the highest probability of electing the best political representatives, and thus one with the highest probability of (indirectly) making correct decisions. However, Mill gives a duty-based argument for citizens not only to acknowledge and endorse the political authority of indirect democracy, but also (by the virtue of democracy itself) to participate in the decision-authorization procedures. Since epistemically the best decision-authorization procedure requires our political participation to function properly, and since we have a duty to exercise power over others and to limit their rights and liberties only on grounds of epistemically the best reasons and arguments, we have a duty to vote in the elections. However, this duty is far more demanding than simply voting every few years. In fact, the duty is mostly focused on how we vote (rather than whether we vote). Well-functioning democracy requires citizens not only to exercise their voting rights, but also to exercise these voting rights responsibly, promoting public instead of private or sectarian interest. Mill thus writes that each citizen should vote as if the election "depended upon himself alone" (Mill 1861, 200), and indicates that individual voter is not given the ballot "to himself for himself," but "by and for the community" (Mill 1861, 199, see also Barker 2015, 1154). Citizens should exercise their voting rights according to 'their best and most conscientious opinion of the public good,' and failure to do so represents a failure to exercise a particular duty toward others.

Institutional arrangements and voting mechanisms can help citizens exercise this duty, but they can also hinder its proper exercise. Mill believed that, in the first half of the nineteenth century, open ballot tended to hinder proper exercise of citizens' duty towards others. Under social and financial pressure (from landlords or factory owners) citizens were in danger of retribution if they voted having in mind the public interest, and not the private or sectarian interest of individuals or groups exercising social and financial power over them. Open ballot was not a desirable voting system in such conditions. When huge social and financial inequalities are in place, and when some citizens exercise financial and social power over others, secrecy can help us exercise our duty toward others. However, in different circumstances (e.g., in the second half of the nineteenth century, according to Mill), when social and financial inequalities are reduced or when they do not support power structures in which members of one group are dependent upon members of the other, secrecy might not be so desirable. Under such conditions, citizens' "self-corruption" (Mill 1977a, 491) becomes the main problem.[17] Namely, Mill thinks that citizens will give "dishonest and mean votes from malice, from personal rivalry and from the interests of a class or sect far more readily in secret than in public" (Mill 1859b, 47). For this reason, for example, the parliament practices open ballot, and no one approves secret ballot in the parliament. Namely, members of the parliament would often promote their private interests, and publicity acts as a mechanism that prevents them from promoting private instead of public interest. Similarly, publicity increases responsibility in citizens since it forces them to give account of their conduct, which gives citizens strong reasons to "adhere to conduct of which some decent account can be given" (Mill 1859b, 44). It compels deliberation and forces citizens to think what the right thing to do is, as well as how they will argue and defend their vote when called to account for their actions.

Mill's argument for open ballot can be summarized with one important quote, when Mill claims that "man's share of public interest is . . . not enough to make him do *his duty* to the public without other *external inducements*" (Mill 1859b, 45, emphasis added). Publicity of one's vote is one of these external inducements that help citizens properly exercise their duty toward others. Mill thus attempts to "look inside a black box of the voter and to control their responses through publicity" (Barker 2015, 1155). Open ballot thus helps citizens vote responsibly and take the public interest into account, as well as to resist "self-corruption" through epistemic vices (such as negligence and intellectual laziness) and private and sectarian interests. It helps citizens elect the best representatives and (indirectly) make epistemically the best (most correct, just, efficient) decisions, thus exercising their duty to only limit other citizens' rights and liberties on the grounds of best reasons and arguments. Though Mill is appealing to a distinct moral (and not epistemic) duty we have toward others (to coerce them only by what can be considered the most correct or the most just laws and policies), he emphasizes that democracy (characterized, among other things, by open ballot) is the best instrument to exercise this duty. His argument thus represents an instrumental epistemic argument for democracy in general and for open ballot in particular.

Pledges and Campaign Promises

The level of representatives' autonomy shapes and determines both the filtering quality of representation and the epistemic value of indirectness. If representatives' autonomy is too small (and citizens can decide how their representatives will argue, deliberate or vote), the filter will be too thin, and the epistemic value of indirectness will be reduced or even completely lost. Tocqueville (2000, 236) thus writes that having political representatives too dependent on the will of their constituencies is "the same thing as if the majority itself held its deliberations in the market-place." On the other hand, if representatives' autonomy is too big (and they do not answer citizens for what they say and how they vote in the parliament), the filter might be too thick, and the epistemic value of inclusiveness might be in danger. Having representatives who answer to their constituencies in no sensible way will resemble a form of oligarchy and the beneficial effects of democratic control will be lost.

Mill's account of advocacy entails two components: representative's passionate link to the electors' cause, and representative's relative autonomy of judgment (Urbinati 2000, 733). While the first injects conflict and a "spirit of controversy" in political deliberation, the second directs political processes toward decisions. The former introduces a form of democratic control (i.e., when electors recognize that a representative no longer shares their cause, they can vote for someone else in the next elections) while the latter introduces competence in the decision-making process (i.e., enables representatives to use their superior competences and form opinions different from those held by their constituencies). Just like in many other cases, Mill holds that a proper balance has to be struck—balance that will enable us to enjoy both the epistemic benefits of indirectness and the epistemic benefits of democratic control.

How should this balance, according to Mill, be achieved? Hanna Pitkin's reading, in which she compares representative's role in Burke's and Mill's political though, can lead us to a wrong conclusion. Pitkin argues that, for Mill, political representatives are not superior in wisdom or other moral and intellectual capacities to their constituencies. Furthermore, she argues that, following Mill's theory of representation, members of parliament should represent and promote personal or local interests of their constituencies, acting as agents whose political actions are fully dependent on the will of citizens who voted for them (Pitkin 1969, 21, see also Urdanoz 2019, 9–10). The first two claims are discussed and rejected in other parts of the book[18]: Mill, in fact, held that political representatives should be superior in wisdom to their constituencies (but not necessarily in technical knowledge), and argued they should represent citizens' ideas and perspectives with regard to general interest, and not citizens personal or sectarian interests. Third claim, one regarding the full dependence of political representatives on the will of their constituencies, seems just as wrong as the other two. Mill emphasizes that full deference of elected officials to the will of the voters is the "one and only danger of democracy" (Mill 1977f, 74, see also 1977a, 511).

There are (at least) three sets of arguments Mill uses in favor of the greater autonomy of political representatives. They also help us understand how exactly the balance between indirectness and democratic control should be established. Finally, though only the first set of arguments directly addresses the quality of political decisions, all three are needed to keep the democratic system in an epistemically favorable state, i.e., in a state that enables the production of correct laws and policies, as well as the development of citizens' capabilities.

First, as argued earlier in this chapter, Mill believes that some citizens are more qualified to rule than others. Competences they have acquired through education, training and experience affect their ability to participate in the decision-making and decision-authorization processes. Furthermore, indirect democracy enables some citizens to deliberate in epistemically favorable conditions (e.g., in the parliament), devoting more time and energy to public matters than an average citizen. Finally, some citizens will have access to partisan associations and other organizations in the informal political sphere that will give them better access to experts in various fields and enable them to develop better and stronger arguments. Indirect (representative) democracy is epistemically superior to direct democracy because it enables better use of citizens' (representatives') moral and intellectual qualities, as well as better use of epistemic conditions in which formal political deliberation takes place. Pledges and campaign promises remove the epistemic benefits of indirectness by binding the "views of professional stateman to those of the amateur" (Mill 1982b, see also Barker 2015, 1156). There is no place for the division of epistemic and political labor when all public decisions simply reflect the direct will of the citizens. To properly harness the epistemic benefits of indirectness (and the division of labor), political representatives should enjoy a relatively high level of autonomy. Of course, they should be responsible to their electors, deliberate and vote to promote the general interest, approaching it from the perspective of their constituencies. At the end of their turn, citizens will be able to assess their work and (formally) give them another turn of remove them from the parliament (1977a, 501–503). Of course, citizens will (and should) also be able to communicate their opinions and influence the representative's opinion in the informal political sphere, through media or public rallies (Mill 1977a, 535). Nonetheless, indirectness is preserved because there is no formal mechanism to shape the representative's opinion in accordance with the will of his electors. Democratic control is preserved as well since citizens evaluate representative's work at the end of his term, and participation in the informal political sphere enables them to influence the representative's opinion with good reasons and arguments, but not to coerce him or to ask him to endorse their will.

Second, Mill believes that political representatives' greater autonomy will enable them to resist sectarian interests of their constituencies (Mill 1977b, 318–320). In a delegate system, where political representatives hold minimal autonomy and have mandate only to convey the direct will of their electors, the political arena becomes a battleground of various conflicting (private and sectarian) interests. Political representatives are discouraged from deliberating and acting for the common good of the nation, but are instead urged to argue and vote in favor of their electors' sectarian interests, making strategic compromises with representatives from other groups not because such compromises are in the real interest of the entire population, but because they facilitate the achievement of their sectarian goals. This can weaken the perceived legitimacy of democratic procedures since the minorities will no longer have a reason to endorse a decision (one they substantively disagree with) because it was produced by epistemically the best procedure. Namely, under such conditions, democracy will be epistemically adequate only to determine what is in the interest of the majority, and not what is in the interest of the entire population. For these reasons Mill indicates that political representatives should judge the conditions of their constituencies taking into account the real interest of the whole country (Mill 1977a, see also Urbinati 2000, 777). Political representatives can do so only when their autonomy is guaranteed, and when they can deliberate and vote without having to defer to the will of their constituencies. Rejecting pledges and campaign promises thus brings important epistemic benefits: by giving representatives a greater level of autonomy and by reducing the electors' direct influence on representatives, sectarian interests can be prevented from entering the formal political sphere. Though this does not guarantee that formal politics will remain free of such influences, Mill is convinced that, by putting together this and other similar filters, such a feat can be approximated.

Third, as indicated earlier in this chapter, Mill acknowledges that the parliament has a very important educative role, even calling it "a grand institution of national education" (Mill 1977c, 348). Citizens can follow parliamentary debates and learn a lot not only about the political opinions of those who disagree with them, but also about their own views and the reasons and arguments supporting them. However, this is not all they can learn. Since citizens' representatives share a passionate link to their cause but deliberate in epistemically favorable conditions and have at least equal (and probably better) moral and intellectual competences than average voters, citizens can learn what follows from their own opinions and perspectives when these are evaluated and discussed in epistemically favorable circumstances. Pledges and campaign promises endanger this learning opportunity: if political representatives have to follow, argue and vote in favor of their electors' opinions, although these opinions are formulated under unfavorable epistemic conditions (and by citizens of average or below average capacities), then citizens cannot learn from parliamentary debates since these will simply mirror the debates in the informal sphere.

Filtering Mechanisms and Universal Suffrage

Unlike Hare, who was focused primarily on the quality of political outcomes and allowed some property requirements for the suffrage,[19] thus excluding from franchise "five out of six adult men" and leaving "most of the working class without the franchise" (Kern 1998, 169), Mill called for almost-universal suffrage. As indicated in previous chapters, Mill held that in perfect representative system "every adult human being should have the means of exercising, through the electoral suffrage, a portion of influence on the management of public affairs" (Mill 1859b, 21). However, Mill does not sacrifice the quality of political decisions for some other political value (e.g., education or participation). He offers an instrumental justification of universal suffrage and argues that disenfranchisement of any group within population (and particularly disenfranchisement of larger groups, such as the working class) can seriously undermine democratic procedure's epistemic value, i.e., its ability to produce correct, just or efficient laws and policies. Disenfranchisement of any particular group can deprive the society of an epistemically valuable perspective but can also diminish the protective role of democracy since "those who have no voice will be postponed to those who have" (Mill 1859b, 21, also Mill 1977a, 470). Furthermore, Mill argues that universal suffrage can have an important educational effect, claiming that "exercise of personal, and electoral, rights is one of the chief instruments both of moral and intellectual training of the popular mind" (Mill 1859b, 22, also Mill 1861, 164–165).

Mill does, however, allow some exceptions. These exceptions are grounded in "the prevention of greater evils" (Mill 1861, 166) and the extension of suffrage limited in this way represents another filtering mechanism of popular will. *First*, Mill calls for a minimal level of education (being able to read, write and perform the common operations of arithmetic), stressing that such minimal level of education should be "within the reach of every person," either available free of charge or cheap enough that even the poorest citizens can afford it. Disenfranchised citizens would be, under such conditions, excluded from universal suffrage not by the society, but by their own laziness (Mill 1977a, 470). Such citizens are unable to contribute and improve the epistemic quality of collective decision-authorization procedures, and their political participation will not have the desired educational effect on their minds. It seems that, though the minimal education criterion addresses citizens' intellectual capacities, Mill is actually using it to assess citizens' moral capacities. While lacking some basic intellectual competences (like being able to read and write) can significantly reduce one's epistemic contribution (and make one more prone to vote for incompetent representatives),[20] lack of such competences in the conditions where one could have easily acquired them points in another direction and indicates a serious moral flaw in one's character. Mill thus believes that citizens who lack the desire to improve themselves neglect the "permanent interests of man as a progressive being" (Mill 1859a, 24), and as such are not fit to exercise any influence on the management of public affairs. The more stressing problem is thus not their lack of basic intellectual competences, but their lack of "the commonest and most essential requisites for taking care of themselves; for pursuing intelligently their own interests, and those of the persons most nearly allied to them" (Mill 1861, 166). Furthermore, since such citizens have already expressed their disinterest in education and self-improvement, their political participation would have negligible educational effect. In fact, Mill held that disenfranchisement of citizens lacking minimal education, combined with the plural voting proposal, represent important preconditions democracy needs to fulfil its educative role (Miller 2003). Of course, Mill argues that everyone should get the chance to acquire education—this is primarily a duty parents have towards their children, and when parents cannot fund their children's education, the state should subsidize the cost (Mill 1965a, 947–950, see also Ryan 2011, 661–662). In the end, only those who have willingly decided not to get any education will be disenfranchised.

Second, Mill holds that citizens who pay no (direct) taxes should be excluded from franchise, as well as those receiving parish relief.[21] As before, these exclusions are not permanent and citizens can acquire franchise by starting to pay their (direct) taxes, by keeping clear of poor relief and by paying all their debts in time. Mill insists that these conditions should be such that all citizens "ought to be able to fulfil [them] if they choose [to]" (Mill 1861, 171). Again, unlike Hare, Mill wants to extend suffrage to almost all adult citizens, excluding only those who, by their own free will, have not acquired minimal level of education or are unable to provide for themselves.[22] While some might argue that this argument is based in justice or reciprocity (e.g., only those who pay the taxes should have some influence in the decision-making process on how money thus accumulated will be spent), I believe this criterion is grounded in the desire to improve the quality of democratic decisions. First, Mill argues that not paying taxes while still deciding how this money will be spent might have a bad influence on a voter's mind, giving such voter "every motive to be lavish, and none to economize" (Mill 1861, 169). Second, Mill holds that citizens who refuse to work and provide for themselves lack moral qualities needed to participate in the decision-making process that affects others since they "either do not care sufficiently for it" or are in "a general condition of depression and degradation" (Mill 1861, 170). Giving such citizens direct political influence (franchise), as well as giving it to those who have refused to acquire even the minimal level of education, represents a danger for the security of others. This danger is not (primarily) due to their lack of intellectual competences or their unfair treatment, but due to their lack of moral competences. Such citizens are not "in the normal condition of a human being" (Mill 1861, 171) since they lack the desire for their own progress and self-development. Electoral laws should thus employ filtering mechanisms that will inhibit such citizens from having a direct (and potentially harmful) political influence on others.

Third, Mill discusses whether some citizens convicted of a crime should be excluded from universal suffrage and gives a mixed answer.[23] Although some argue that Mill clearly sets criminal offenders outside the boundaries of democratic citizenship (Manza and Uggen 2004, 491, Planinc, 153–154), I believe that this does not stand for all relevant cases. On the one hand, as argued earlier in this book, Mill holds that practicing franchise can help develop citizens intellectual and moral capacities. Criminal offenders, just like all other (and perhaps even more than other) citizens, need a chance to improve these capacities, so giving them voting privileges might help in that regard. On the other hand, Mill is reluctant to give voting privileges to citizens who refuse to acquire even the minimal level of education, although it might seem that such citizens could profit from the educational function of franchise. Similar arguments can thus be used to discuss Mill's filtering mechanism concerning citizens convicted of a crime. Unlike with the citizens lacking the most basic education, Mill believes convicted felons' direct political influence (through voting) would be negligible and would not significantly affect the quality of government. However, Mill (1859b, 21) believes that depriving such citizens of voting privileges might help "giving a moral character to the exercise of suffrage" and act as a "part of the sentence," thus exercising a good influence on the minds of other citizens and reminding them that voting is a moral act that should be taken seriously. Finally, citizens convicted of serious crimes (and insane persons) might lack the ability to improve their moral capacities. In such cases, giving these citizens voting privileges will not help fulfil the educative role of political participation. However, this is the case only of citizens convicted for "crimes evincing a high degree of insensibility to social obligation" (Mill 1859b, 21). Thus, most misdemeanors and petty crimes (e.g., simple drug possession or disorderly conduct) should not disqualify one from the franchise, while most felonies and serious crimes (homicide, rape and arson) should.

Limiting the extension of suffrage is a method of filtering the public will, and while Mill, convinced of the positive impact that political participation has both on the quality of decisions and the development of citizens' moral capacities, uses it to the minimal extent, it can still be considered as one of filtering mechanisms he employs. Voting privileges can thus be denied to some citizens, provided that such disenfranchisement is necessary to prevent greater evils, such as the creation of incorrect, unjust or inefficient laws and policies on important public issues. Furthermore, voting privileges can be denied upon demonstration of a low standard of political morality, in cases where active political participation cannot be expected to have a positive influence on citizens' self-improvement and the development of their capacities.

Local Government

There is some disagreement on the role of local politics in John Stuart Mill's political thought. Should local government be free to make autonomous decisions within its jurisdiction or should it be just a simple extension of the central (national) government? Also, which areas of public life should fall under local, and which under national government? Mill himself clearly indicates the dangers of allocating too much power either to local or the central government and argues that we have to 'steer carefully between these two errors' (Mill 1981a, 203, also emphasized in Kurer 1989, 291). As in many other instances, Mill argues that a proper balance has to be achieved.

While most philosophers agree that Mill's plural voting proposal, his endorsement of Hare's voting system as well as his rejection of pledges and secret ballot constitute some of the important formal mechanisms used to limit and shape the popular will, many (Krouse 1982, Hollander 1985) believe Mill tries to compensate for these mechanisms by encouraging mass participation at the local level. After all, if competence is in the focus of national government (and can be guaranteed by these filtering mechanisms) then citizens' participation and education through participation should be in the focus of local government (which should strive to foster mass participation and avoid filtering mechanisms that limit and shape the popular will). Kurer (1989) gives a great overview of this discussion and presents some interpretations that support the earlier characterization. Krouse (1982, 531), for example, claims that Mill endorses local autonomy and decentralization in order to facilitate mass participation and to realize the principle of participation and the educative role of democracy (Thompson 1976). Similarly, Hollander (2015, 181) indicates that Mill was hostile to centralization and argued in favor of the extensive autonomy of a local government. Finally, Baccarini (1993, 74) goes even further and indicates that, at the local level, political participation was so important for Mill that he was ready to sacrifice competence to foster participation.[24] Though I recognize and affirm the principle of participation in Mill's political thought, and though I agree it is properly realized (at least in part) at the local level, I believe his claims on the role of local government can be seen as one additional filtering mechanisms limiting the popular will.

Mill (1981a, 203) acknowledges that Tocqueville's writing on the history of democracy in America inspired some of his thoughts on the role of national and local government. Tocqueville's argument against centralization largely resembles Mill's own argument against benevolent despots (Baccarini 1993, 70) and can also be examined by appealing to Thompson's (1976) principle of participation and principle of competence. Tocqueville claims that assigning greater level of autonomy to local government can have two sets of beneficial consequences. First, it can help citizens make better policies and decisions at the local level since the local population can have better insight into its own interests, as well as some specific knowledge not available to benevolent foreign experts. Second, local government enables citizens to participate in collective deliberation of public issues (Tocqueville 2000, see also Kregar 1998), which is "one of the most effectual means of training the societal feeling and practical intelligence of the people" (Mill 1977e, 168–169). Mill was particularly focused on the second set of beneficial consequences and even considered local government as "the chief instrument of public education" (Mill 1977a, 535). Namely, local government gives many citizens a chance to participate and to fill some of the numerous local offices, and citizens holding these positions "have to act for the public interest, as well as to think and to speak [which] cannot all be done by proxy" (Mill 1861, 276). As we can see, Mill wholeheartedly endorsed Tocqueville's argument based on the educative role of the local government. However, he did not share Tocqueville's optimism regarding the competences of such government. As a reaction to the Poor Law Amendment Act of 1934, Mill writes that every branch of local administration should be "closely and vigilantly looked after by the central government" (Mill 1982a, 206). He is skeptical of local government's ability to produce correct, efficient and just local policies and decisions, and worries that, when left unsupervised, local government might endanger citizens' right to have their lives governed by competent persons (Mill 1977a, see also Brennan 2016). For these reasons Mill indicates that "in the comprehension of the principles even of purely local management, the superiority of the central government, when rightly constituted, ought to be prodigious" (Mill 1861, 290). The central government is epistemically superior because it is composed of individuals with greater intellectual and moral capacities, as well as because it has access to knowledge relevant for good governance throughout the country, as well as from abroad. Local bodies, on the other hand, "might generally have the advantage in the details of [local] management" (Mill 1861, 290), yet this does not imply that local government should have significant autonomy or a decisive role in decision-making processes focused on local issues. Furthermore, Mill considered local government more prone to become a rule of a few influential individuals (local magnates and landlords) promoting their personal or sectarian interests. He thus writes that popular control "never acts purely, intelligently or vigorously, except on a large scale" (Mill 1982a, 206). To better comprehend how central government functions as a filtering mechanism on local popular we have to determine which issues the central government addresses, and which functions it performs.

Oskar Kurer (1989, 294–296) again gives a very useful overview. According to him, Mill indicates that activities of national interest include management of jails, local police and local justice (Mill 1977a, 541), poor laws, sanitary regulation and education[25] (Mill 1977a, 542), as well as local tax system and modes of taxation (Mill 1977a, 544). Furthermore, Mill leaves under authority of national government all and any issues of "general interest" or "universal concern." Purely local activities, on the other hand, mostly concern "paving, lighting and cleansing of the streets of towns" (Mill 1977a, 541), and these seem to be the only activities where the national government should not interfere, though it should still act as a teacher or a guide, providing information and suggestions, as well as publicly condemning (though not prohibiting) some negative practices. This implies that, following Mill, local government has authority only in a few purely local interests. However, participation in decision-making processes of such a narrow scope cannot effectively help develop citizens moral and intellectual capacities, nor can it help harvest the epistemic value of diverse perspectives among the local population. For these reasons, Mill introduces a third type of activities: those of both local and national interest, where local government can help with the implementation of directives and policies coming from the national government. Some activities from the first list can be found here, including management of jails, local police and local justice, as well as sanitary regulation and education, provided that these are under close supervision by the central government (Mill 1977a, 542, 544). Kurer (1989, 295) thus rightfully concludes that the "local government is reduced to an administrative appendix of the center" and characterizes Mill's system as a form of deconcentration (and not decentralization), where authority is delegated to the local government, which is nonetheless under strict supervision from the central government (Kurer 1989, 297). Local government thus becomes little more than an extension of national administration, tasked with implementing and executing decisions and policies created by the national government. Mill's claim that "localities should do little more than execute the laws and instructions laid down by the legislature of the empire" (Mill 1977a, 606) clearly supports this interpretation and indicates that Mill was skeptical regarding the competences of local governments to produce correct, just and efficient decisions.

A very limited scope of activities under direct and full jurisdiction of local government was one of the many filtering mechanisms Mill introduced to limit the authority of popular will and to prevent the harms that unrestricted popular will could cause. Aware of political participation's positive impact of moral and intellectual capacities of citizens, he tried to encourage it by delegating some tasks from national to local government, but concerned for the lack of relevant competences at the local level, he settled with a system in which "policy-making is centralized and administration is mainly localized" (Kurer 1989, 298). Mill's division of labor between the local and the national government can thus be seen as another filtering mechanism used to limit direct popular will and to preserve the epistemic qualities of indirect democratic government.

CONCLUDING REMARKS

Mill claims that (in developed nations) democracy represents the best form of government. It surpasses other forms of government both in its ability to produce correct, just and efficient political decisions and in the ability to improve the intellectual and moral capacities of citizens under its jurisdiction. However, to have any of these epistemic qualities, democratic government has to be structured in a particular way—it has to incorporate the epistemic advantages of both the division of epistemic and political labor and of the distinction between deliberative and executive stages in the decision-making process. Not every democratic regime can have this epistemic value. Direct democracy, for example, might encourage the participation of citizens in the decision-making processes, yet in doing so it diminishes both its educative function and its ability to produce correct, just or efficient decisions. A well-structured democratic government thus has to be characterized by a form of indirectness, and the institutional mechanisms have to be adjusted to support the epistemic advantages of both the division of labor and (spatial and temporal) of the division between various stages of the decision-making and the decision-authorization processes. Furthermore, institutional mechanisms should have a positive influence on the voters' minds, reminding them that participating in elections is a moral act that affects others as well as themselves.

Mill introduces a group of institutional and procedural filtering mechanisms that can help safeguard democratic procedures and improve the epistemic aspects of democratic processes. His rejection of secret ballot and pledges and campaign promises, as well as his qualified rejection of universal suffrage (characterized particularly by the minimal education requirement) and attribution of very limited power and authority to local government are some of the filtering mechanisms that can help democracy attain the adequate level of epistemic value. However, these are not all of the filtering mechanisms that Mill has in mind. Plural voting proposal and the idea that all adult citizens (except for, of course, those below the minimal level of education and those unable to provide for themselves) should have a voice, but not an equal voice, is probably one of the best examples how citizens' can be filtered to accommodate Mill's high epistemic standards. The next chapter addresses the epistemic value of plural voting proposal and its proper role in Mill's political thought. Similarly, partisan associations and political parties can be seen as an excellent example of institutions and organizations that filter public will and shape collective deliberation. Their epistemic role as one of Mill's filtering mechanisms will be discussed in one of the following chapters.

NOTES

1. Of course, Mill considers democracy the best form of government for developed western nations, where citizens have already acquired certain skills, competences and virtues that enable them to properly participate in a democratic society. In some underdeveloped nations other forms of government might be better in meeting the regulative ideal, i.e., producing the best consequences through moral and intellectual development of citizens and creating efficient and correct policies. See the fourth and the eighteenth chapter of Consideration of Representative Government for details (Mill 1977a, 413–421, 562–577).

2. This characterization, albeit quite a recent one, was already used by David Estlund (2003) and Gustavo Dalaqua (2018a). Helene Landemore (2017, 76) somewhat follows this line of thought and characterizes Mill as an "epistemic democrat with a strong elitist twist."

3. Deliberative function is removed from citizens in the formal political sphere as vast majority of citizens do not participate in parliamentary debates. However, citizens can (and should) deliberate in the informal political sphere, and their deliberation can (and should) influence the deliberation taking place within the formal political sphere.

4. Austrian political economist Joseph Schumpeter offered a market model of democracy, where politicians offer their services and compete for citizens' resources (votes). There is a strict division of labor: citizens vote and elect their political representatives but do not participate in the process of creation of laws, policies and political decisions. This is left for experts, whose work is evaluated every few years in the elections, when they are re-elected or replaced by a new group of experts, those whom the citizens consider more competent and efficient. For a comprehensive overview of this model see Schumpeter (2008), but also Elliott (1994) and Brooker (2010).

5. Jorge Urdanoz (2019, 5) warns us that Mill does not argue in favor of "proportional representation" since such a system, although still better than the "Originating" (Colomer 2007, 265) electoral system in Mill's time, would allow political parties to dominate the public discourse. Instead, Urdanoz follows Thompson (1976) in arguing that Mill defended "personal representation" as a device against party representation. There is no "majority" or "minority" as a homogeneous group defending some ideas and principles before the elections—these categories are determined for each borough

after elections, where they represent electors who have (or have not) acquired a representative in the parliament. Contrary to Urdanoz's reading, I follow Urbinati (2002), Dalaqua (2018a, 2018b) and others who focus on Mill's agonistic approach, where proportionality serves to inject epistemically valuable conflict in public deliberation. I give some arguments for this reading in the chapter on epistemic value of partisanship in Mill's political philosophy.

6. It seems that active citizens can also indirectly participate in the decision-making process. As Mill (1861, 275) indicates, "reading newspapers, and perhaps writing to them, public meetings, and solicitations of different sorts addressed to political authorities, are the extent of participation of private citizens in general politics." Citizens can thus indirectly participate both in the decision-authorization process (not only by voting in the elections, but also by influencing their political representatives through activities in the informal political sphere, see Dalaqua 2018a, 6) and in the decision-making process (by influencing the experts through activities in the informal political sphere). It is important to emphasize, however, that citizens' participation is never direct and decisive—it is one among many things that influence decision-making and decision-authorization processes.

7. Mill argued that a well-functioning government has to follow both democratic and bureaucratic principles: it has to balance between the best aspects of both participation and competence (Miller 2003, 647). Some (Halliday 2004, 134, Baccarini and Ivanković 2015, 148) follow this interpretation but emphasize that parliament's balancing power realizes itself in the decision-authorization stage, and not earlier, during the decision-making process. While this seems correct, Mill also had in mind that political representatives *indirectly* shape the decision-making process by indicating the general direction the society should move in. He agrees that we should "leave the business of legislation to the professional legislators, *except* on questions involving political principles and interests" (Mill 1861, 102, emphasis added). Furthermore, Mill argues that the parliament can give directions on how to prepare the law (and that these directions are imperative to the Commissioners), as well as that "the Commission has no power of refusing its instrumentality to any legislation which the country desired" (Mill 1861, 101). Somewhat similar ideas can be found in contemporary discussion on the division of epistemic labor, in works by Thomas Christiano (2012) or Philip Kitcher (2011).

8. Again, this does not imply that citizens do not participate at all in decision-making processes, nor that they participate in decision-authorization processes only during elections, once every few years. Mill emphasizes that political participation takes place both in the formal and in the informal political sphere (Mill 1977a, 423). Thus, for Mill, being outside of the representative assembly does not deprive a citizen of political power (Holmes 1988, 233, Urbinati 2000, 766, Dalaqua 2018a, 5). However, citizens' political power becomes less direct and decisive since it is filtered through various mechanisms.

9. Miranda Fricker (2007) warns us of testimonial epistemic injustice, when members of some social groups, due to negative identity prejudices related to their group, receive less credibility than they should have received. David Coady (2010), on the other hand, introduces a concept of distributive epistemic injustice, when members

of some social groups, due to financial, social or cultural conditions often related to that group, receive inadequate and unfair amount of epistemic resources (e.g., access to education, knowledge). Both forms of epistemic injustice cause serious social and political problems for the members of these groups, making them unable to properly communicate what is meaningful to them (as well as to properly support their positions with reasons and arguments other groups will find persuasive). Epistemic injustice might thus seriously undermine their political influence. Baccarini and Ivanković (2015, 147) indicate that "it does not seem that labourers of Mill's time suffered from this kind of injustice, at least if we follow Mill's own testimony about events." In fact, Mill seems worried regarding the growing political influence of the working class and introduces plural voting proposal as a measure to reduce this influence and to prevent class legislation. I agree that Mill is not worried that the members of the working class, once universal suffrage is established, will have trouble expressing their will and their interests in the public deliberation. However, as Mill emphasizes in more than one occasion, political deliberation should be about citizens' ideas, opinions and perspectives, not on their (individual or class) interests. In his discussion with Lorimer, Mill indicates that "whenever [citizens' interests are] not identical with the general interests, the less they are represented, the better," and warns us that "what is needed is a representation, not of men's differences of interest, but of the differences in their points of view" (Mill 1977c, 358). In a "false" democracy, interests of one class might dominate the political arena while its epistemically valuable perspective remains misrepresented. Not having adequate epistemic resources (sufficient knowledge and skills, as well as credibility in the eyes of others) due to unfair social and economic conditions and identity prejudices might be a case of epistemic injustice. Mill was aware of this when he argued that workers should elect members of other classes (intellectuals, progressive industrialists, merchants and shipowners) to represent them in the parliament (Mill 1977a, 401). Representatives from these classes will have adequate skills and competences to properly explain, support and defend the workers' ideas and perspectives, and members of other classes will not have negative identity prejudices towards them.

10. Of course, Austin (2015) is just one in the long line of authors who defended similar claims, with Plato (2000) as the most notable example.

11. Austin argues that unbalanced democracy has a tendency to prevent the formation of class of such "fit-to-rule" elite. Mill (1977c, 346) agrees that in some cases this can be a problem, but argues that properly exercised democracy can foster representatives' competences to rule.

12. Partisan associations and political parties are another way how opinions and perspectives of some groups and classes of lower social and economic status can be strengthened and better represented in the deliberative assembly. For more information on this argumentative line see the chapter on Mill and the epistemic value of partisanship.

13. In late 1850s and early 1860s, when Mill was writing most of his works on representative government, the House of Commons of the Parliament of the United Kingdom was composed of 658 members. See Hart (1992, 24–25) and Urdanoz (2019, 3).

14. This remedy is not necessarily related to the parliament. Other democratic innovations (which nonetheless take form of representative democracy), like mini-publics, where a group of citizens is randomly chosen (and not elected by the people) to deliberate on laws and policies, can uphold continuous consultation with the experts. For more information on mini-publics see Wright (2010).

15. Again, this does not imply that citizens should not participate in the decision-making process. It only shows that citizens should not participate directly, and even when their participation is indirect, it should go through several filters and not have a decisive role. Partisan associations, non-governmental institutions focused on political issues, policy institutes and think tanks can all enable citizens to participate in the decision-making process and improve the quality of their contribution, as well as the quality of final political outcomes. It is important to stress, however, that these types of associations function in the informal, and not in the formal political sphere.

16. Duty-based justification of democracy somewhat similar to Mill's account can be found in Estlund (2008). An alternative duty-based justification can be found in Claassen (2018).

17. Mill has this in mind when he rejects Hare's proposal to allow electors to vote at home. Hare proposal was to have electors fill-in and sign their voting paper at home and bring it personally to the polling place. Since Hare's system enabled and encouraged citizens to write many names on the voting paper and to arrange them in the order of preference, there is no surprise that Hare allowed citizens to fill-in their voting papers at home. Mill believes this can be a dangerous problem: "at home the eye of the public is absent, but the hand of the briber is not" (Mill 1977c, 336). Though Mill later acknowledges that the advantages of Hare's system outweigh this disadvantage, he nonetheless sees lack of publicity as a "serious objection."

18. For additional information on moral and intellectual superiority of political representatives in Mill's political thought, see the chapter on the epistemic value of partisanship. What should the members of parliament represent (citizens' interests or citizens' perspectives) is addressed earlier in this chapter.

19. Hare suggests that ten-pound franchise established in 1832 is appropriate and "just about right" (Kern 1998, 169).

20. Mill seems to believe that there is an important difference between citizens who lack minimal education when such education cannot be provided for all and citizens who lack minimal education due to their disinterest and laziness. The first case represents a hardship where some citizens are disenfranchised (and thus harmed) due to no fault of their own, but because the society failed to perform its duty. However, in order to prevent greater evils, such citizens should remain disenfranchised until they acquire minimal education. Society is, of course, under strong and urgent obligation to make acquiring minimal education available to all. There is no hardship in the second case. When minimal education is available to all citizens yet some refuse to acquire it, there is no one to blame for their disenfranchisement but themselves. Some contemporary philosophers strongly reject this claim: Amartya Sen (1984, 307–324, 1995, 259–273) and Martha Nussbaum (2000, 111–166), for example, argue that people who live in poor and depriving conditions might form adaptive preferences and end up not desiring some basic human good (e.g., education). They might claim

that, under such conditions, deprived citizens who lack the desire to acquire (minimal) education should not be blamed for this decision. In fact, the society is to blame for allowing them to grow up and live in such poor conditions. However, Mill seems to be aware of adaptive preferences and the problems they might cause. He gives an example how depriving conditions and unfair distribution of power "enslave minds" (Mill 1984b, 271–272) and make women develop preferences that are not in their interest as progressive beings. Therefore, Mill's claim that those who chose not to acquire education have no one to blame for their disenfranchisement but themselves holds under two conditions: education has to be available to all, and social and economic conditions must not influence one's desire to acquire education. Mill had both conditions in mind, though he explicitly emphasized only the first one.

21. To be more precise, Mill holds that citizens who receive or who have received parish relief within a fixed period of time (for example, five years before the election in question) should be excluded from franchise. Furthermore, he also excludes citizens who are insolvent and unable to pay their debts (Mill 1977a, 472).

22. Again, some might argue that Mill's criteria are too demanding and might disenfranchise citizens through no fault of their own. In many periods in human history some people were unemployed despite actively searching for work, and automatization and technological development might further increase the number of such citizens in the future. However, Mill again applies this criterion only in the conditions where anyone could find meaningful employment provided that one is actively searching for it.

23. Mill's view on disentrancement of criminal offenders is often discussed in the US, where similar laws are in place and where (depending on the state) felony results with (usually temporary) loss of civil rights (Brown 2003, 319–333). A problem arises, however, when disenfranchised citizens are disproportionately members of particular social groups (Manza and Uggen 2008, Siegel 2011), and Mill would probably agree that such cases of disenfranchisement require thorough analysis and deeper inquiry into the roots of the problem.

24. Baccarini (1993, 74) takes into consideration that, for Mill, political participation can establish its educative role only when it brings together "the superior minds of the government" and the local intellectual elite on the one hand and citizens participating in the local government on the other (Mill 1977a, 538). However, the relationship between the national and the local government is grounded not in political authority of the former over the latter, but in the friendly information exchange (Baccarini 1933, 73). Similar ideas are put forward by Ryan who argues that, according to Mill, "knowledge must be centralized and power must be localized" (Ryan 2016, 206–207).

25. Mill allows central government to control and supervise the education system by uniform yearly examinations and certification of teachers. For more information, see Mill (1977d, 303) and Mill (1984a, 214), as well as the chapter on education in this book.

Chapter 5

Plural Voting Proposal

One of Mill's most (in)famous and controversial ideas is his plural voting proposal—idea that, although all qualified citizens should have some political influence, this influence should not be distributed equally. Despite his strong support for the universal suffrage, the inegalitarian character of his plural voting proposal has urged some philosophers to regard him as a non-democrat (Burns 1957),[1] while others have even suggested to call the new hybrid form of government Mill is advocating 'scholocracy,'[2] in order to differentiate if further from democratic procedures (Estlund 2003). This proposal has been thoroughly analyzed and criticized, and both its role in Mill's political thought and its applicability in contemporary western democracy have been addressed in numerous publications. Unfortunately, it seems that Mill's original work is somehow neglected in favor of some notable interpretations, and the emphasis is sometimes placed on the implementation of Mill's ideas in contemporary society without first analyzing and understanding the justificatory process Mill carefully developed to support those ideas. This chapter aims to clarify some of the contested ideas by analyzing the reasons and arguments Mill used to support them, as well as to emphasize how these ideas and arguments are connected into a coherent system. Furthermore, this chapter tries to determine what is the role of plural voting in Mill's argument and how exactly does the plural voting proposal improve the epistemic quality of a democratic decision-authorization process.

The previous chapter introduced a set of mechanisms Mill used to filter public will, including open ballot, rejection of pledges and campaign promises, as well as strong limitations on the scope of local government. These filtering mechanisms serve to protect democracy from two dangers it can succumb to: low grade of intelligence, both within representative bodies or among the citizens who participate in decision-authorization procedures, and class legislation, an unwanted occurrence when a social group sharing similar interests achieves numerical majority and can pass laws without any regard for interests and opinions of the rest of society. Mill reminds us that "though government cannot be better than collective mind of the community, it can do a great deal to uphold or undermine the social influences which either prevent or improve the collective mind (Mill 1977c, 357). The plural voting proposal discussed in this chapter can also be characterized as a filtering mechanism, a useful instrument that can help democracy produce laws and policies of high substantive quality, but also educate citizens and improve their capacities.

The chapter's innovative contribution can be summarized along two lines. First, it argues that Mill intended plural voting to serve not as a temporary, but as a permanent measure. This interpretation characterizes Mill as an inegalitarian with regard to the distribution of political influence and addresses epistemic considerations that ground Mill's inegalitarianism. Having read and understood Mill in this way, we can regard plural voting proposal as an important part of his political thought and cannot simply dismiss it as a mechanism Mill used as a temporary measure. Second, this chapter elaborates Mill's division of political and epistemic labor and explicates how plural voting proposal introduces competence in democratic decision-making process.

The *first* part of the chapter emphasizes Mill's account of voting as a privilege (not a right) and having this in mind analyzes his understanding of political equality. By introducing Berlin's (1969) distinction between positive and negative liberties, I claim that Mill argued only for the equality of negative liberties. Positive liberties, those inherent to a participatory democratic process, are not to be equally distributed. The *second* part reassesses Mill's principles of participation and competence (Thompson 1976) and demonstrates how plural voting perfectly meets both principles by simultaneously inviting (almost) all citizens to participate in the decision-authorization process, yet giving them unequal political influence, in accordance with their perceived competence. This is why Mill believed that everyone should have a say in the decision-authorization process, though not everyone should have an equal say. Furthermore, additional arguments supporting plural voting proposal and its social roles are discussed. Finally, against most contemporary interpretations, I argue that Mill proposes plural voting as a permanent (and not only temporary) measure and show that the key reason for this proposal is neither to prevent class legislation nor to educate citizens but instead to increase the instrumental epistemic value of democratic procedures, i.e., to enable democracy to produce the best possible outcomes. But how does plural voting proposal help improve the instrumental epistemic value of democracy? Where does the competence of the educated enter the decision-making and decision-authorization process? The *third* part answers these questions by comparing Mill's view on experts with the views of Thomas Christiano and Philip Kitcher. While Christiano and Kitcher advocate for equality in the process of setting up political aims (and give greater power to the experts only when discussing the implementation of the already set aims), Mill rejects the idea of equality both in the process of setting up aims and in the process of their implementation.

ELECTORAL SUFFRAGE: RIGHT OR PRIVILEGE?

To properly understand Mill's plural voting proposal, we first have to analyze his views on the voting process and the exercise of political influence. Neglecting these important aspects of his political thought might lead us to some erroneous interpretations of plural voting proposal, including the reading that characterizes it only as a temporary measure.

Mill's Ethics of Voting

One of the important yet often disregarded aspects of Mill's political thought is his moralized understanding of the voting process (Brennan 2012). Grounding his argument in strong liberal foundations, Mill argues that "there is no such thing as a right to power over others" (Mill 1859b, 25). Every adult individual should be free to act however he wishes, provided that his actions do not cause harm to someone else or violate a distinguishable moral duty he has towards others (Mill 1859b, 25). Electoral suffrage, however, is a form of power over others—it gives every citizen a small portion of political influence and enables every citizen to participate in the political process and authorize laws and policies that affect everyone. Mill thus concludes that there is no such thing as an unconditional right to vote. Electoral suffrage should be understood primarily as a privilege or as a conditional right. However, Mill seems to be inconsistent in using this terminology, even when terms are used within the same publication.[3] I believe epistemic interpretation of his work can help us resolve the apparent inconsistency.

Mill is adamant in claiming that, for individual's actions that affect only himself, no one has the moral right to limit his freedom. By extension, no individual has the moral right to limit the freedom of others. Furthermore, when necessary laws, policies and political decisions have to be made, no individual has an inherent right to participate in such decision-authorization process. However, when public decisions affect one's liberties (i.e., when this cannot be avoided and left within individuals' personal sphere), everyone is entitled to have his liberty limited only by epistemically (and morally) the best possible laws and policies, or by laws and policies produced by epistemically the best (or the most reliable) procedures, those having the highest tendency to produce beneficial consequences. Mill considers democracy, characterized by several filtering mechanisms (including plural voting proposal), as the best procedure epistemically—it has the highest tendency to produce correct decisions and, more broadly, to produce the best results. Voting can thus be seen as both a right and a privilege—we are entitled to have political influence in the decision-authorization process (and thus exercise power over others) only because it is epistemically the best instrument for securing that, when anyone's liberties have to be limited, they are limited by laws and policies produced by a procedure with the highest chance of generating the best possible outcomes.[4] Children and uneducated citizens are, for example, denied electoral rights and privileges because their direct participation in the decision-authorization process has a tendency to decrease (and not increase) the overall quality of political outcomes.[5] Of course, this implies a highly moralized conception of electoral suffrage—since, by voting in the elections, we are exercising power over others, we have a duty to exercise it responsibly, in a way that best promotes the epistemic quality of laws, policies and decisions thus produced.

Mill clearly indicates that "voting for a Member of Parliament is a moral act, involving a real responsibility" (Mill 1977c, 366). In his discussion on the epistemic value of ballot, he criticizes secret ballot as it "makes voters free of all sense of shame or responsibility," and later suggests open ballot as an external inducement (filtering mechanism) that helps motivate voters to "do their duty to the public" (Mill 1859b, 47). Similarly, he argues against the practice of collecting votes at home since such voting procedures might encourage those disinterested and incompetent to vote, which might in turn reduce the epistemic value of democracy.[6]

Since citizen's vote is strictly a matter of duty, does this imply that Mill holds citizens should be obliged to exercise their electoral privileges? This is certainly not the case. Mill simply wants to emphasize that, since our voting rights and privileges do not belong to us unconditionally, but because our political participation through the exercise of suffrage has a tendency to improve the epistemic quality of laws and policies and the overall quality of political results, we should not exercise our voting rights and privileges carelessly. Mill thus writes that one should vote not following his whims or personal or group interests, but "according to [one's] best and most conscientious opinion of the public good" (Mill 1861, 198–199). He thus indicates that the "public trust of voting" should only be exercised by those competent and interested to rule (Mill 1861, 211, see also Barker 2015, 1155), since those who do not care whether or in which way they vote "have no moral right to vote at all" (Mill 1859b, 50).

Mill's ethics of voting (and its epistemic interpretation) are of great importance for understanding his political thought in general, as well as his arguments for plural voting proposal in particular. He presents an instrumental and epistemic account of electoral suffrage: our voting privileges are conditional and are grounded in beneficial effects our political participation has both on the quality of political decisions and on the improvement of our own moral and intellectual capacities. However, as we shall see in this chapter, Mill is convinced that widespread voting privileges combined with unequal distribution of political influence represent the optimal formal arrangement for reaching these beneficial consequences.

Equality and Political Influence

Previous paragraphs demonstrated that, for Mill, there are no inherent electoral rights. No one has an inherent right to power over others, nor the right to have political influence through which the power over others can be exercised. Our voting rights and privileges are grounded in their instrumental usefulness: they help society produce better laws and policies, as well as improve the moral and intellectual capacities of its citizens. Since there is no inherent right to political influence, there is also no special right to have equal level of political influence as other citizens. How should political influence be distributed depends primarily on the effects various models of distribution have on the government's ability to produce correct, efficient and just outcomes, as well as on its effects on citizens' minds. In other words, there is no intrinsic argument for the equality of political influence.[7]

Some might argue otherwise by stressing the importance of equality in Mill's political thought, especially in his famous essay *On Liberty* (Justman 1990). Though equality is indeed a very important idea for Mill, we must notice that in *On Liberty* Mill focuses primarily on the idea of negative liberty, i.e., the area within which a subject—a person or group of persons—is or should be left to do or be what he is able to do or be, without interference by other persons (Berlin 1969). Mill's thoughts on positive liberty, i.e., his answer to the question what, or who, is the source of control or interference that can determine someone to do, or be, this rather than that (Carter 2016), are quite different. He explicitly distinguishes between the power that one has over oneself alone and the power one has over others.

> They say that everyone has an equal interest in being well governed, and that everyone, therefore, has an equal claim to control over his own government. I might agree to this, if control over his own government were really a thing in question; but what I am asked to assent is, that every individual has an equal claim to control over the government of the other people. The power that suffrage gives is not over himself alone [i.e., negative liberty], it is power over others also [i.e., positive liberty]: whatever control the voter is able to exercise over his own concerns, he exercises the same degree of it over those of everyone else. Now, it can in no sort be admitted that all persons have an equal claim to power over others. (Mill 1859b, 22–23)

It seems that equality does not play an important role in Mill's thoughts on collective decision-making procedures, though it still plays an important role with regard to the development of individual capacities (Baccarini 2013, Macpherson 2012). It is very important to ensure equal protection of everyone's basic negative liberties (e.g., freedom of thought, speech, press and assembly), but equality should be rejected and opposed when we address positive liberties. It should instead be replaced with competence and (non-equal) participation, because these are the key virtues needed to achieve better quality of political decisions, but also optimal development of citizens' competences.[8]

MILL'S REASONING FOR PLURAL VOTING

Mill writes in the nineteenth century, when only a small percentage of adult citizens was allowed to have and exercise political influence by participating in the electoral process. Although the number of citizens considered eligible to vote doubled both in Reform Act 1832 and Reform Act 1867, it still remained relatively small, with only four million eligible voters in the population of over twenty-nine million (Barker 2015, 1150–1151). Many intellectuals of that time, including Mill, were worried that the sudden rise of franchise might endanger the stability of political community or significantly reduce the quality of new laws and policies. John Austin, for example, warns that the Parliament "returned by universal suffrage would ruin our finances, destroy economic prosperity, [but also] destroy the natural arrangement of society" (Austin 1867, 19, as quoted in Mill 1977c, 349). Thomas Carlyle similarly claims that in democracy a "wise man will never again be able to rule" and extends his warning by arguing that "it is dangerous for some to be free" (Carlyle 1867, as paraphrased in Barker 2015, 1146). However, unlike scholars who unconditionally oppose further extensions of franchise, Mill is cautious but optimistic: he argues that a significant number of citizens (much more than the number set by the two Reform Acts) is already fit for suffrage, and believes that many more (virtually all) will follow as soon as educational reform takes place and all citizens get the opportunity to receive (at least minimal) education.

However, as indicated earlier in this chapter, while Mill argues for (almost) universal suffrage,[9] he emphasizes that political influence should not be distributed equally. This represents the central claim behind his plural voting proposal.

Filtering Mechanisms and Political Suffrage

The distribution of influence within formal political sphere (i.e., how to distribute voting privileges, as well as how to weight individual or group votes) represented one of the most important themes in nineteenth-century political philosophy. The debate was set between two extremes: an inegalitarian (undemocratic) account that attributed all political influence to a single individual (i.e., despotism) and an egalitarian (democratic) account that distributed political influence equally among all citizens ('one person, one vote' democracy[10]). Mill approaches this discussion from the utilitarian standpoint, using the two criteria of good government (its ability to produce good, efficient and just decisions and its ability to improve citizens' existing moral and intellectual capacities) to assess the instrumental quality of different models of political influence distribution. His argument against (benevolent) despotism was discussed in earlier chapters, and we can simply summarize it here and conclude that Mill thinks despotism fails to adequately meet both criteria of good government. It fails to harness and organize the existing knowledge in society thus failing to produce laws and policies of optimal substantial quality, and it hinders the development of citizens' capacities by making them passive and disinterested in public issues. Mill is unsympathetic towards the other extreme as well. His worries are primarily directed towards dangerous laws, policies and decisions that might be produced by a government characterized by universal suffrage and equal distribution of political influence. However, Mill sometimes has other worries: equal distribution of political influence might have a harmful effect on citizens' minds impeding the optimal development of citizens' capacities. He indicates two motives for an unequal distribution of political influence: (i) to prevent one group of people from being able to control the political process without having to give reasons in order to have sufficient support, and (ii) to avoid giving each person an equal chance to influence political decisions without regard for their merit and intelligence. Mill indicates that "in this stage of things, the great majority of voters . . . are manual laborers; and a twofold danger, that of too low a standard of political intelligence, and that of class legislation, would still exist in a very perilous degree (Mill 1861, 171–172).

More than one account can be assigned between the two above mentioned extremes. We can, for example, try to preserve the quality of political decisions by keeping the suffrage limited only to well-educated citizens (e.g., university graduates), or we can opt for a form of census suffrage, where only citizens earning above some fixed sum of money are allowed to vote (and hope that such citizens will be, in general, more competent to participate in collective decision-authorization processes than those below the census). This is an *exclusive* approach, one that answers the problem of citizens' low political intelligence by narrowing the electorate, thus removing the suffrage from unqualified citizens and excluding them from a decision-authorization process. The electoral system in mid-Victorian England corresponded to this model, with majority of citizens having no voting rights, which were reserved for the competent few. However, the "few" in question were not a small group of nobles or experts, but instead a group of approximately two and a half million citizens (relatively rich men) of the twenty-four million population.[11] Accounts developed by Thomas Carlyle and John Austin followed this model. Although Mill wants to steer between the two extremes, he clearly rejects this exclusive approach. We can follow his two criteria of good government to establish and organize arguments he uses to reject this account. *First*, this exclusive approach fails to harness the existing knowledge in the society, and thus fails to produce political decisions, policies and laws of optimal epistemic quality. Mill indicates that, when the (formal) political influence is withheld from some, the interests of "those who have no voice will be postponed to those who have" (Mill 1859b, 38–39), and their valuable opinions and perspectives will be ignored in the collective representative body (Mill 1977a). Withholding franchise from workers[12] or women, for example, results in a government that is both unable to make use of the knowledge these groups have and unfit to produce unbiased laws and policies that will properly address the common interest. *Second*, this approach also fails to improve citizens' existing moral and intellectual capacities. Mill indicates that, when large groups of citizens are disenfranchised, "they themselves have less scope and encouragement to [use] their energies for the good of themselves and of the community" and reminds us that "the maximum of the invigorating effect of freedom upon character is only obtained, when the person acted on either is, or is looking forward to becoming, a citizen as fully privileged as any other" (Mill 1861, 58, 65). He sees franchise as a "school of public spirit" (Mill 1861, 69) and argues that withholding this form of education from the majority of citizens represents a great evil and cannot be a feature of a good form of government. As we can see, Mill firmly believes that Carlyle's and Austin's accounts, although they represent a path between the two extremes, are not the correct path.

Instead of the exclusive approach, the one that attributes political influence in the formal political sphere only to a (relatively) small number of competent citizens, there is an alternative path between the two extremes. A more inclusive account, one endorsed by Mill (but also Lorimer, Cecil and others), attributes political influence to (virtually) all adult citizens. Every citizen can participate in the decision-authorization process. The problem of citizens' low political intelligence is not solved by narrowing the electorate, but by attributing citizens unequal political influence, in proportion to their competence to participate in the decision-authorization process. While all citizens are allowed to vote in the elections, their votes carry unequal weight and some citizens have political influence that is two, three or more times greater than the influence of other citizens. This inclusive approach, typically regarded as a plural voting proposal, still acts as a mechanism for filtering the public will but does not suffer from common objections other exclusive approaches are subject to. It enables all relevant interest (but also all opinions and perspectives) to be represented in the Parliament, harnessing the knowledge widely distributed in the political community and ensuring the protection of everyone's interests, improving the quality of laws, policies and political decisions. Similarly, this inclusive account enables and encourages (almost) all citizens to participate in the political process, fostering their public education and the development of their moral and intellectual capacities. However, an important question remains: what is the relevant criterion for the unequal distribution of political influence?

Plural Voting Proposals

As indicated earlier in the chapter, there is more than one criterion for the unequal distribution of political influence. Mill was not the only proponent of plural suffrage—James Lorimer and Robert Cecil advanced similar mechanisms, though their proposals differ from Mill's in some important aspects. To properly grasp the key divisions between these proposals we first have to differentiate between substantive and procedural criteria for the allocation of additional votes. Approaches grounded in *substantive* criteria are typically inegalitarian and distribute political influence in accordance with some external goods (like education, wealth or social status). These approaches have to argue that having the good in question improves citizens' competence to participate in the political process, and thus citizens having more relevant good (more wealth, better education, higher social status) should have greater political influence in the formal political sphere. Approaches grounded in *procedural* criteria are typically egalitarian and distribute political influence following the will of the citizens, who are regarded as equals in the first stage of the procedure. Citizens then (as equals) determine who is more competent and who should have greater political influence in the later stages of decision-authorization procedure.[13]

James Lorimer (2017) seems to offer a plural voting mechanism grounded in procedural criteria for attributing additional votes. Following Mill's (first) interpretation, Lorimer argues that "the office of the suffrage is to give political expression to the social powers actually existing in the community" (Lorimer 2017, as paraphrased in Mill 1977c, 355). A similar position in contemporary debates is introduced (though not strictly endorsed) by Trevor Latimer (2018), who suggests two-stage elections, where the first stage is strictly egalitarian and serves to determine citizens who receive additional votes, and the second stage is inegalitarian and characterized by plural voting, with every citizen having at least one vote but some (those recognized and elected in the first stage) having more than one. While Lorimer (at least according to Mill's reading) builds a descriptive account,[14] one that tries to determine how political influence is distributed in society and how to mimic such distribution in collective decision-authorization procedures, Latimer seems to suggest a normative account. His intention is to offer an egalitarian account of plural voting: while the mechanism has egalitarian foundations, it seems to have epistemic aspirations—to improve the quality of collective decision-authorization processes, as well as the subsequent quality of political outcomes. Mill would probably reject this proposal on epistemic grounds, arguing that it fails to differentiate between social influences that pervert and those that improve the collective mind (Mill 1977c, 357), but also that it fails to promote the epistemic value of agonism (Mill 1977a, 479). However, further evaluation of Latimer's procedural criterion for plural voting proposal goes beyond the scope of this chapter. Some advantages Mill sees in his own plural voting proposal, as opposed to a more egalitarian Latimer's proposal, are discussed later in this chapter.

There are a few plural voting mechanisms grounded in substantive criteria for attributing additional votes, and they differ with regard to the quality they identify as grounds for unequal distribution of political influence. Robert Cecil,[15] for instance, argues that additional votes should be attributed to rich citizens—those who pay more taxes and thus contribute more money to the public budget should also have greater say in public matters and have additional influence in the formal political sphere. He uses an example of a joint-stock company where every stakeholder has a number of votes in proportion to the number of shares he owns, and draws analogy with the state, arguing that the same principle should apply in collective decision-authorization procedures. Again, Mill rejects this proposal and offers several objections: unlike joint-stock company, the state is concerned with not just property, but with the entire welfare of citizens (Mill 1977c, 354–355), and more importantly, it is dubious that such substantive criteria would improve the epistemic qualities of decision-authorization procedures (Mill 1977a, 474–475). Finally, since wealth is not a reliable indicator of competence, citizens would be unable to comprehend and perceive such mechanism as just. But what are the qualities that indicate voter competence? And what substantive criteria can be endorsed (and be perceived as just) by all citizens?

Mill's own proposal also grounds additional votes in a substantive criterion, but unlike Cecil he is adamant that "the only thing which can justify reckoning one person's opinion as equivalent to more than one, is individual mental superiority" (Mill 1861, 175). Of course, this feature has to be verifiable and measurable, and Mill suggests that the nature of a person's occupation, as well as their acquired formal education could be reliable indicators of their mental faculties. Furthermore, Mill calls for a system of voluntary examinations which should allow citizens with no formal education to claim privileges of plurality of votes. Contemporary authors often regard formal education as Mill's primary (or even only) indicator, and this seems to be a valid interpretation. After all, Mill writes that "if there existed such a thing as a really national education, or a trustworthy system of general examination, education might be tested directly," and other markers (like occupation) are introduced later to compensate for the absence of the former indicators (Mill 1861, 175). He is convinced that, unlike wealth or social status, this substantive criterion and plural voting proposal grounded in it "would not be repugnant to any one's sentiment of justice" and could be endorsed by all citizens (Mill 1861, 177, see also Estlund 2003, 57–58). But what are the reasons for this claim? Why would plural voting proposal, which attributes political influence according to mental superiority, improve the quality of government?

Plural Voting Proposal and the Quality of Political Outcomes

Following Mill's two criteria of good government, plural voting helps organize the existing capacities within political community to promote and facilitate the creation of the best laws, policies and decisions. It achieves this is two ways. First, it prevents class legislation, thus blocking one class from passing laws that promote only its own class interests (and not the common good), but also encouraging epistemically fertile agonist deliberation within representative bodies. Second, it gives additional votes to well-educated citizens, thus distributing political influence in favor of more competent citizens while still giving suffrage to (almost all) citizens. Mill's inegalitarian ideas and his epistemic arguments for plural voting proposal deserve close consideration.

The danger of class legislation was one of the main reasons why many mid-Victorian thinkers (including Mill) feared uncontrolled universal suffrage. Giving electoral privileges (and equal influence in the formal political sphere) to all citizens would result in one group of people (i.e., the working class) having, due to its enormous size when compared to other social groups, a position of permanent dominance in the political process. Furthermore, since members of this group share many interests (class interests), which are often in conflict with the interests of minority groups, the dominant group would be able to rule while ignoring the interests (but also opinions) of smaller groups, thus leading to a democratic tyranny of the majority. Since the dominant group would not be incentivized to argue for laws and policies in terms of public interest and the common good, the resulting political outcomes would promote sectarian or class interests and would thus lack the appropriate epistemic qualities.[16] However, since (primarily in Mill's time, but to a certain degree even today) higher levels of education are typically acquired by wealthier citizens, plural voting proposal would effectively (though not declaratively) attribute greater political influence to the members of minority groups. Plural voting makes each class "strong enough to make reason prevail, but not strong enough to prevail against reason" (Mill 1861, 182), and puts political power under "the necessity of appealing to the reason" (Mill 1859b, 24). In a society divided in two or more classes, plural voting proposals injects constructive conflict in the formal political sphere by shaping the composition of the Parliament in a way that no class can make political decisions without having to justify them to others. Of course, in order to be justifiable to others, political decisions have to be grounded in public interest and appeal to the common good. Thus, when we consider Mill's views on the epistemic value of political conflict, we can see that even the protective function of plural voting proposal has epistemic justification. Plural voting proposal fulfills its protective function when it protects political conflict in the formal political sphere, preventing the domination of a single group and the tyranny of majority. However, the same can be said for Robert Cecil's plural voting proposal—the mechanism he suggests would prevent class legislation and thus force political representatives to make political decisions that promote public (and not class) interest. Though this can have epistemic benefits (e.g., lead to substantively better, more just or more efficient decisions), it does not represent the entirety of Mill's view on the danger of class legislation. Even if all members of the dominant class think in terms of the common good, class legislation still leads to epistemically sub-optimal results.

Mill's case for plural voting proposal can also be seen as an argument based on the constructive epistemic value of systematic political agonism. By preventing class legislation, plural voting proposal is blocking the dominance of one group of people (e.g., the workers), who usually share not only the same class interests but also the same perspective and similar worldviews, in the political process. However, since this proposal gives some political influence even to those who have poor and barely adequate education, it blocks class legislation from the other side (e.g., those well-educated) as well. Mill warns us that "those who are supreme over everything, whether they be One, Few or Many, have no longer need of the arms of reason; they can make their mere will prevail; and those who cannot be resisted are usually to well satisfied with their own opinions to be willing to change them, or listen without impatience to anyone who tells them that they are in the wrong" (Mill 1861, 181–182). The epistemic value of deliberation, just like the epistemic value of diverse perspectives and political agonism, is thus lost when one class exercises total domination in the political arena. To prevent this, plural voting proposal gives some political influence to each group, yet prevents each class from ruling by itself, without having to justify its opinions and policies to the other. It protects the members of each group from the tyranny of the other (Baccarini and Ivanković 2015). However, by distributing political influence in such way, plural voting proposal is also institutionalizing conflict in the formal political sphere. While *On Liberty* (1859a and 1977d) allows and encourages political agonism with regard to negative liberties (freedom of thought, press, speech and assembly guarantee that we can create, express and promote confliction opinions), there is little mention of conflict and its encouragement with regard to positive liberties (e.g., in the electoral process or in the Parliament)—while we can infer that it would be desirable, it is unclear how it can be guaranteed. There is no mention of elections, quotas, boroughs or parliamentary debates in *On Liberty*, primarily because the arguments there do not address positive liberties. The arguments there focus on negative liberties and address some conflict-enabling practices that should not be prohibited, yet say little of practices that should actively encourage or foster political conflict, especially in the formal politics. *Considerations on Representative* Government (1861 and 1977a) resolve this problem by protecting and fostering epistemically valuable political conflict in the formal sphere. We can see this when Mill argues that "opinions and wishes of poorest and rudest classes may be very useful as *one influence among others* . . . on Legislature" (Mill 1858b, 42–43, emphasis added), and again when he adds that his proposal makes each class "strong enough to make reason prevail, but not strong enough to prevail against reason" (Mill 1861, 182). This value of diverse perspectives is best introduced through deliberation (in Parliament), yet to achieve sufficient diversity in the representative assembly the aggregative mechanism (electoral process) needs to be shaped in inegalitarian fashion to achieve the desired result.

Following this argumentation, one could be led to believe that Mill's only (decision-oriented) reason for plural voting is to attain a balance between groups or classes. This balance would then force them to deliberate instead of simply asserting their will, thus using the epistemic value of public deliberation to improve the quality of political outcomes. While this represents an important part of Mill's argument, it does not represent the whole argument.

"Mental superiority," often measured by the level of attained education, plays an important role in Mill's plural voting proposal. Though attributing additional votes using wealth as the relevant criteria might help prevent class legislation, it fails to account for inequalities in citizens' intellectual and moral capacities. Mill was strongly influenced by the classical political philosophy, and his plural voting proposal can be seen as a combination of Plato's epistocracy and Aristotle's democracy. Following Plato, Mill emphasized the value of greater wisdom of the few, while following Aristotle he embraced the value of diverse perspectives for political decision-making (Estlund 2003, 57). While Mill never embraced Plato's epistocracy (because it denied the value of diverse perspectives for decision-making, as well as because it was not compatible with the account of moral and intellectual improvement of the people), he considered the idea that competence should have greater weight than incompetence to be very appealing (Cerovac 2016b). Mill's argumentation aims to maximize individual liberty, but this liberty can be limited when our actions have impact on lives of other individuals. As long as we make decisions that are within our private sphere, neither majority of the people nor (moral) experts should have an authority to limit our liberty. Things change, however, when our decisions influence other people beside us, just like all political decisions do:

> There would be no pretense for applying this doctrine to any case which could with reason be considered as one of individual and private right. In an affair that concerns only one of two persons, that one is entitled to follow his own opinion, however much wiser the other might be than himself. But we are speaking of things that equally concern them both; where, if the more ignorant does not yield to the guidance of the wiser man, the wiser man must resign to more ignorant. ... No one but a fool, and a fool of peculiar description, feels offended by the acknowledgement that there are others whose opinion, and even whose wish, is entitled to a greater amount of consideration than his. (Mill 1861, 172–173)

Giving greater political influence to the voice of an expert in such situation can be legitimate. In fact, as indicated in the final chapter of this book, in such cases we have a duty to distribute political influence unequally (see also Miller 2015, 410–411). Mill thus indicates that:

> When two persons who have a joint interest in any business, differ in opinion, does justice require that both opinions should be held of exactly equal value? If ... one is superior to other in knowledge and intelligence, the judgment of a higher moral or intellectual being is worth more than that of an inferior: and if the institutions of the country virtually assert that they are of the same value, they assert a thing which is not. One of the two, as a wiser or better man, has a claim to a superior weight. (Mill 1861, 172)

As we can see from the quotes above, Mill endorses the *truth tenet*, arguing that political decisions can be right or wrong according to some procedure-independent standard (i.e., consequences they produce), but also the *knowledge tenet*, affirming that there are people with superior knowledge in politics, those who know what should be done better than others, and the *authority tenet*, claiming that such people should have greater political influence (and greater authority) in the formal political sphere.[17] His plural voting proposal has a distinct instrumental (and epistemic) justification: distributing political influence unequally is the best instrument for creating political outcomes (laws, policies and decisions) of optimal epistemic quality.

Dale Miller (2015, 410) seems to endorse this interpretation yet argues that there is "an even more fundamental consideration than these issues of good policy." This important consideration is justice and, if unjust, plural voting could not be justified despite its "contributions to the effectiveness and educational power of government" (Miller 2015, 410). Miller acknowledges that, for Mill, the principles of justice are grounded in utility, and proceeds to emphasize that voting is a privilege and exercise of power over others. However, precisely for these reasons, it seems that the educated are given additional votes because giving them greater political influence increases the overall quality of political decisions, and when we have to exercise power over others, we have a duty to do so in the epistemically optimal way. Were it not contributing to the overall quality of results, for the purpose of attributing additional votes education would be just as irrelevant as wealth or social influence.

Plural Voting Proposal and the Education of Citizens

Mill holds that plural voting also helps improve citizens' existing moral and intellectual capacities. While the educational effect of participation has already been addressed in earlier chapters, we still have to analyze how (and why) the unequal distribution of political influence positively affects citizens' capacities. Mill (1861, 180) thus indicates that he considers equal voting "in principle wrong," because it exercises "a bad influence on the voter's mind." He then proceeds to add that "it is not useful, but hurtful, that the constitution of the country should declare ignorance to be entitled to as much power as knowledge" (Mill 1861, 180). Plural voting thus plays an important institutional role since it "shapes the national character" and teaches citizens about the value of education (Miller 2015, 409). However, plural voting fulfills its educational role in two additional ways.

First, by preventing class legislation, plural voting fosters deliberation and epistemically fertile agonism. Since no social group can impose its will upon others and promote only its class interest, citizens and their political representatives are forced to deliberate, to defend their own views against criticism and to think in terms of the common good and the public interest. Mill reminds us that "the position which gives the strongest stimulus to the growth of intelligence is that of rising into power, not that of having achieved it," and proceeds to add that "the one which promotes the best and highest qualities is the position of those who are strong enough to make reason prevail, but not strong enough to prevail against reason" (Mill 1861, 182). Plural voting proposal creates a balance between classes and thus fosters favorable social conditions for deliberation and the use of reason, and thus for the improvement of citizens' intellectual and moral capacities.

Second, by promoting opinions and perspectives of well-educated citizens, plural voting ensures that these ideas will be thoroughly discussed in representative bodies, but also in the informal political sphere (media, social movements and rallies, political campaigns). This will bring "inferior minds in contact with superior," which contributes "more than anything else to keep the generality of mankind on one level of contended ignorance" (Mill 1861, 281–281). Plural voting thus plays an important role in national education since it raises the overall level of political debates and enables epistemically fertile interaction between citizens with various levels of education[18] (Miller 2003).

Plural Voting: Temporary or Permanent Measure?

Many scholars (often following the republican tradition) seem to believe that the main motive Mill had to suggest plural voting was to stop the tyranny of the majority in a form of class legislation (Brink 2013, Brilhante and Rocha 2013, Urbinati 2002, Honohan 2002, Justman 1990, Gutmann 1980). After all, introducing plural voting and giving the educated (i.e., the minority of voters) more than one vote might look like an attempt to defend the republican value of non-domination (Pettit 1999). For example, Brilhante and Rocha (2013, 62) claim that "Mill would not have favored inequalities that implied undue power over others because this would undermine the autonomy that was a central value in his political philosophy," and add that he "advocated the plural voting system on the assumption that it would increase general happiness by preventing the tyranny of the majority." Similarly, Amy Gutmann (1980, 51) writes that Mill finds equal voting "appropriate in the future when each person's potential as a progressive being is realized," and Nadia Urbinati (2002, 77) agrees by indicating that the aim of plural voting was to "preserve pluralism and to offset the power of the majority." The danger of too low standard of political intelligence is often neglected, and the entire plural voting proposal is regarded as a temporary solution Mill used "in [his] stage of things" to answer the problem of British electorate in the nineteenth century. However, there are good reasons to consider Mill's plural voting account as a permanent solution.[19]

In fact, Mill's own words oppose those who think that plural voting is only a temporary solution that should not be considered as an important part of his political thought. Namely, Mill emphasizes that he does not "propose the plurality as a thing in itself undesirable, which, like the exclusion of a part of the community from the suffrage, may be temporarily tolerated while necessary to prevent greater evils" (Mill 1861, 180). It is clear that Mill's main reason for plural voting is not class legislation, the 'greater evil' from the previous quote. Even in a society where there is no fear of one class or group of people being able to control the political process without having to give reasons in order to have sufficient support, Mill would still opt for plural voting and against the equality of votes.

> I do not look upon equal voting as among the things which are good in themselves, provided they can be guarded against inconveniences. I look upon it as only relatively good, . . . but in principle wrong, because of recognizing a wrong standard, and exercising a bad influence on the voter's mind. It is not useful, but hurtful, that the constitution of a country should declare ignorance to be entitled to as much political power as knowledge. (Mill 1861, 180)

Mill is very clear when he assets that plural voting is not just an instrument that can be used to prevent class legislation. He thinks that unequal distribution of political influence represents an important feature of a well-functioning democracy, and grounds this claim in epistemic foundations. Namely, democracy has to implement a plural voting mechanism to achieve optimal results, i.e., to produce political decisions of optimal quality and to best improve citizens' intellectual and moral capacities. Even if all citizens acquire decent education, some differences in their level of education will still exist. Even the most egalitarian interpretations of Mill's political thought do not include arguments for equal distribution of education (only for equal distribution of capability for education).[20] He thus believes that, even in the ideal future society where (almost) all citizens have acquired decent level of education, some will be better educated and more competent than others. Since there will always be inequalities in citizens' competences, plural voting will always play an important role. Its epistemic and educational functions will be relevant as long as there are inequalities in citizens' competences.

THE EPISTEMIC ROLE OF PLURAL VOTING

Mill is well aware of the defects that any form of government might have. He points out that the worst defects a democratic government might face are its inability to produce good decisions and its tendency to be influenced by particular interests of dominant groups (Mill 1977a, 436). Plural voting was introduced as a means to counter these defects: its main purpose was to ensure that the representative government produces high quality outcomes, and that no group has exclusive right to the benefits of social cooperation by the power of votes alone (and without having to deliberate and convince others to support the decision in question).

It is unclear, however, how exactly was plural voting proposal supposed to counter the first defect of democratic government, i.e., to ensure that the procedure produces good decisions. How was plural voting supposed to achieve its purpose? Baccarini and Ivanković (2015, 147–149) claim that plural voting proposal seriously threatens the quality of outcomes. It is unclear at which stage of the decision-making process does the epistemic value of plural voting help us create better policies and decisions. They analyze the problem stage (where political values are expressed and some problems are detected), the proposal stage (where the educated commission drafts laws and policies), and the approval stage (where the Parliament chooses to pass or reject a certain law proposed by the commission) and claim that plural voting proposal does not bring epistemic value in any of the stages mentioned above. Similar objections are raised by Gaus (2008) and Peter (2012), who claim that it is very difficult to determine who are the experts regarding some political issue and add that the relevant competences for making or authorizing political decisions are often so widely dispersed that the (epistemic) distinction between citizens and experts is small and irrelevant, just like the (epistemic) distinction between procedures characterized by equal suffrage and those characterized by plural voting.

This part of the chapter tries to answer why Mill thought plural voting proposal had epistemic value, and in which stage of the decision-making process did this epistemic value manifest itself. In order to answer these questions, we must first analyze the sophisticated structure of democratic government and the key stages of democratic decision-making process, as well as different concepts of expertise.

Moral and Technical Knowledge

As indicated in the first chapter, Thomas Christiano introduces a useful distinction between technical and moral knowledge. Technical knowledge regards crafts, skills and disciplines like engineering, medicine, carpentry, physics, law or computer sciences. Most people can see this knowledge as useful and some educational institutions can be publicly seen as reliable sources of this knowledge. However, there is another kind of knowledge, one that regards what is right and what is wrong. This is moral knowledge, and it is about values. It is not as public as technical knowledge since we have a widespread disagreement on the moral issues, including disagreement on who the experts in morality are (Christiano 2008 and 2012). Mill agrees that the technical knowledge is probably more public that the moral knowledge, but unlike Christiano he thinks that we can still determine those whose "opinions and even wishes" (Mill 1861, 173–174) should be given greater consideration. Mill does not set strict constrains on education (he does not insist that only philosophers, or only experts in political science or economics, have greater political influence), nor does he name the exact profession one has to have in order to have more than one vote. His main idea is that people who have dedicated some time and effort to improving their intellectual and moral capacities are generally more capable of knowing what is more valuable in life (they are better acquainted with higher pleasures), and therefore are more capable of setting valuable aims for the society in general.

Plural Voting and Division of Labor

Mill firmly believed in the idea of epistemic division of labor and consequently, that laws and political decisions should be made by the most competent members of a society (i.e., experts). He saw division of labor as one of the central reasons for rejecting direct democracy, but did not believe that parliament should make laws, public policies and political decisions. This task was to be appointed to small expert bodies (commissions), while it was the task of the Parliament to discuss and deliberate on proposed laws and decisions, as well as to accept or refuse proposals made by such commissions (Mill 1977a, 424). Unlike expert bodies, Mill did not think that the Parliament should be composed primarily of experts:

> [Members of parliament] are not a selection of the greatest political minds in the country, from whose opinions little could with certainty be inferred concerning those of the nation, but are, when properly constituted, a fair sample of every grade of intellect among the people which is at all entitled to a voice in public affairs. Their part is to indicate wants, to be an organ for popular demands, a place of adverse discussion for all opinions relating to public matters, both great and small. (Mill 1861, 106)

Therefore, considering the division of labor and a purely deliberative function of the Parliament, Mill did not have in mind that plural voting will directly ensure more competent lawmakers and policymakers. The (technical) competences of lawmakers and policymakers can be similar both under monarchical and democratic rule (Mill 1977a, 438–439). Plural voting is introduced to give additional strength to opinions and even wishes of those better educated, and to increase the number of people representing these opinions and wishes in the Parliament. If small expert bodies (commissions) are those who devise practical means (laws, policies, decisions) to achieve a desired political end, it is the Parliament who sets these political ends, and in setting them, the parliament represents the general public. However, plural voting enables the Parliament to put a greater emphasis on ends that well-educated people consider valuable (because their opinions are better represented in the parliament). Plural voting thus improves the quality of political decisions not by improving the technical process of finding best practical solutions to designated problems, but by improving the quality of political aims we as a society want to achieve. To answer Baccarini and Ivanković's question, the epistemic value of plural voting is introduced primarily in the problem stage of democratic decision-making process. What we define as a problem in a society depends on the values and aims we want to pursue. For example, if we want to protect the traditional family with father as breadwinner and mother as caretaker (Kristol 1995), having a 30 percent unemployment rate will not be a serious political problem, as long as those unemployed are women. Similarly, if our political aim is full employment, even a five percent unemployment rate can be considered a serious political problem. Mill believes that the plural voting proposal will affect the quality of aims and values set by the citizens and the Parliament, and this will improve the quality of laws and policies since they will now be designed to achieve more valuable aims.

Mill's view is radically different from the thoughts of many contemporary political philosophers and epistemologists who discuss the role of experts in a democratic society. Philip Kitcher and Thomas Christiano, for example, agree that it is the role of a democratic process to set up important aims, and the role of experts to devise means for achieving these aims (Kitcher 2011, Christiano 2012). We should be democratic egalitarians when discussing political aims, and advocate expertise only when we discuss practical means for achieving those aims. Mill clearly disagrees and rejects democratic egalitarianism: there are those who are more competent in setting valuable aims and they should have greater political influence in a democratic decision-making and decision-authorization process.[21] Of course, this does not imply that *only* those more competent should participate in the process of defining valuable aims, since that would reintroduce the danger of class legislation, but also damage the epistemic value of diverse perspective. In order to have an epistemically optimal system we need to combine political participation of (virtually all) citizens with unequal distribution of political influence (grounded in citizens' competences).

CONCLUDING REMARKS

The relevance of plural voting proposal in Mill's political thought has often been disputed. The proposal has even been characterized as one of the few inconsistencies in Mill's philosophical project, a mechanism that casts elitist shadow on his otherwise liberal and progressive ideas. We must, however, resist an increasingly common trend of interpreting Mill's ideas from the standpoint of contemporary liberal thought, especially when such interpretations contradict the very statements Mill made himself. Plural voting proposal plays an important role in Mill's philosophical thought—it puts together and connects various principles and values Mill considered important for a good collective decision-authorization process. This process does not rest on the idea of political equality, but on the complex structure that incorporates both the epistemic value of diverse perspectives and the epistemic value of expertise. Consequently, it stresses both the importance of political participation and the importance of unequal political influence citizens should have. We can discuss how Mill's ideas could be implemented in a contemporary liberal philosophy, yet we should not forget Mill's basic ideas and the utilitarian justificatory process behind them.

NOTES

1. James Burns thus writes that Mill's viewpoint is not, in a strict sense, the "viewpoint of a democrat" (Burns 1957, 294).

2. Estlund characterizes scholocracy as a collective decision-authorization procedure in which each and every citizen has some political influence and can participate in the decision-authorization process. However, citizens' influence in the formal political sphere is unequally distributed, with well-educated citizens having larger formal influence than those who have received poor or average education. In effect, all citizens have (at least) one vote, yet those with better education have more than one (Estlund 2003, 57–58).

3. While he often refers to voting as a privilege (Mill 1977a, 411, 469–471, 474, see also 1977b, 333), he also sometimes speaks of citizens' voting rights (Mill 1977a, 415, 451, 481, 1977b, 339).

4. Furthermore, many (Thompson 1976, Krouse 1982, Wolfe 1985, Baccarini 1993, Cohen 2000) will stress the protective function of voting rights and privileges. Suffrage gives (virtually) all citizens a say in collective decision-authorization process, enabling them to voice their concerns, present their arguments and protect their interests. While I agree on this with other authors, I consider protective function as an element of more basic and unifying epistemic function. Namely, a procedure accomplishes its protective function when it produces outcomes of optimal procedure-independent epistemic (and moral) quality, i.e., when it produces "the greatest amount of beneficial consequences, immediate and prospective" (Mill 1861, 54).

5. This, of course, does not imply that their perspectives and opinions are epistemically worthless and should as such be disregarded by lawmakers and policymakers. The fact that one's opinions and wishes might be useful as one influence among others does not automatically imply that one should, regardless of one's "present state of moral and intelligence, . . . be admitted to the full exercise of suffrage" (Mill 1859b, 42–43).

6. However, Mill is quick to add that this filtering mechanism should be fine-tuned since it risks discouraging interested and competent citizens from voting, provided they live too far from the voting poll. Similarly, it risks discriminating against some social groups which might, in turn, prevent an epistemically valuable perspective from entering public deliberation. For more information on this filtering mechanism see *Thoughts on Parliamentary Reform* (Mill 1859b and 1977b).

7. However, there might be an intrinsic (justice-related) argument for inequality of political influence. This argument is addressed later in the chapter. Also, for additional information see Miller (2015).

8. To additionally stress this point, it might be useful to point out important differences between Mill's approach and the approach of those who base democratic legitimacy on the idea of equality. For example, Thomas Christiano (2008) builds his theory on a basic claim that human beings are authorities in the realm of value because (i) they are capable of recognizing, appreciating and producing value, and because (ii) their exercise of this authority is itself intrinsically valuable. Christiano further claims that equal status of persons is based on the fact that human beings all have essentially the same basic capacities to be authorities in the realm of value (Christiano 2008). Mill (1977a, 1977b), on the other hand, believes that there are obvious differences in people's capacity of appreciating intrinsic values (his version of 'higher pleasures' utilitarianism), and that differences in this capacity should produce differences in status. He explicitly states that citizens' rights should *not* be equally distributed "until all are equal in worth as human beings" and proceeds to argue that "it is a fact that one person is *not* as good as another" (Mill 1859b, 23). Of course, this does not imply that those who are better educated should direct the private lives of those who are not (Mill clearly stresses this point in *On Liberty*), nor should they have absolute power in political arena (this is pointed out in *Considerations on Representative Government*). The underlying reason for this is not equality, however, but the idea that intellectual and moral qualities of all human beings should be cherished and improved, and this would be impossible if other people direct our every action. It does not imply, however, that everyone should have an equal say in a collective decision-authorization process (see Cerovac 2016b).

9. As indicated in earlier chapters, Mill thinks not all citizens are fit for the exercise of suffrage, i.e., not all are fit to have influence in the formal political sphere. Those who have not received even minimal education (being able to read, write and do simple arithmetic), those who pay no taxes and those who receive welfare support from the state should not be allowed to exert power over others. However, after comprehensive educational reform Mill was arguing for, the total share of such (unfit for suffrage) citizens would be minimal. For additional information see Mill (1977a, 467–481).

10. Interestingly, *one person, one vote* democracy shifted from what was considered an extremist position in min-Victorian period to what can be considered the political mainstream in the twentieth century.

11. Egland had a population of 24.397,385 in 1881 (Wrigley and Schofield 1981, 208–209), and there were 2.338,809 registered voters in 1880 (Craig 1977, 623). This implies that approximately 10 percent of total population had electoral rights, and this

percentage would go higher when applied to the number of adult citizens. This was not so different from the suffrage in Athenian democracy, where "probably no more than 30% of the total adult population" were allowed to participate in the (formal) political process (Thorley 2005, 74).

12. Mill asks whether "the Parliament, or almost any of the members composing it, ever for in instant look at any question with the eyes of the working man?," and proceeds to argue that, although he is not suggesting that the working men's view is in general nearer to the truth than the other, "it is sometimes quite as near; and in any case it ought to be respectfully listened to, instead of being, as it is, not merely turned away from, but ignored" (Mill 1861, 56–57).

13. For additional information on procedural and substantive criterion in plural voting models see Latimer (2018).

14. Mill indicates that Lorimer builds a descriptive account instead of focusing on how the political influence ought to be distributed (Mill 1977c, 357).

15. For additional information on mid-Victorian debates on parliamentary reform see Conti (2019) and Quinault (2011).

16. Mill indicates that ideal representative system has to be organized in a way that "two classes, manual laborers and their affinities on one side, employers of labor and their affinities on the other [are] equally balanced" (Mill 1861, 129).

17. For additional information on the three tenets see Estlund (2008) and Cerovac (2020).

18. Mill believes this interaction will be useful both to those lacking proper education and those well-educated though, of course, not to the same degree. Nonetheless, since political agonism has beneficial epistemic effects (e.g., produces constant challenges and prevents correct beliefs from becoming a dogma), even citizens with best education will profit from interaction with others. See Mill (1977d) and Latimer (2018).

19. This interpretation is endorsed by Chin Ten (1980) and Chris Baker (2015). Dale Miller (2015) and Ivan Cerovac (2016b) focus their papers precisely on this point.

20. Requiring or even promoting equal education for all citizens would limit their autonomy and thus seriously endanger the epistemic value of personal liberties.

21. These ideas are grounded in his differentiation between higher and lower pleasures (Mill 1985a) and are addressed earlier in this book, in the chapter on education and competence.

Chapter 6

The Epistemic Role of Partisanship

The previous chapters discussed Mill's account of political representation and its beneficial effect on the quality of political decisions. Representation facilitates and improves all three functions of public deliberation.[1] *First*, deliberation can have its transformative function and forces us to reflect on our beliefs and opinions, preferably leading to their transformation in the light of better reasons and arguments, only if we deliberate with citizens holding different political views. Deliberation with like-minded people loses much of its transformative potential. Proper political representation thus serves as a precondition guaranteeing that all relevant social voices will be expressed and, hopefully, heard. *Second*, deliberation can have its constructive function and help us construct new positions and arguments only if different social perspectives are included in the deliberative process. Repeatedly discussing the same issues with with people belonging to the same social group we belong is not going to construct new positions but will instead reinforce our existing biases and prejudices. Diversity of perspectives in public deliberation can only be secured through proper political representation, reflecting all relevant social perspectives. *Third*, deliberation fulfills its epistemic function when political debate aims at acquiring knowledge and producing the best and most just political decisions.[2] Again, to properly discharge this function, public deliberation has to avoid the dangers of group polarization and crippled epistemology (Talisse 2009, Sunstein 2011), which can significantly reduce the quality of its outcomes. Representing all relevant social groups and, even more importantly, all relevant social perspectives (Mill 1977c, 358) is required in order to discuss and justify laws and policies in terms of good reasons and arguments, those leading to correct, efficient or just political decisions.

However, having a proper system of political representation is not enough to establish and sustain transformative, constructive and epistemically fertile deliberation in democratic societies. A political system has to be organized to shape public deliberation in a way that enables and promotes these functions. A few important questions thus remain unanswered. Once we have acknowledged the beneficial effects of political representation, how should we organize and moderate public deliberation, both among political representatives in the formal political sphere (e.g., in the Parliament) and among citizens in the informal political sphere (e.g., trade unions or interest groups)? Also, how can we properly link the deliberation taking place in the formal political sphere with the one in the informal political sphere, thus securing continuous interaction between representatives and their constituencies, as well as between the political system, informal public sphere and civil society? Finally, how can we manage and contain conflict that inevitably arises in liberal and democratic societies, but also ensure that public deliberation reaches high epistemic standards? In other words, once we have adopted a system of political representation, how can we make it work? These are serious challenges for all deliberative (and epistemic) democrats, and Mill's answer to these challenges represents the central theme of this chapter.

European political tradition typically answers this challenge by appealing to political parties and other partisan associations—they are seen as proper instruments that can manage and organize political conflict, adequately integrate political representation, ensure decent quality of political discussion and the subsequent outcomes (laws, policies and decisions), as well as connect formal and informal political sphere. There is no surprise that Mill, just like many other political thinkers of his time, reflects on the role of partisanship in liberal and democratic societies and discusses some of the advantages and disadvantages of party system. This chapter follows and reinterprets Mill's political thought on partisanship, emphasizing the epistemic role these associations can (and should) have in democratic decision-making and decision-authorization procedures, as well as the dangers partisanship introduces in democratic politics.

This chapter provides innovative contribution to the ongoing debate by characterizing partisan politics as one of Mill's mechanisms for filtering the public will. Evaluating political parties and partisan associations in this way, as organizations introducing both spatial and temporal indirectness in the decision-making processes, enables us to focus on Mill's thoughts regarding the epistemic (instrumental) value of partisanship. Furthermore, the analysis of Mill's critical attitude towards the party system of his time enables us to answer which features partisan associations should (and which they should not) have in order to improve the epistemic quality of democratic process.

The chapter is divided in two parts, gradually building and reinterpreting Mill's justification of partisanship. The *first* part addresses the fact that partisanship was often neglected by philosophers arguing in favor of deliberative democracy (Rosenblum 2008), and presents an overview of how various philosophers (mis)interpreted Mill's account on political parties. It proceeds by reconstructing Mill's definition of a political party (Kinzer 1981, Mill 1982a) and enlisting Mill's principles for assessing the nature and quality of influence of any organization, association or institution on democratic politics. This will help us assess the criteria we can use to evaluate the party system and determine whether it improves or hinders public deliberation and the epistemic value of political conflict. Finally, in the *second part,* some epistemic advantages of the party system are analyzed and supported by Mill's views. Parties are characterized as "discursive architects" (Ypi and White 2010), but also as vehicles (Tinnevelt 2015) and catalysts (Habermas 1996) for deliberation. They facilitate representation by shaping people's visions of the future and reflecting the key cleavages in public opinion (Mill 1977a, Rosanvallon 2008), but also promote and structure public deliberation (Biezen and Saward 2008) and filter the content that enters the public sphere. Furthermore, political parties are valuable instruments that help us institutionalize and manage political conflict (Dalaqua 2018b), introduce competence in democratic deliberation (Thompson 1976, Christiano 2012), strengthen the underrepresented classes through political education and organization (Kinzer 1981, Ypi and White 2016) and create a deliberative link between civil society and the state (Lawson 1988, Teorell 1999). All these advantages are, in a more or less direct way, already discussed and emphasized by Mill, and his assessment of these advantages is built upon his epistemic justification of democracy.

MILL, PARTISANSHIP AND PUBLIC DELIBERATION

Though representative democracy is widely accepted and affirmed as a decision-making and decision-authorization procedure with considerable legitimacy-generating potential, not all representative institutions have a good reputation. Political parties have often been thought of as subversive elements that endanger both the moral and the epistemic qualities of democratic decision-making procedures: they organize citizens in order to promote the private, but not the public good (Rousseau 1997), they have a damaging effect on their members' epistemic capacities (Atchison 2012), they polarize the democratic society (Layman, Carsey and Horowitz 2006) and even lead to de-stimulation of voter turnout (Brady, Ferejohn and Harbridge 2008). Though these critiques come from proponents of both aggregative and deliberative democracy, the latter have traditionally been more hostile towards partisanship, sometimes completely ignoring the need for partisan associations in the electoral representative democracy, and sometimes removing deliberation from conventional political arenas, elections and parties and placing it inside alternative deliberative arenas (e.g., mini-publics[3]) where the participants are non-partisans (Rosenblum 2008).

However, in order to answer whether any political institution increases or decreases the quality of democratic decision-making and decision-authorization process, we should first formulate a set of criteria according to which we shall evaluate the effect of this institution on a democratic society. Considering that we are focusing on Mill's evaluation of partisanship, we should start from his own evaluative criteria.

Mill's Criteria for Evaluation of Political Institutions and Organizations

The two criteria of good government, as well as their philosophical justification, have already been discussed and analyzed in the first chapter of this book. The first focuses on the government's ability to improve moral and intellectual capacities of its subjects, while the second addresses the government's ability to organize citizens' existing moral and intellectual virtues to the best possible effect (Mill 1977a, 390–392). Furthermore, I have already argued in the first chapter that both criteria are instrumental and epistemic in nature, and contribute to the shared common goal, the production of correct laws and policies that produce the greatest amount of beneficial consequences (Mill 1977a, 404). However, a question remains whether we can apply the same criteria for the evaluation of other political institutions and organizations, not only the government itself.

I follow Thompson (1976), Kinzer (1982) and many others who argue that Mill applies the same criteria for evaluation of all political institutions, including the system of partisan political associations. Political parties and other partisan associations are thus seen as good if they expand the ability of a political system to improve and organize citizens' existing moral and intellectual capacities. They are, of course, portrayed as harmful if they diminish the political system's ability to produce such consequences. The key question thus becomes how political parties affect collective deliberation? Mill emphasizes this when he argues that, "though Government cannot be better than collective mind of the community, it can do a great deal to uphold or undermine the *social influences* which *either prevent or improve the collective mind*" (Mill 1977c, 357, emphasis added). Party system is one of such social (and political) influences, a filtering mechanism that can be considered good or bad depending on whether it improves or reduces the quality of public deliberation.

Having established that, for Mill, political conflict can have considerable epistemic value, we have proceeded by analyzing how political institutions and filtering mechanisms can fuel and moderate political conflict, making it epistemically fertile. The central question now becomes how political parties, understood as one of these filtering mechanisms, influence the epistemic value of political conflict? Do they moderate it successfully, thus increasing its epistemic potential? Or do they fuel the conflict but fail to contain it, thus decreasing its epistemic value and making it counterproductive? To answer these questions, we should (temporarily) abandon Mill's two vague principles and ground our evaluation on a list of more explicit criteria (that are, nonetheless, based on Mill's two principles of good government). Dennis Thompson (1976, 13–90, see also Zakaras 2009, 181–182) distinguishes between principle of participation and principle of competence, and attributes educational and protective function to each of the principles. The political institution has a good social impact if it increases citizen participation, and in doing so improves citizens' moral and intellectual capacities and ensures that everyone's interests are protected. Similarly, political institution has good social impact when it makes proper use of existing competences in a society, thus protecting everyone's interests from the disastrous public effects of ignorance and setting an example from which all citizens can learn.

We can evaluate political parties in this light, and in doing so we should answer the following four questions: first, do political parties increase citizen participation in a way that improves moral and intellectual capacities of their members and sympathizers? Second, do they increase participation in a way that enables members of underprivileged classes to voice their perspective and protect their interests? Third, do they organize the existing competences of their members in a way that facilitates production of the best political decisions? And fourth, do they set good examples for citizens and create an environment in which citizens can acquire new competences? If we can answer positively on all four questions, we should conclude that political parties have a beneficial role in the political system. However, if most or all of these questions are answered negatively, we should be led to conclude that political parties decrease the quality of democratic decision-making process.

Having set forth clear evaluative criteria, we can turn our inquiry to Mill's own assessment of partisan politics. However, before proceeding we should briefly address the dominant interpretation of Mill's stance on partisanship and articulate why it does not represent a coherent approach to Mill's position on political parties.

Mill on Partisanship: A Dominant Interpretation?

It comes as no surprise that many contemporary philosophers share quite a negative view when they discuss the role of partisanship in Mill's political thought. Henry Sidgwick (2012), for example, indicates that Mill did not consider partisan organizations as a normal feature of representative institutions, while Dennis Thompson (1976, 118–120) emphasizes that Mill was hostile towards party government and did not consider it necessary for stable and effective democracy. This reading is clearly inspired by Mill's writings on representative government (1977a, 1977b, 1977c), where Mill endorses Hare's (2015) electoral system. Hare opposed the idea of electoral boroughs and argued that the entire state should be a single electoral unit, and Mill saw this system as an excellent instrument for improving the quality of the personnel in the parliament, often selected not on the basis of their competence but on their material wealth or their willingness to follow party leaders (Mill 1977c, 362–363). The mid-Victorian party system was clearly in conflict with Mill's principles of participation and education, as it was not fulfilling its educative and protective function. Thompson and Sidgwick are right to conclude that Mill did not support the party system of his time. In fact, Mill would probably agree that it is better to have no parties at all than to have a party system like the one in nineteenth-century England. Nonetheless, even though Mill clearly articulated a few serious flaws of party politics, he also believed that Hare's electoral system can remedy these flaws. As Kinzer (1981, 107) skillfully indicates, Mill's hostility was not directed towards the idea of partisanship or the principle of party politics, but against the existing party system. He had developed a normative theory of political parties[4] and had a clear idea of what a party should be. The existing party system in 19th century England, characterized by petty party warfare empty of ideological content, was far from Mill's ideal system, one where structured political agonism transforms existing beliefs, creates new positions and produces better political decisions. Mill's apparent negative stance towards political parties, indicated by many contemporary philosophers (Sidgwick 2012, Thompson 1976), actually represents his critique of the current party system in 19th century England, and not of the normative idea of partisanship. However, before proceeding we should turn to the distinction between Mill's descriptive and normative conception of partisanship. What did Mill think of the party system in his time, and what he believed a political party should be?

Mill's Evaluation of mid-Victorian Party System

Mill's approach to political parties somewhat changed throughout the years, and his view was influenced by the existing party system in nineteenth-century England. Two dominant parties (Conservative or Tory Party and Liberal or Whig Party) fought for political power in the Parliament, yet their struggle was empty of any meaningful ideological content. Mill firmly believed that each of these parties should follow a set of principles (order and stability for Conservatives and progress and reform for Liberals) built upon solid intellectual foundations. Tories should thus hold that "the real model of government lies somewhere behind us in the region of the past" and argue in favor of "the subjection and dependence of the great mass of the community ... upon the hereditary possessors of wealth and ... the Church," while Whigs should see "the perfect model of government ... before us and not behind us, ... not in the direction of some new form of dependence, but in the emancipation of the dependent classes" (Mill 1988a, 28–31). Mill held that the political conflict between these two elaborate perspectives would thus be creative and epistemically fertile, and the laws and policies produced through this structured conflict would be grounded upon the best reasons and arguments, those that can withstand serious criticism. However, as Mill (1972) often emphasized, members of both parties were completely unaware or did not understand the principles that should have served as the intellectual and organizational foundation of their parties. Partisanship thus turned into mere factionism[5], with political activists focused on their personal or class interests and not on the common good or the political values their party should have promoted.

Besides the obvious ignorance and ideological unawareness of party members, Mill held that the party system of his time was introducing a few harmful effects that were severely crippling the epistemic quality of democratic decision-making procedures. We can arrange these harmful effects in two groups: those preventing many citizens distinguished by their virtue or intelligence from being elected as Members of the Parliament, and those affecting the reason and autonomy of those already elected.

Mill was concerned that the party system of his time was not improving but was instead deteriorating the quality of political representatives. In his evaluation of Hare's electoral model (Mill 1977c), Mill was thrilled with the innovations Hare had suggested and offered several arguments indicating why this system represents a far better model than the existing one, based on the Reform Bill of Lord Aberdeen's Government (Mill 1977b). The first advantage Mill discusses is the ability of Hare's model to improve the personnel in the Parliament. Namely, England was divided in many boroughs, and each of these electoral units was sending a single representative to the Parliament. This prevented many distinguished men from being elected since their supporters were dispersed and local grandees (often men of questionable intellectual and moral capacities), whose influence and reputation were limited to a small area, got elected since they had local support. Following this observation, Mill notices that party leaders often choose to support local grandees as candidates in the parliamentary elections. Even among local grandees, party leaders favor wealthy candidates willing to spend money during the election process and candidates who will blindly follow party leadership and local opinion (Mill 1977b, 362–363). Finally, other party members and sympathizers in an electoral unit are thus forced to support the candidate appointed by party leadership, even when they disagree with the decision of party leaders and think the appointed candidate is not the best person to represent them in the Parliament. Refusing to support the appointed candidate produces a risk of dividing the party and giving victory to the other side. This was the first serious disadvantage of the party system in Mill's time: instead of supporting the best candidates whose novel perspectives and intellectual contribution can improve the quality of discussions in the Parliament, the party system (supported by the existing electoral model) supported local grandees and wealthy candidates dependent on party leadership. Not only were such candidates lacking intellectual and moral capacities to adequately contribute to the discussions in the Parliament, they also came from similar social backgrounds and were often alienated from the citizens they represented. Such party system was epistemically deficient and was unable to harness the available intellectual strength of the country and prevented the representative assembly from containing "the elite of the nation" (Mill 1977b, 362). Mill believes that Hare's model could easily tackle this problem. Party leaders would be forced to select the best candidates since their electors could vote for another party candidate somewhere else, in some other borough. Party leadership would thus be pushed to appoint "the best and most distinguished men on their own side" (Mill 1977b, 363), those who could find local support but also receive stray votes from other boroughs.

The second danger Mill saw in the party system of his time was the epistemically disastrous effect it could have on representatives' reason and autonomy. Political parties often require a substantial degree of discipline and obedience from their members, and this degree becomes even more demanding when applied to political representatives in the Parliament. Members of deliberative assembly were often required not only to vote, but also to argue and publicly speak in favor of laws and proposals they had found inadequate or even repugnant. This was a serious problem and Mill discussed it on several occasions, especially considering that he himself served as a Member of the Parliament from 1865 to 1868. First of all, Mill did not believe that such a high degree of party discipline is justified. He served as an "independent" Liberal (Kinzer 1982, 114) and argued that party members elected as political representatives should follow the principles that stand as the intellectual foundation of their parties, yet should not let themselves "be muddled under the pretense of keeping a Government in" and should always "vote as they thought best . . . and take their chances of whatever might be the result of a full and free discussion" (Mill 1988b, 34). Second, Mill believed that Hare's electoral model could remedy this problem as well. Since political representatives who did their part in the Parliament well could be re-elected even without direct support from the party leadership, they would be free to argue and vote according to their conscience and not following the orders of party leaders.

Mill was convinced that political parties can have a negative impact on the quality of deliberation in the Parliament. First, they prevent candidates of superior intellectual and moral qualities from being elected in the deliberative assembly, and second, they reduce the autonomy of political representatives and often urge them to argue or vote against their better judgment. However, Mill believed that these shortcomings can be overcome by Hare's electoral model. This model would force party leaders to support the best candidates and would weaken the party discipline that was severely limiting the autonomy of political representatives. Hare's model was thus seen as an adequate solution that would end the mediocrity of mid-Victorian parties and set foundations for a proper party system (Kinzer 1982, 113). Mill's arguments in *Considerations on Representative Government* and *Recent Writers on Reform* that show the perceived epistemic danger of a party system, often quoted by philosophers who argue that Mill was hostile to the idea of partisanship (Sidgwick 2012, Thompson 1976), are directed against the existing party system in nineteenth-century England, and not against the idea of partisanship. As we can see, Mill was eager to improve the existing party system and believed Hare's electoral model can help remove some of its shortcomings.

Mill's Normative Account of Partisanship

Although Mill had many doubts and did not believe that the mid-Victorian party system can have a positive impact on democratic decision-making processes, he did not abandon the idea of a well-functioning party system. In fact, he held that epistemically fertile public deliberation would be unattainable without some form of political organization, one that facilitates political participation and increases the deliberative capacities of its members. As Mill (1982a, 165) famously argues, "no body of men ever accomplished anything considerable in public life without organized cooperation." When people share some common values and principles and believe that these are important for the wider political community, they have to find means they can use to present these values and principles (as well as laws and policies following from them) in the deliberative assembly in the best possible manner. They should apply a form of division of labor, with some members focusing on recruitment or education of citizens, some working on implementation of these principles and values at the local, and some at the national level, while others might engage in administration, public relations or the intellectual work on the justification of the principles in question. A political party is thus "a means of giving organized political expression to ideological commitment" (Kinzer 1982, 107). It is instrumentally valuable since it represents the best means to achieve the desired end, i.e., to arrange the society in accordance with the principles and values we find important. Furthermore, it is epistemically valuable since it enables us to produce the best reasons and arguments to defend our principles (and laws and policies that implement them) in a deliberative assembly and, provided that the other side also uses the best available reasons and arguments, to produce correct and just political decisions.

As we can see from the previous paragraph, Mill considered political principles and values as core elements of a political party. They give unity and coherence to political parties, but also provide justification for laws and policies the party will argue for. Principles are the essence of a party (Kinzer 1982, 112). A huge problem arises when a political organization starts producing loyalties independent of principles that lie in its essence. This is the main reason for Mill's negative stance towards political parties in nineteenth-century England. Instead of improving the quality of public deliberation both by promoting the best candidates and through the division of epistemic labor, mid-Victorian parties were reducing the quality of deliberation (and the subsequent quality of political outcomes, laws and policies) by supporting candidates of average or below-average capacities and by turning public deliberation in petty party warfare. Mill thus firmly believed that parties are not (and should not be) vehicles for self-interested individuals or groups, but collective sources of knowledge and experience that can be improved and used to produce better political decisions. Like Rosenblum (2000, 816), Mill thought of political parties as "forums for reasonably deliberative collective decision-making about public life." Parties and partisanship had an important epistemic role to play, and the party system of nineteenth-century England failed to play this role.

This part of the chapter showed us that there is a huge difference between Mill's normative account of partisanship and his view of the mid-Victorian party system. When they play their role properly, partisan associations can improve the quality of public deliberation. However, when their political role is distorted, and parties become interest groups (factions) organized around private interests of their members instead around guiding political principles, parties can greatly reduce the quality of public deliberation. However, a question remains. How partisan associations, when they function properly, moderate political conflict and how can they improve the epistemic quality of deliberative procedures?

THE EPISTEMIC VALUE OF PARTISANSHIP

Political parties and partisan associations simultaneously fuel political conflict and contain it within liberal democratic institutions (Tinnevelt 2015, 11).

They realize the truth by reconciling and combining the opposites and do so within a system of contained struggle (Mill 1977d, see also Tinnevelt 2015). However, to systemize Mill's arguments in favor of partisan associations, it would be prudent to evaluate them along the lines of four questions indicated earlier, when we addressed Thompon's (1976) differentiation between the educative and the protective component of principle of participation and principle of competence. Do political parties increase citizen participation in a way that improves moral and intellectual capacities of their members and sympathizers? Do they increase participation in a way that enables members of underprivileged classes to voice their perspective and protect their interests? These first two questions address the influence partisan associations have on the capacities of their members. However, there are two more questions to be answered. Do political parties organize the existing competences, both of their members and the citizens in general, in a way that facilitates production of the best political decisions? Do they set good examples for citizens and create environment in which citizens can acquire new competences? These second two questions address the effect partisan associations have on the political system and its ability to produce correct and just decisions.

This part of the chapter provides affirmative answers to the above mentioned questions, indicating that properly structured system of political parties and partisan associations can be a valuable filtering mechanism. Furthermore, though it sometimes refers to arguments put forward by contemporary authors to demonstrate that partisanship can meet the normative criteria set by Mill, it also argues that Mill himself was aware of these arguments. It thus traces Mill's influence in many contemporary views on partisanship.

Partisan Associations and Citizens' Moral and Intellectual Development

One way to attribute epistemic value to some social or political institution is to claim that this institution improves citizens' knowledge-producing competences or generally helps them acquire knowledge. Furthermore, an institution can have epistemic value if it helps promote social values related to tolerance and deliberative ethos, which are in turn needed for citizens' moral and intellectual development.

Mill believes that political parties "provide civic education to the masses" (Kinzer 1981, 121). They disseminate political knowledge, as well as relevant political skills and competences, among their members enabling them to participate in the political process. Partisan associations can help citizens who lack the access to education in general, or to political education in particular, to gain new information and skills to make their political views more coherent. Similar ideas can be found in some contemporary authors. White and Ypi

(2016), for example, bring our attention to the story of Etienne Lantier, the protagonist of Zola's Germinal, who is taken to be a great example of such political education. Lantier starts as a poorly educated, rebellious and unemployed young man who, through his participation in epistemically enriching partisan associations, turns into an intellectually sophisticated activist (Zola 1983). Mill had this in mind when he expressed doubts regarding the political competence of political representatives from the working classes. He believes that workers should elect people from other classes (provided that such citizens are more competent to participate in the political process) to represent their views (Mill 1977c, 352, see also Urbinati 2000, 776), and partisan associations should help transfer some of these competences to the members of the working classes, enabling them to take more demanding political functions in the long run.[6] Political parties and related associations (political foundations, think tanks, informal groups or even trade unions) can be great platforms for systemizing and spreading political knowledge as well as for improving some relevant skills (verbal and non-verbal communication, networking, management and leadership skills). Partisan associations have a unique ability to connect citizens and experts who otherwise would not come into contact. Since partisan associations (unlike factions) gather around some central values (and not around private interests of group members), they often include members from various backgrounds and fields of expertise. Their joint political effort and focus on the same political aims, combined with partisan forums as means for inter-party deliberation and learning, ensures that complex views and topics requiring technical knowledge can become available to all citizens (Christiano 2012, see also Cerovac 2019).

However, and probably even more important, apart from being institutions of non-formal political education, partisan associations can serve as means for self-improvement through political participation. Mill emphasizes that being outside of the representative assembly (at the national level) does not deprive one of political power (Dalaqua 2018a, 6). First, he indicates that private citizens can participate in general politics (between parliamentary elections) by "reading newspapers, and perhaps writing to them, public meetings and solicitations addressed to political authorities" (Mill 1861, 275). Second, citizens can "be elected and fill one or other of the many local executive offices," and the participation in these "carries down the important political education" (Mill 1861, 276). In both cases, Mill argues that political participation and deliberation on various public issues can improve citizens intellectual and moral capacities.[7] Political parties with democratic internal structure can also be important sites of participation and deliberation. Members are invited to vote for party leadership, but also to participate in discussions on political ideas and values the party is organized around, as well as their application in real-world politics. Intra-party democracy can thus serve as another platform where citizens can, by participating in discussions and by taking place in various bodies, boards and offices, deliberate on public issues thus improving their intellectual and moral capacities.

Partisan Associations and the Protective Function of Participation

While the former section addressed how political parties can improve citizens' moral and intellectual capacities, this section shows that partisanship can help protect the public interest in general. Namely, partisan associations can strengthen underprivileged social groups and classes and organize them to participate in the political arena, thus enabling them to protect their own interests and values (Kinzer 1981, 121). This is, in turn, necessary for the protection of the public interest since we cannot hope that it will be properly determined or properly protected if some social groups lack any political influence (Mill 1977a, 404). Following Mill, protective function thus helps us create correct, just and efficient laws and policies since epistemically the best political system is the one that enables us to harvest valuable political input from all citizens and precludes the tyranny of the majority, where one group rules without having to use reasons and arguments to defend its views and policies grounded in them.

Mill is aware that much of the collective will-formation takes place outside formal political institutions, in the informal political sphere, sometimes referred to as "agora of the moderns" (Mill 1977a, as quoted in Dalaqua 2018a, 6). Social and economic inequalities often spill over to the informal political sphere thus making some groups unable to participate in democratic procedures. Members of powerless groups will be disadvantaged not only in regard to the access to political education and specialized (expert) knowledge but also in access to the resources needed to convey their political message to the wider public. These inequalities in political influence impair the epistemic value of democratic procedures when they prevent constructive conflict and advance ideas of a single group (Mill 1977d). There is little difference between one group having no voice in the Parliament (formal political sphere) and the same group having no voice in the media or in the other areas of public life (informal political sphere). In both cases, a valuable perspective is precluded from properly entering the public deliberation, thus demonstrating its strengths and indicating weaknesses in other perspectives. The epistemic value of political conflict is realized in both formal and informal political sphere, and huge inequalities in the distribution of wealth can prevent it from properly fulfilling itself in the informal sphere.

Partisan associations can help their members acquire epistemic resources (political education, skills and competences needed to participate in the democratic decision-making process, access to experts and policymakers, access to mass media) that will help them protect their interests and principles in democratic deliberation. Furthermore, partisan associations can help remedy hermeneutical epistemic injustice by enabling partisans to create new hermeneutic resources or to achieve a collective understanding of an injustice that affected each of the individuals, yet none had the hermeneutic ability to define what was wrong about that particular practice. Miranda Fricker (2007, 160–173, see also Medina 2013, 99–106) uses an example of 'sexual harassment,' a notion coined in 1960s to describe a practice that was going on for thousands of years. Nonetheless, only after coming together at university seminars and activist group meetings (composed primarily or exclusively of women participants) were those affected by that practice able to formulate what was exactly morally wrong with it, to coin a new term that can describe the practice appropriately and to plan political and legal action to prevent such practices from occurring in the future. Just like activist groups, political parties and partisan associations often gather citizens holding similar political principles, but also citizens facing similar social and political problems. Their joint deliberation within partisan associations can help them clearly articulate these problems, create new hermeneutical resources needed to describe some practices and phenomena, and plan collective political action to formulate and advance appropriate laws and policies. Though discussion on hermeneutic epistemic injustice takes place in the past decade, similar ideas can be found in Mill's letters to Harriet Taylor, where he considers the beneficial effects of the Convention of Women in Ohio (and later in Massachusetts) to claim equal rights. Mill proceeds to claim that these conventions, composed mostly of women participants, and where "most of the speakers are women," give him hope that he will live to see some of his and Taylor's ideas implemented into political practice (Mill 1850, as quoted in Hayek 2015, 163). These conventions enabled women to articulate the problems they were facing as a social group, but also to plan political action and to acquire support from the media and other social groups holding similar political values and principles. New York Tribune and other newspapers reported favorably on these conventions, and they were supported by many men, including slave abolitionists and Afro-Americans. We can thus see that Mill, similarly to Fricker almost 150 years later, believed that closed deliberation (within university seminar, activist group or partisan association) can have epistemic (and protective) function—it can help members of a social group to articulate their problems and to plan future political action. Parties thus provide "a concert for mutual aid among those who agree" on some political principle (Mill 1981b, 315). However, closed deliberation can only be fruitful when it is followed by public deliberation where all relevant perspectives are included. While the former can have some epistemically beneficial consequences, it cannot fully realize the educative and the protective function without the latter.

Furthermore, Mill is aware that "means of communication in a mass society can preclude public and critical debate once they start to propagate the ideas of only one group" (Mill 1977a, as paraphrased in Dalaqua 2018a, 7). This usually happens when the means of communication (media and publishing houses) in the informal political sphere are owned and controlled by the members of a single social group. Partisanship can reduce the impact of power asymmetries on agents' capacities to participate in reason-giving and decision-making processes. It does this task by cutting the link between social and economic power, and the access to political education and expert knowledge. Mill clearly hints in this direction, and Ypi and White build upon his idea by arguing that partisanship plays this role by offering certain irreplaceable epistemic resources. Partisan forums (including party conventions, branch meetings, assemblies, protests, blogs and websites) can then be seen as learning platforms for citizens. They empower disadvantaged citizens and give them epistemic resources needed for political participation. Furthermore, partisan forums have an important motivational role—they show disadvantaged citizens that they are not alone in their political struggle. Therefore, partisanship "plays an important role in ensuring the sustainability of shared political projects when epistemic challenges are at stake" (White and Ypi 2016, 90). It helps partisans remain true to their political principles by structuring public deliberation and offering hermeneutical resources (but also expert knowledge) needed to uphold the partisan commitment.[8] Of course, this can have epistemically beneficial consequences when it is practiced to a proper measure (it can give partisans epistemic resources to defend political principles they uphold), as well as epistemically disastrous effects when practiced excessively (when it leads to group polarization and crippled epistemology). However, when practiced properly, partisan associations can help protect and uphold faith in some political ideas to a healthy degree. Furthermore, they can protect the underprivileged classes from having their political will dispersed due to the lack of proper epistemic resources to defend their political principles. Though this argument looks similar to the former one (the one regarding moral and intellectual development of citizens), we have to take into account that giving epistemic resources to the members of the worst-off classes has a protective function as well since it enables them to protect their interests to make their voice heard in the informal political sphere.

As we have seen, Mill recognizes the instrumental value of political parties. They reduce the impact of power asymmetries on agents' capacities to participate in decision-making processes by helping their members acquire epistemic resources needed to protect their interests and perspectives in democratic deliberation. Recent work by Ypi and White supports Mill's argument and shows that partisan associations should help reduce the negative epistemic effects of power asymmetries in the informal political sphere. By organizing within political parties and other partisan associations, underprivileged social groups can acquire epistemic and political resources to participate in the political process, to give their valuable epistemic contribution and to help create epistemically optimal political outcomes.

Partisan Associations and the Organization of Citizens' Competences

While some arguments for the epistemic value of partisanship take indirect route and demonstrate how political parties can improve the intellectual and moral capacities of their members, thus improving the quality of the political discourse and the subsequent quality of laws, policies and decisions, some take a more direct approach and argue that partisan associations can help us organize the existing competences present within our political community to produce the best results. These arguments are discussed in this part of the chapter. Building on the central book from the chapter on the epistemic value of agonism, I follow Mill (but also Kinzer, Dalaqua, Tinnevelt and others who build upon Mill's argument) to argue that partisan associations can have an important epistemic role since they create, manage and institutionalize political conflict (which can be instrumentally valuable since it helps us acquire and uphold true beliefs). Furthermore, I discuss a few additional arguments Mill uses to support the epistemic value of partisanship, including its role in facilitating the interaction between representatives and citizens, as well as in improving the conduct of politicians. Finally, I argue that partisan associations can also help political representatives monitor and evaluate the work done by experts in the executive government.

Mill was aware that the epistemic quality of the deliberative process in which opposing views are articulated, evaluated and modified depends on the epistemic quality of the conflicting views themselves. The conflict of considered and well-argued judgments will epistemically be far more fertile than the conflict of rash and ill-considered judgments. To properly harness the epistemic value of political conflict, we should organize our epistemic (and political) practices to ensure that the views in the political arena are well-argued, but also to secure that objections and critiques are well-founded and clearly articulated. This can be achieved by allowing (and encouraging) like-minded citizens to collaborate in order to make their views grounded on the best possible reasons and evidence, before these reasons enter public deliberation and are confronted with opposing views held by others. Mill thus argues that "no body of men ever accomplished anything considerable in the public life without organized cooperation" (1982a, 165). Furthermore, he proceeds to claim that "truth . . . is so much a question of the reconciling and combining of opposites, that . . . it has to be made by the rough process of a struggle between combatants *fighting under hostile banners*" (1859a, 86, emphasis added). These combatants should be organized in partisan associations that will help them produce the best reasons and arguments to support their views, as well as find the best objections against the views of others.

Political parties have a demanding task: they have to structure and focus public opinion to make it appropriate for deliberation and democratic decision-making. Furthermore, they have to shape public opinion and prevent it from becoming too fragmented (as emphasized in Rosanvallon 2008), thus serving as "discursive architects" (Ypi and White 2010, 819). In other words, partisan associations play an important role as mechanisms filtering the public will, making political conflict epistemically fertile. Mill believes that political parties thus accomplish two important functions. First, they map the principal divisions in a democratic society through political representation. In order to attract popular support, parties have to advocate for political values and principles that at least some citizens consider important. Since citizens endorse conflicting values, political parties transfer this conflict into the formal sphere, and other partisan associations transfer it into the informal political sphere. Furthermore, political representation enables parties to map the conflict and properly emphasize important social divisions and issues that divide the public. Second, political parties structure, moderate and shape political conflict. Autonomy of representatives' judgment enables parties not merely to mirror existing social divisions but also to facilitate creative and transformative functions of public deliberation. They can negotiate and make political compromises that would be unattainable in systems characterized by the direct participation of citizens in decision-making and decision-authorization procedures (Mill 1977a, 1977c, also Urbinati 2002 and 2014). Mill thus believes that political parties simultaneously inject conflict in public deliberation and shape it to make it epistemically fertile (Dalaqua 2018b).

There are two further advantages of a party system. First, as we know from the previous chapters, Mill sees the Parliament as "the great council of the nation" (1977a, 534) and indicates that its members have greater moral (and not technical) knowledge than average citizens (1977b, 324). Parliament's role is to monitor and discuss the laws and policies produced by the executive government, a body composed primarily of experts with specialized technical knowledge (Mill 1977a, 433). However, an important question arises. How can political representatives monitor and properly discuss the laws and policies created by the executive government if they lack the technical knowledge to properly understand the reasons and arguments experts in the executive government use to argue in favor of these laws and policies? While the representatives are more than competent to discuss "the general affairs of life" (Mill 1977b, 324), a great majority of them will lack technical knowledge in some specific field relevant to a particular policy or decision produced by the executive government. Lacking the relevant technical knowledge, representatives will have to consult with the experts in the field before they can properly address the issue at hand in the Parliament. Partisan associations can facilitate the consultation process (Mill 1981b, 315), as well as knowledge transfer from scientists and experts to political representatives. While Mill does not discuss this in detail, this idea is elaborated by Thomas Christiano (2012) who emphasizes that representatives will find it much easier to believe the experts with whom they share similar political values and principles. While a left-wing representative might want to dismiss the information gained from a right-wing expert (e.g., economist or social worker) thinking that the expert wants to manipulate her to endorse some conservative policy), she will be less inclined to do so with the information gained from a left-wing expert. Since they share similar political values and ideals, she will find no reason (or at least no direct reason) to believe that she might be the target of manipulation. Political parties and partisan associations gather members with expertise in many different areas, and since they are united around a shared set of political values and principles, the knowledge transfer will be facilitated within such associations (Cerovac 2019). Furthermore, it is not easy for a political representative to assess and evaluate the credibility of experts he or she is consulting with. While she might be able to recognize the relevant experts in a few specific fields, she is very unlikely to be able to evaluate experts in all the possible areas of public life. Partisan associations can be quite valuable here since they can, through a joint effort of many members with some expertise in different areas, create a list of trustworthy experts that representatives can use when they need to acquire relevant technical knowledge on some specific topic. Finally, some partisan associations (institutes, foundations, think tanks) engage directly and systematically in consulting the political representatives, and even publish policy analyses and other documents to help representatives grasp the technical issues at hand.

Second, Mill believes that a properly implemented party system can be used to monitor and sanction the conduct of politicians and experts within partisan associations. When he discusses the advantages of Hare's proposal, Mill indicates that such system would force party leaders to remove the political influence from incompetent but rich candidates and assign it to "the ablest and most distinguished men on their own side" (Mill 1977c, 362–363). Parties rely on the knowledge of experts and competent politicians to produce public policies and political decisions (when in power) or to raise constructive criticism of existing policies and decisions (when in opposition). When the party in power makes a policy that fails to bring about the aims that it was supposed to bring about, the party can shame or demote the experts and politicians who participated in its creation. Similarly, a party in opposition can degrade party experts who have consulted representatives to argue and deliberate against a particular law or policy, when in the end it turned out that the law or policy was beneficial and in line with the party's aims (Christiano 2012, 41–42). Furthermore, a party can shame or demote experts who have abandoned the party's central political principles or have started producing policies based on their personal interests instead on the common good and party's political values. This can serve to motivate experts within partisan associations to produce the best possible policies but can also enable partisan associations to relieve and replace a team of experts that has failed to deliver. Finally, party can help create "linkage chain" (Lawson 1988, 16) and the relation of mutual accountability between citizens, experts and political representatives.

As we have seen, following Mill's political thought and supporting it with some contemporary arguments, the party system organizing citizens' existing competences and shaping the decision-making and decision-authorization processes has three beneficial effects on the quality of political results. First, it organizes political struggle and simultaneously injects and contains conflict in public deliberation. Second, it facilitates knowledge transfer from experts to political representatives, thus improving the epistemic quality of parliamentary debates. Finally, it creates a system of mutual accountability between experts, representatives and party members (regular citizens) which facilitates intra-party deliberation, as well as deliberation between citizens participating in debates within formal and those participating in debates within informal political sphere.

Partisan Associations and "the Spirit of Compromise"

Apart from the beneficial effects that public deliberation can have on the development of citizens' moral and intellectual capacities in a democratic party system, partisanship can also positively affect the perceived legitimacy of political decisions.[9] The previous part of the chapter demonstrated how, following Mill, political parties can help increase normative legitimacy of political decisions—since they have tendency to improve the (instrumental) epistemic quality of collective decision-authorization and decision-making procedures, as well as the epistemic (procedure-independent) quality of laws, policies and decisions, there are good reasons to acknowledge the legitimacy-generating potential of decision-making procedures within a democratic and representative party system. However, Mill also believes that party system can help increase the descriptive (perceived) legitimacy of political decisions—partisan associations can improve the quality of public deliberation, and citizens will know and understand that the laws and policies were endorsed by their representatives because they were supported by the best available reasons and arguments, and only after they were able to resist criticisms by the best reasons and arguments from the other side.[10] When discussing the beneficial effects of representation, Mill (1861, 104) stresses that it enables every person to find "somebody who speaks his mind, as well or better than he could speak it himself . . . to be tested by adverse controversy; where those whose opinion is overruled, feel satisfied that it is heard, and set aside not by the mere act of will, but for what are thought to be superior reasons, and commend themselves as such to the representatives of the majority of the nation." While an independent representative can probably advocate for the opinion of its constituencies better than they can do themselves, he could advocate for their opinion even better in collaboration with other like-minded individuals, including other representatives and experts in various fields, but also other party members who might lack relevant technical or moral knowledge, but might be useful to advise and motivate the representative to stay true to the party's central political principles. Epistemic advantages of a party system can thus increase the perceived legitimacy of political decisions since the citizens know that these decisions have passed a rigorous critical scrutiny and are supported by the best reasons in a system that increases the (instrumental) epistemic quality of public deliberation. Of course, just like before, Mill is aware that partisanship, when characterized by group polarization and crippled epistemology, can also reduce the descriptive (perceived) legitimacy of political decisions. However, when properly institutionalized and exercised, the party system can increase the perceived legitimacy of political decisions.

Similarly, the party system can enhance and promote "the spirit of compromise" (Mill 1977c, 344), which is needed not only to ensure the stability of democratic government, but also to enable epistemically fruitful deliberation among political rivals. Mill quotes Austin and agrees that "all successful government, and all prosperous society, is carried on and maintained by a mutual give and take" (Austin 2015, 6, see also Mill 1977c, 344). Political representatives, as well as citizens, have to be aware that there are conflicting interests and opinions within a democratic society. However, realizing that they are not infallible, and that public deliberation can help them acquire better and more accurate beliefs, citizens should embrace their differences and stop making their opinions and interests the sole basis of political decisions (Mill 1977a, see also Dalaqua 2018b). The party system can help accomplish this goal. First, partisan associations map and shape social cleavages, but also moderate public deliberation in the informal political sphere, thus informing citizens on the variety of conflicting opinions in a society. Second, as indicated earlier, indirect democracy facilitates the process of political negotiation and compromise, and political parties and partisan associations can serve as a middleman between the government and the citizens (see also Habermas 1996) explaining why compromises are needed and justified from the standpoint of their political principles (but also political principles of their constituencies, who might not initially agree with the compromising solutions in question).[11] Political parties thus become both the facilitators and the protectors of "the spirit of compromise."

CONCLUDING REMARKS

To properly understand Mill's view on political parties we need to introduce the distinction between a normative and a descriptive account of partisanship. Without this distinction, his writings might appear dispersed and even inconsistent since he seems to consider political parties both a necessary condition for a well-functioning democratic representative system and an intrusive element that reduces the (epistemic) quality of democratic decision-authorization procedures. Descriptively, Mill held that the party system of mid-Victorian England produced more harm than help for the representative politics: political parties were mere factions and interest groups, devoid of all political ideals, and party leaders supported and promoted rich members of average or below-average moral and intellectual virtues. This is why, in *Consideration on Representative Government* and other writings, Mill endorses Hare's proposal—it will demolish the way political parties used to function in Mil's time and force parties to change substantively. However, Mil did not think partisan associations should be abolished altogether. They should instead be pushed to function in accordance with their normative ideal. Parties should help structure and improve the quality of political deliberation, facilitate democratic representation and participate in the wide political education of citizens. Thus, even though Mill offers an evaluation of the mid-Victorian party system, the relevant philosophical contribution is his moral ideal of a party (Kinzer 1981, 121).

Agonism and conflict play a very important (epistemic) role in Mill's political theory. Conflict can be epistemically fertile and can help us acquire new and to better understand existing true beliefs, but it can also help us make better laws, policies and political decisions. Political parties are a living representation of this conflict: they fuel conflict and map key divisions in a society. Just like all other political institutions and organizations, parties can decrease or increase the epistemic quality of political decision-authorization process. They can make conflict destructive, reinforce group polarization and undermine the stability of a social system, but they can also make conflict creative and productive, improve public deliberation and foster "the spirit of compromise." Partisanship, when properly structured and institutionalized, can greatly improve the epistemic quality of political deliberation, thus improving the (instrumental) quality of political outcomes as well as the moral and intellectual capacities of citizens.

NOTES

1. Many deliberative democrats have proposed slightly different (yet quite similar) functions of public deliberation. As indicated in previous chapters, I am using Ronald Tinnevelt's (2015) formulation since it captures all relevant considerations and fits well with Mill's approach to deliberative democracy.

2. I have argued that both transformative and constructive functions of public deliberation can be understood as subsets of its epistemic function. In both cases, the transformation of your beliefs and preferences, as well as construction of new positions and arguments, serve the epistemic goal of acquiring true and justified beliefs. If transformative and creative functions of public deliberation would lead us to generally adopt epistemically worse and less justified beliefs, these functions would not be desirable. For a detailed account on how transformative and creative functions ultimately fall into a wide reading of epistemic function see earlier chapters of this book, but also Estlund (1997, 2008) and Cerovac (2016a, 2020).

3. For a detailed account of mini-publics, including their epistemic strengths and weaknesses, see Wright (2010).

4. Tinnevelt (2015, 1) explicitly rejects this idea, claiming that Mill recognized the legitimate role of political parties within democratic societies, yet did develop a normative theory of partisanship. I cannot properly address and reject this claim here, but it will be answered by the end of the chapter.

5. For a detailed distinction between a faction and a party see Ypi and White (2016).

6. This seems to be one of Mill's long-term goals: he indicates that members of the poorest and rudest classes, "in their present state of morals and intelligence" (Mill 1977b, 334), should not be admitted to the full exercise of suffrage (though, of course, their opinions might be useful as one influence among others). Partisan associations, along with other instruments of education, can be of great help in elevating the moral and intellectual capacities of members of such classes, thus making them suitable for political participation.

7. For a detailed overview of the educational role of political participation see the third chapter of this book.

8. Ypi and White (2016, 94) discuss a case of Rosa, a socialist living in West Europe in 1989. Due to political and social changes affecting her country, she suddenly has to decide whether to abandon her socialist ideas or to change them to fit the new political reality. The latter is much harder when one is not a partisan. In order to keep her faith in socialism and formulate how her political principles can be reconciled with the political situation of that time, Rosa needs to deliberate with her fellows, citizens who defend similar political ideals. Partisan associations can help her create new hermeneutical resources and gather relevant epistemic (and not merely psychological) support for her views. See Ypi and White (2016) and Cerovac (2019) for details.

9. It is important to emphasize that, though the party system can increase the perceived legitimacy of democratic decisions, it can have a completely opposite effect. Mill is quite aware of the danger of group polarization and crippled epistemology (Talisse 2009, Sunstein 2011), and acknowledges that "the tendency of all opinions to become sectarian is . . . often highlighted and exacerbated by [free discussion]," and adds that the truth that should have been seen is often "rejected all the more violently because proclaimed by persons regarded as opponents" (Mill 1859a, 94). Public deliberation in a representative party system can thus have both positive and negative effects on the decision-making procedure's descriptive legitimacy. The effect it will have depends on the implementation of the idea of partisanship. However, Mill is convinced that, when properly realized, partisanship will increase decision-making procedure's perceived legitimacy.

10. For a detailed account on how parliamentary debates can have an educative function see the chapter on the epistemic value of democratic deliberation.

11. Gutmann and Thompson (2014) warn us that this is usually not the case. In fact, nowadays partisanship and campaigning tend to polarize the society and undermine the spirit of compromise. While this seems to be the case, we should not forget that Mill focuses on the normative idea of the party, arguing what a political party should be and what it should do.

Chapter 7

Filtering Mechanisms and Antipaternalism

John Stuart Mill is an author of numerous publications, books, essays, newspaper articles, and his intellectual work stretches into various scientific fields and addresses a wide variety of topics. In this, Mill introduced many novel ideas and sophisticated proposals which lead to a specific type of objection targeting his political thought—the apparent lack of consistency. One of the common objections targeting Mill's political thought addresses the apparent inconsistency between his strong antipaternalist stance in *On Liberty* and his alleged paternalist justification of democracy and, in particular, justification of institutional mechanisms Mill uses to filter the public will, in *Considerations on Representative Government*. Authors like Richard Arneson (1982), David Brink (2013) and Eunseong Oh (2016), for example, argue that Mill's opposition to state paternalism in debates on personal liberties seems incompatible with his endorsement of plural voting proposal (and other filtering mechanisms) in the electoral process. Namely, if we argue in favor of a plural voting proposal and ground our justification of such mechanism in the beneficial results it produces (political decisions of optimal quality, as well as positive influence on citizens' intellectual and moral capacities) for the political community in question, we are actually introducing paternalist considerations that limit the community's collective sovereignty, and we introduce these considerations with the intention to improve the well-being of this political community. To avoid the inconsistency objection Mill would have to argue that there is some relevant difference between *political* decision-making process, where some forms of paternalism introduced by mechanisms such as plural voting proposal are appropriate, and *personal* decision-making process, where any form of paternalism is unjustified.[1] His critics, of course, argue that there is no such relevant difference.

The chapter's innovative contribution goes is two directions. First, it demonstrates that Mill's epistemic justification of democracy, just like his arguments for various filtering mechanisms, can be defended on non-paternalist grounds. The chapter demonstrates that we cannot simply characterize these mechanisms as paternalistic and then discard them as inappropriate.[2] Second, the central argument helps us reconcile individual freedom with democratic decision-making process. Focusing on epistemic justification of government can help us determine the proper scope of both democratic decisions and laws protecting individual rights.

The first part of this chapter analyses the inconsistency objection. Namely, some critics argue that Mill's plural voting proposal is grounded in paternalist considerations and is not compatible with his otherwise antipaternalist sentiments. Following this reading, Mill attributes greater political influence to better educated citizens in order to protect minority groups and to educate the majority of population. He thus limits the collective sovereignty by reducing the political influence of democratic majority in order to educate the citizens and to improve the quality of political decisions. This certainly looks like a form of paternalism: one's sovereignty is reduced for one's own good. I defend the consistency of Mill's project and argue that plural voting proposal (as well as other filtering mechanisms Mill employs) can be justified on non-paternalist grounds. This type of justification fits well within Mill's project and there are good reasons to think Mill indirectly offered similar arguments. To properly grasp this line of thought, the *second* part discusses the educative role of the plural voting proposal. Though Mill clearly endorses improvement of citizens' capacities as one of its important goals, this goal does not have to be paternalistic. Educating citizens and improving their capacities can be a valuable instrument to improve the epistemic quality of democratic procedures, thus increasing the quality of subsequent political decisions. We can defend plural voting for its educative role without the need to ground this defense in the positive effect education has on citizens' well-being. However, a problem remains. Even if plural voting's educative role can be interpreted as a means for improving the epistemic quality of democratic procedures and for producing better results, this does not help us escape the paternalist objection. The *third* part addresses this concern and evaluates whether the quality of political outcomes can be a non-paternalist reason to limit collective sovereignty. Using the recent arguments on normative consent, the idea that in some circumstances consent (or non-consent) can be null, enables us to argue that in some cases the majority's non-consent can be null. For example, when a political community makes a decision that affects all its members (both those who agree with the decision in question and those who do not, i.e., both the majority and the minority), requiring the use of decision-making (and decision-authorization) procedure that has the highest tendency to produce correct, just or efficient decisions does not have to be grounded in paternalist consideration, but in a duty we have towards others. We can thus legitimately limit political community's collective sovereignty in order to protect the minority from incorrect or unjust decisions. Finally, the *fourth* part briefly addresses Mill's publicity requirement and his claim that plural voting proposal should be grounded in considerations all citizens can consider just.

PLURAL VOTING AS A PATERNALIST MECHANISM

Many authors indicate antipaternalism as one of the key features of Mill's political thought (Baccarini 2013, Estlund 2003, Feinberg 1987, Hudlin 1985). Appeals to inconsistency within his philosophical project usually target the apparent conflict between antipaternalism and utilitarianism (Ten 1980, Primorac 1986, Cressati 1988, as paraphrased in Baccarini 2013, Cohen-Almagor 2012, Bell 2020), as well as the conflict between antipaternalism and Mill's political economy (Claeys 2013). These appeals, despite being important for the overall discussion, are not in the focus here. The chapter instead addresses the apparent conflict between antipaternalism and plural voting proposal, addressing a famous critique by Richard Arneson's (1982).

Mill on Paternalism

Paternalism is usually defined as any sort of "interference with a person's liberty of action justified by reason referring exclusively to the welfare . . . of the person being coerced" (Dworkin 1988, 16). Mill clearly rejects and condemns such practices in *On Liberty*, where he indicates that it is (almost) always wrong to use coercion to limit the freedom of sane adults for the sake of their own well-being (Mill 1859a and 1977d). Individuals should not be prohibited from performing self-regarding actions, not even when they make such actions for morally or epistemically flawed reasons, or when they are harmed by the actions in question. Of course, one's liberty can be denied when one's actions cause (direct or indirect) harm to non-consenting others. The state can thus legitimately prevent a factory owner from harassing her employees or from unleashing a dangerous chemical in the local environment. While the state uses coercion to limit individual's liberties, this form of state action can be justified by its aim to prevent the individual from harming other citizens. While some (Feinberg 1985) claim that Mill's harm principle might be used to justify censorship of thought, speech and press, arguing that some exercises of freedom of speech and press might (indirectly) offend other's moral or religious sentiments and harm them by reducing their happiness and producing negative emotions such as anger, disappointment or disgust, Mill is adamant that these cases do not represent a valid reason for censorship or any other form of coercive state action.[3]

There are two important exceptions—cases when an individual does not directly or indirectly harm others, yet the state can legitimately exercise coercion to prevent the individual from performing some action or to motivate the individual to perform some action. *First*, Mill holds we are allowed to (in fact, we have a duty to) interfere with one's freedom when one's action is clearly harmful for the individual *and* when we have good reasons to believe that the individual lacks some relevant knowledge that would persuade him not to perform the harmful action in question, or we sincerely believe the individual temporarily lacks relevant intellectual capacities the employment of which would result with the rejection of the harmful behavior.[4] Mill's gives a famous bridge example and indicates that

> if either a public officer or anyone else saw a person attempting to cross a bridge which had been ascertained to be unsafe, and there were no time to warn him of his danger, they might seize him and turn him back, without any real infringement of his liberty; for liberty consists in doing what one desires, and he does not desire to fall into the river. (Mill 1859a, 172–173)

This and similar cases represent an exception to the general rule and can be applied only when certain conditions are in place. Exercising coercion is justifiable only when there is no other way of warning (or informing) the individual and only when we know that the individual lacks the relevant information. Once we have informed the individual of the danger ahead and he still wants to risk crossing the bridge, no coercive measures should be applied since "no one but the person himself can judge of the sufficiency of the motive which may prompt him to incur the risk" (Mill 1859a, 173). Similarly, we can limit one's freedom when the individual temporarily lacks relevant decision-making competences or is in a state of diminished capacities and is going to perform some clearly harmful action. However, in both cases these infringements can only be temporary and would not be justified had the individual been in normal epistemic circumstances. *Second*, and also more relevant for this chapter, Mill holds that the state can legitimately exercise coercion and prevent an individual from performing an action that does not harm any other person, provided that performing such action would put the individual in state in which she would be unable to perform some specific duty toward other citizens or the public in general. If a parent, for example, adopts a harmful and extravagant lifestyle that makes him unable to properly exercise the duty he has towards his children, the state has every right to punish him. However, he deserves the punishment for failing to fulfil a specific duty to others, not for his extravagant lifestyle. Similarly, though no one should be punished for being drunk, a policeman or a soldier should be punished for being drunk on duty. Mill thus concludes that "whenever there is a definite damage, or a definite risk of damage, either to an individual or to the public, the case is taken out of the province of liberty and placed in that of morality or law" (Mill 1859a, 147). These two types of cases are only exceptions when the state can intervene and limit one's freedom even when one's actions cause no (direct or indirect) harm to others.[5]

The Apparent Inconsistency

As indicated earlier in this chapter, Mill takes a strong antipaternalist stance in *On Liberty*. As long as their actions affect only themselves (and as long as they have access to relevant information and are not violating a duty they have to others), individuals should be left to freely decide how they want to act and live. The state should not interfere with, promote or suppress any particular practice, activity or lifestyle, provided that the individual undertaking it does not harm any other non-consenting person. Similarly, the state should not impose strong autonomy-threatening filtering mechanisms to ensure that citizens make correct decisions: while it might advise, provide information and even educate its citizens, no coercive mechanism should be employed when citizens make decisions that affect only their own well-being. Individuals have (almost) full individual sovereignty with respect to activities and practices affecting only themselves.

However, some authors (Arneson 1982, Brink 2013) emphasize that the same does not apply when Mill discusses collective sovereignty in *Considerations on Representative Government*. Mill does not hesitate to put strong constraints both on the scope of democratic decisions and the majoritarian decision-making (and decision-authorization) procedure used to create them. He gives a list of mechanism that can be used to filter public will, withdrawing the actual decision-making process from the public and putting a strong emphasis on the role of experts (Mill 1977a, 1977b, see also Garforth 1980, Ravlić 2001, Estlund 2003, Baccarini and Ivanković 2015, Cerovac 2016b). For example, his strong appeal for a representative system without pledges and campaign promises, where electors are unable to recall their representatives in mid-term, is one such filtering mechanism limiting the collective sovereignty. Giving the Parliament an almost exclusively deliberative function, while tasking the government and the expert commissions with the creation of laws and policies, can be seen as another similar example. Finally, Mill's plural voting proposal which assigns greater political influence in the formal political sphere to better educated and more qualified citizens is also a form of filtering mechanism that limits the collective sovereignty: well-educated minority can thus sometimes outvote the majority of citizens or at least oppose and block the legislation that would be easily passed in one-person, one-vote system.[6] These filtering mechanisms shape political procedures and move citizens (except perhaps at the local level) away from *direct* decision-making and decision-authorization practices. Mill is very clear about this intention when he endorses Tocqueville's thought that we should carry into practice a form of democracy which "on the one hand, most exercises and cultivates the intelligence and mental activity of the majority; and, on the other, breaks the headlong impulses of popular opinion, by delay, rigor of forms, and adverse discussion" (Mill 1977e, 189). Mill's aim is to limit the collective sovereignty and shape decision-making and decision-authorization procedures to attribute greater influence to experts and well-educated citizens, thus ensuring that the unqualified (or poorly qualified) majority cannot pass legislation without the consent of the minority. These filtering mechanisms improve the epistemic quality of results (laws and policies) since they simultaneously prevent class legislation and introduce competence in the decision-making and decision-authorization process. Arneson (1982) and Brink (2013) think that this epistemic criterion is clearly paternalistic. We impose some decision-authorization processes upon a political community to improve the quality of decisions it produces, and we reduce political influence of the majority (thus reducing its collective sovereignty) to improve its well-being. Mill thus defends individual sovereignty, which is endangered when we limit one's freedom for one's own sake, while he completely neglects collective sovereignty, which is endangered when, instead of the majority of citizens, political decisions are disproportionately made and authorized by experts and well-educated citizens.

Similarly, following his two criteria of good government, Mill assigns another task upon these filtering mechanisms—they have to facilitate the improvement of citizens' intellectual and moral capacities. Rejection of pledges and campaign promises enables political representatives to deliberate freely and to change their opinions in the light of better reasons, thus fostering epistemically fertile deliberation which serves an important educative role. Open ballot forces citizens to think about the public good and to provide reasons (when asked) justifying why they voted the way they did. Plural voting proposal, as argued in the previous chapters, also has an important educative role, since it simultaneously promotes education and raises the overall level of political debates. Richard Arneson (1982) argues that Mill's focus on education also represents a paternalist turn in his political thought: if education is something good for the citizens and if the state, using filtering mechanisms to shape the political process and to limit some of their liberties, promotes education to improve citizens' well-being, it adopts a paternalist methodology. Again, Mill faces that same problem: while he defends individual sovereignty and holds that the state should not limit one's liberty for one's own good, he simultaneously introduces and defends filtering mechanisms (and some of them seem to limit collective sovereignty) for their educative effect and the beneficial effect they have on the well-being of citizens.

The following two parts of the chapter discuss in detail these two apparent inconsistencies and demonstrate why Mill's defense of filtering mechanisms does not necessarily rest upon paternalist considerations.

PATERNALISM AND POLITICAL EDUCATION

Mill puts great emphasis on government's ability to provide political education for its citizens and even writes that "the most important point of excellence which any form of government can possess is to promote the virtue and intelligence of the people themselves" (Mill 1861, 30). As noted earlier, some authors think this represents an obvious paternalist criterion. Richard Arneson, for example, indicates that Mill's idea that "government is responsible for educating and uplifting those under its jurisdiction" represents a "clearly paternalistic reason" (Arneson 1982, 48). Favoring Mill's antipaternalist ideas from *On Liberty*, he proceeds to wonder "why should government be responsible for the moral betterment of adult citizens," beyond simply making opportunities for education available to all adult citizens (Arneson 1982, 48).

If we take Mill's second criterion for good government (i.e., its ability to educate the citizens) as a purely intrinsic quality (one which serves no additional instrumental purpose, but is valuable only for its own sake), Arneson's conclusion can hardly be avoided.[7] However, as indicated in the earlier chapters, Mill is clear that the unifying criterion of good government are "beneficial consequences, immediate and prospective" (Mill 1861, 54). Improving citizens' intellectual and moral capacities is both intrinsically (as a constitutive part of beneficial consequences) and instrumentally (as a prerequisite for creating other beneficial consequences) valuable (see Mill 1977a, 406–412). To focus on the latter, Mill argues that democratic government's ability to produce correct, just or efficient decisions depends (in part) on the citizens' existing education and (moral and intellectual) capacities. He thus considers education not only as something valuable in itself, but also as an important means for creating (and authorizing) correct political decisions, those leading to the best political outcomes (Cerovac 2017).

Can we use this (partial) instrumentalist reading to resist the paternalist interpretation? When applied to the level of individual sovereignty, that can hardly be the case. When the state actively promotes education (and withholds some liberties from individuals who have not received such education) in order to enable them to make better choices and decisions that affect only themselves, the state is still acting in a paternalist manner. Mill clearly rejects this form of paternalism when he indicates that the state should not limit one's freedom regarding actions that affect only oneself (Mill 1977d). If an adult individual wants to drive a car in his possession despite lacking relevant knowledge and competences to do so properly and has a huge flat yard surrounded by a strong fence preventing those outside from entering and those inside from accidentally leaving (e.g., by losing control and breaking through the fence), the state should not interfere and limit one's freedom to drive in his yard, even when such behavior might cause him direct bodily harm. The state can inform such individual that this action involves a high risk of severe injury and might even require from car manufacturers to warn the customers that non-proficient use of their product might be dangerous for the person using it, but it should not limit one's freedom to drive a car under such conditions. However, things substantively change when we apply instrumentalist reading to other-regarding actions. The state can require that individuals driving cars in streets and on roads, where they can harm other non-consenting people (pedestrians, by-standers and other drivers), acquire the education needed to drive safely and with minimal risk to others. The state can make one's liberty to drive a car in public spaces conditional on one's education and competences, and it can do so without the appeal to their own well-being typical for paternalist justification. Mill believes our participation in decision-making and decision-authorizing procedures resembles this example. One's exercise of political privileges (e.g., voting in the elections) affects not only the individual performing that political action, but also other persons who have participated in the decision-authorization process, as well as those who did not participate (e.g., passive and disinterested citizens) and those who cannot participate (e.g., children and people with severe mental disorders). Participating in collective decision-authorization procedures is a kind of action that affects (and can harm) other people around us, and not just ourselves.[8] Making political participation conditional on acquiring some level of education and competence can be defended on non-paternalist grounds, to prevent the harm one's participation in the electoral process can inflict on others (by reducing the quality of decision-authorization procedure as well as the quality of final outcomes).

Furthermore, recall that, for Mill, the state can legitimately limit one's freedom to perform an action when such action would put that individual in a state in which one would be unable to properly fulfil some duties towards others. The state can limit police officer's freedom to drink alcohol or to use strong drugs and other addicting substances since such actions significantly reduce officer's ability to perform his or her duty. This would not be grounded in paternalist considerations since the justification does not address police officer's health or well-being, but officer's ability to perform a clearly ascribed duty. Recall that Mill looks upon electoral suffrage not as a right but as a privilege, a "moral act involving a real responsibility" (Mill 1977c, 366) by which citizens do their "duty to the public" (Mill 1977b, 337). When we participate and vote in the elections we have a duty to make the best contribution we reasonably can. Rejecting most forms of education and opportunities for self-improvement and the advancement of our capacities will reduce the quality of our potential contribution, and possibly make us violate the duty we have towards other citizens and the public in general. Mill clearly indicates that voting privileges should be withheld from citizens who have not acquired a minimal level of education, as well as from citizens who try to exercise their electoral suffrage while intoxicated (Mill 1977b, 316, see also Sturgis 2005). He argues that, in both cases, individual freedom is limited not for one's own good, but to prevent the harm this particular action might cause to others, as well as to prevent the individual from entering the state in which he will be unable to fulfil his duties towards others. As we can see, Mill's second criterion of good government and his idea that the state should promote education and improvement of citizens' capacities can be justified without the appeal to (that particular citizens') well-being.[9] Since laws, public policies and political decisions affect and can harm others, our participation in decision-making and decision-authorization procedures falls not within the area of blameless liberty, but in the area of law and morality. Mill's second criterion is thus justified not only because education represents something good for us, but because incompetent political participation can make us harm non-consenting others (by producing inefficient or unjust laws and policies). Since our working definition of paternalism regards "interference with a person's liberty of action justified by reason referring *exclusively* to the welfare . . . of the person being coerced" (Dworkin 1988, 16, emphasis added), we can see that Mill's focus on education is not paternalistic. There are also other-regarding reasons for his second criterion of good government.

Even if voting privileges should be conditional on one's education, additional questions arise. How can we defend unequal distribution of political influence on non-paternalist grounds?

PATERNALISM AND THE QUALITY OF DECISIONS

As demonstrated in earlier chapters, Mill introduces a list of filtering mechanisms (and plural voting proposal in particular) for two reasons: to better organize citizens' competences and thus improve the quality of political decisions, and to improve citizens' existing competences by providing a specific form of political education. While some argue that the second reason endorses a form of paternalism, we have seen that improving citizens' competences can also be valuable instrumentally, as a means for creating and authorizing correct, just or efficient decisions. While this temporarily removes the burden of paternalism from the second criterion (by arguing that education is a means for improving the quality of political outcomes), it remains conditional on demonstrating that the first criterion (i.e., the quality of outcomes) is non-paternalistic. If we can show that the justification of the first criterion is not grounded in paternalist considerations, we can finally conclude that Mill's argument for filtering mechanisms (and especially for plural voting proposal) is non-paternalistic.

Alleged Paternalism in Mill's Epistemic Argument

Mill traditionally (and explicitly) offers two arguments to defend plural voting proposal.[10] First, the protective argument points out that plural voting proposal can help us prevent the tyranny of the majority characterized by class legislation, when citizens pass legislation to pursue their individual or class interests instead of the general interest and the common good. When the majority of citizens are also members of some social group (e.g., working class), distributing political influence equally might result in aggregative decision-making processes where the representatives of the majority group have no need to defend their opinions or make compromises since they can always outvote the opinions held by the minority. Plural voting proposal can thus help us secure that no social group make political decisions without having to defend them within collective deliberative procedures. Second, the epistemic argument addresses existing differences in citizens' moral and intellectual competences and defends unequal distribution of political influence (within formal political sphere) in organizing these competences in an epistemically optimal way. As argued earlier, both arguments should be understood from the consequentialist point of view[11]: if the majority group is pursuing its own class interests and starts outvoting the minority, eliminating the need for collective deliberation, and if democratic procedures fail to acknowledge and make use of unequally distributed competences, our decision-authorization procedures will result in substantively bad (incorrect, unjust or inefficient) political decisions, resulting in harmful consequences for the entire political community.

Philosophers who point at Mill's allegedly paternalist justification of plural voting proposal typically focus on his epistemic argument. Discussing Mill's protective argument, Richard Arneson (1982, 56) writes that "the goal of preventing the violation of minority rights and [thus] limiting the freedom of the majority in order to protect a dissenting minority is clearly non-paternalistic." However, he quickly adds that the epistemic argument "appears to be clearly paternalistic" since it defends against the danger of "inept policies" (Arneson

1982, 56). Following this reading, Mill can remain anti-paternalist and keep his plural voting proposal only if he abandons the epistemic argument and the idea that unequal distribution of political influence can be justified because it improves the quality of political decisions. However, epistemic justification represents an important, and maybe even central point in Mill's political thought. Furthermore, Mill finds abandoning the epistemic argument and focusing on preventing class legislation as the sole reason for plural voting proposal unacceptable, since he considers the epistemic argument as the dominant reason for his proposal. As indicated earlier, Mill (Mill 1861, 180) is adamant that he does not advance "the plurality as a thing in itself undesirable, which, like the exclusion of part of the community from the suffrage, may be temporarily tolerated while necessary to prevent greater evils" (e.g., class legislation). Instead, he looks "upon it as only relatively good, but in principle wrong, because recognizing a wrong standard, and exercising a bad influence on the voter's mind" (Mill 1861, 180). Mill cannot simply remove the quality of political decisions and overall political results from his argument (nor can he ground plural voting proposal only in prevention of class legislation), and thus has to address the critics and demonstrate why epistemic argument does not rest upon paternalist considerations.

Of course, one can argue that, since political decisions usually affect all citizens, plural voting mechanism can be seen as a filtering mechanism protecting the minority from the majority's incompetence. After all, minorities can be wronged, and harmful legislation can be passed even when there are no individual or class interests in play. A benevolent yet uneducated or unqualified majority can make and authorize harmful laws and policies even when it tries to think and argue in terms of the common good. Mill (1861, 172–173) endorses a clear anti-paternalist stance with regard to private matters, writing that "there would be no pretense for applying this doctrine to any case which could with reason be considered as one of individual or private right." He argues that, in affairs which concern only one person, "that one is entitled to follow his own opinion, however much wiser the other may be than himself" (Mill 1861, 173). This is Mill's anti-paternalism in *On Liberty*, where he presents epistemic arguments for freedom of thought, speech, press and assembly, but also for other liberties one needs to be able to live a free and autonomous life, one from which we can learn the most. However, public issues do not fall within this category. Laws and public policies represent "things which equally concern both [a person that is superior in virtue, knowledge or intelligence, and a person that is inferior]" (Mill 1861, 173). In such cases we cannot simply fall back to the individual sphere since we have to make a public decision that will affect all citizens, regardless of their competences. When opinions on laws and policies are in conflict and a final decision has to be made, some opinions inevitably have to give way to others. Enforcing such laws and policies thus represents exercise of power over others, and Mill is convinced that a simple procedure characterized by one-person, one-vote principle should not be applied. When citizens disagree on public matters and have to make a political decision that some citizens (either majority or minority) will unavoidably disagree with, and when their competences are unequally distributed, we should endorse the principle that differences in citizens' epistemic (and moral) capacities imply unequal distribution of political influence. When we cannot avoid some form of political coercion (i.e., when a law or political decision has to be made and citizens disagree on what should be decided), it is better to coerce those less competent (even when they are in the majority) than those more competent (even when they are in the minority).

Critics find this idea highly implausible. In fact, they often consider it as the very source of Mill's alleged paternalism. Richard Arneson (1982, 58), for example, indicates that "if someone's choice must be overruled, it is less paternalistic for the many to coerce the few than for the few to coerce the many" (of course, provided that the majority decision does not infringe minority rights). Arguing that "if paternalism is bad, then more paternalism is worse and less paternalism is better," he concludes that "there is more coercion of persons for their own good against their will when a small number of experts have power to enact a government policy thought to be for the good of all including a vast recalcitrant majority, than when the same vast majority has the power to enact a government policy likewise thought to be for the good of all including a small minority of recalcitrant experts" (Arneson 1982, 58). In other words, when citizens have to make a collective decision and some coercion is unavoidable, it is better (there is less coercion) when the final decision follows the opinion of the majority. Mill argues for a decision-authorization procedure characterized by plural voting proposal and embraces paternalism since this procedure entails more coercion that the egalitarian (one-person, one-vote) alternative. If we want to reduce unavoidable paternalism to the minimal level, we should favor egalitarian procedures that distribute political influence equally among all citizens. Any inegalitarian distribution of political influence (including Mill's plural voting proposal) leaves open the possibility that the number of people coerced exceeds the minimal (unavoidable) number of coerced people. Coercion of the minority over the majority remains a viable option. Critics such as Richard Arneson thus conclude that Mill's epistemic argument for plural voting proposal must be paternalistic since it argues for the state in which more people are coerced for what is considered to be the common good than in the state in which all citizens have equal political influence.

While this represents an innovative and insightful objection, there are some reservations regarding its ability to characterize Mill's epistemic justification of plural voting proposal as paternalistic. Recall that Mill emphasizes that some forms of coercion can be justified. Individual's freedom can be limited when one performs actions that harm other non-consenting individuals, or when they (due to inappropriate exercise of this freedom) fail to uphold some clear duty they have towards others. These limitations are non-paternalist since they entail coercion grounded not in the well-being of the individual in question, but in the prevention of harm that the individual can inflict upon others (or upon the entire political community). Can we thus claim that equal distribution of political influence should be rejected due to the harm that ill-educated majority can inflict upon the well-educated majority? Can we argue that, by upholding egalitarian distribution of political influence, citizens are violating some duty they have towards others? Mill would have to give an affirmative answer to at least one of the above mentioned questions in order to ground his plural voting proposal in epistemic (and not only in protective) argument. I believe Estlund's idea of normative consent to political authority (Estlund 2008, 151–156) will help him greatly in this task.

Coercion and Normative Consent

All (or almost all) philosophers agree that consent to authority can sometimes be null. For example, when threatened by a person with a firearm, we can temporarily consent to that person's authority and follow her directives. However, null consent does no impose moral duties and rights that would otherwise come out of valid consent. We have no moral duty to submit to the authority of the person threatening us with a firearm just because we were coerced to consent. In this and similar cases our consent is null and the person threatening us cannot appeal to a particular moral duty our earlier consent has imposed upon us. However, non-consent can also sometimes be null.[12] If a serious traffic accident occurred in front of our eyes, there are several injured persons and we can help them without any risk for ourselves or the others, we have a moral duty to do so. Furthermore, if a physician is present at the crash site (and we have no reason to doubt her qualifications, competences and good will), we have a moral duty to follow the physician's instructions since that represents the best course of action to discharge our duty towards those injured. We can, of course, withhold our consent and choose not to follow physician's instructions, yet this seems morally problematic. In this particular case our non-consent is null. Refusing to consent to physician's authority is morally wrong since, by doing that, we are throwing away the best means for discharging our duty towards others (Estlund 2005).

There is, of course, a huge difference between our non-consent when we have a duty towards others and our non-consent when no such duty exists. Suppose that a physician is more competent to make correct decisions regarding our health than we are. However, mere competence does not give her moral authority over us.[13] Mill discusses similar examples in *On Liberty*—even when others are more competent than we are, they should not be allowed to interfere with our freedom as long as our actions affect only ourselves. Similarly, while we should take into account advice from those more competent than us, we have no moral duty to follow it (Mill 1977d). If we refuse physician's advice regarding treatment of some non-contagious disease that affects us (e.g., cancer, cardiovascular diseases, diabetes) and in doing so we pose no threat for the others (nor do we violate some duty we have towards others), we have no moral duty to follow the physician's advice (although that might be prudential). In such cases the physician has no moral authority over us. However, if we are at the crash site with many injured persons, we have a clear duty towards others. Similarly, if we participate in collective decision-authorization procedures (those discussed in *Considerations on Representative Government*), we have a clear duty not to harm others around us (by making incorrect, unjust or inefficient decisions). In both cases, provided that we can agree on who the experts are, we have a duty to endorse their authority or, to be more precise, to use decision-making (or decision-authorization) procedure that has the highest tendency to produce the best results. Such procedure will be instrumentally justified since it represents the best means for discharging our duty towards others, and our non-consent to that procedure will be null.

Recall that for Mill political coercion (limiting one's freedoms without one's consent) can sometimes be justified. When a citizen fails to discharge a duty he has towards others, and when this failure results with harm inflicted upon others, his non-consent becomes null, and the state can legitimately limit some of his liberties. This approach avoids paternalist considerations since it introduces coercive policies to prevent harm one individual can inflict upon others, and not to increase that individual's well-being. Mill can thus easily avoid the objection characterizing his epistemic argument for plural voting proposal as paternalistic—all Mill has to do is to demonstrate that there is a particular duty towards others in the electoral process, and that egalitarian voting system prevents us from adequately discharging this duty.

As argued in earlier chapters, Mill is adamant that there is such a duty. Since the exercise of our electoral privileges can harm others (by electing incompetent representatives we indirectly participate in authorization and even creation of inefficient, unjust or incorrect decisions), we have a moral duty not only to vote conscientiously but also to endorse a decision-authorization procedure that has the highest (instrumental) epistemic quality, i.e., a procedure that has the highest chance of producing good outcomes. The same rationale applies when we establish our duty to follow physician's instructions at the crash site. We have a duty to follow results of a decision-making procedure that represents the best means for the discharge of our duty towards those injured. Since a physician is a technical expert who knows how to treat injuries far better than we do, and since collective deliberation is not appropriate for the situation, we can discharge our duty towards those injured far better by following physician's instructions than by making relevant decisions by ourselves or using a democratic procedure characterized by equal distribution of political influence. Mill follows this analogy when he refers to executive government: since the creation of good laws and policies requires technical expertise and "professional knowledge" (Mill 1861, 252), they should be made by small groups of experts. However, Mill does not consider technical expertise relevant with regard to representative government: members of the Parliament need to have "knowledge of the general interests of the country," and not (unless by occasional accident) professional knowledge related to some branch of public administration (Mill 1861, 252). When citizens elect their political representatives, they give their votes to those they consider moral (and not technical) experts. The best procedure for electing these moral experts is characterized by (almost) universal but unequal participation. Instead of having an individual or a small group of people establishing who the experts are, and instead of egalitarian democratic process where all citizens participate as equals in the electoral process, Mill argues for filtered democracy[14] where (almost) all citizens have some political influence, but some citizens have more political influence than others. As demonstrated in earlier chapters, Mill provides epistemic arguments both for democracy and for filtering mechanisms such as plural voting proposal—these instruments lead to optimal political results and thus help us discharge our duty towards others better than any other decision-authorization procedure.[15] While Mill's epistemic argument remains debated and highly contested (see Estlund 2003, Lister 2014, Brennan 2016), we can nonetheless agree that Mill strongly believed that filtered democracy represents a decision-authorization procedure with the highest (instrumental) epistemic value. Therefore, plural voting proposal represents a means for discharging our duty towards others. We can thus preserve consistency in Mill's political thought arguing that his epistemic argument for plural voting proposal does not rest upon paternalist considerations, but upon the citizens' duty towards others.

Apart from simply preserving consistency in Mill's work, the central argument in this chapter has important implications for the ongoing debate on the proper scope of political decisions produced by democratic decision-making procedures, as well as on the proper role of experts in the political process. While we can disagree with Mill on the epistemic value of democracy and the instrumental value of various filtering mechanisms, a duty-based approach to political justification requires us to use epistemically the best decision making (and decision-authorizing) procedure available whenever we make decisions that affect others. Authors coming from Rawlsian tradition will use this duty-based approach, along with the liberal criteria of legitimacy and the idea that coercive political power must always be justified to those it is applied upon, to disqualify most other forms of government and to embrace epistemic democracy characterized by equality of political input (Estlund 2008, Peter 2011, Cerovac 2020). However, Mill did not simply fail to think of the publicity requirement.

PUBLIC JUSTIFICATION AND PLURAL VOTING PROPOSAL

Why would citizens endorse unequal distribution of political influence in the formal political sphere? And even if citizens agree that political influence should not be equally distributed, why would they endorse distributive mechanism that focuses on education, and not on some other feature? Can plural voting proposal meet publicity requirement and be justifiable in terms all (qualified) citizens can accept?

Mill acknowledges that plural voting proposal needs to be generally acceptable rather than simply correct. While authority might follow from expertise, legitimacy must be grounded in some form of (hypothetical) consent - citizens must be able to see the advantages of such proposal and thus accept the idea that wiser citizens should have greater political power. Furthermore, citizens should be able to agree on the feature that will shape the distribution of political influence, as well as how to measure such features. He warns us that "it is only necessary that this superior influence should be assigned on grounds which [all] can comprehend, and of which [all] are able to perceive justice" (Mill 1861, 174). This is why Mill has to find a criterion for expertise that can be reasonably accepted by everyone. The problem is, of course, the fact that there is reasonable disagreement on who counts as wise.[16] However, the idea that good education improves the ability to rule more competently is uncontested. Mill thus writes that "[The distinctions in voting power] are not made arbitrary but are such as can be understood and accepted by the general conscience and understanding." They are based on something that "would not necessarily be repugnant to any one's sentiment of justice" (Mill 1861, 177). Finally, Mill believes that all should be able to see that plural voting proposal increases the overall quality of political outcomes, thus being a model that "is most for the interest of both [the ignorant and the wiser man] (Mill 1861, 173). Since Mill believes that good education improves our ability to rule more wisely (i.e., to make better decisions), and since he believes that everyone shares (or can share) this belief, he presents plural voting proposal as a mechanism that attributes greater political influence according to criterion all citizens can accept and see as just. Finally, since all citizens can see plural voting proposal as the best means for discharging their duty towards others, all citizens can endorse it, as well as unequal distribution of political influence the proposal establishes.

This chapter addressed a famous critique that focuses on some apparent inconsistencies in Mill's political thought. Scholars such as Arneson and Brink worry that Mill's epistemic arguments for various filtering mechanisms (and particularly plural voting proposal) introduce paternalist considerations in his justification of democratic procedures. Their suggestion is to preserve consistency by abandoning these epistemic arguments. Filtering mechanisms should be justified in a non-epistemic way, for example by focusing on how to prevent class legislation and the tyranny of majority. I defend Mill's epistemic justification of various filtering mechanisms and argue that it need not be grounded in paternalist considerations. Whenever we make collective public decisions we are interfering with the freedom of our fellow citizens. Therefore, when political decisions have to be made, we have a duty to make these decisions using epistemically the best decision-making (and decision-authorization) procedure available. Using any other non-optimal procedure induces a risk that some citizens (i.e., the minority) will be unjustly harmed by our ignorance or incompetence. Since plural voting proposal improves the epistemic quality of democratic procedures, citizens have an other-regarding duty to use it when making political decisions. Therefore, since its justification is grounded (at least in part) in a duty towards others, epistemic argument for plural voting proposal does not rest upon paternalist considerations. There is no real inconsistency in Mill's political thought—epistemic justification of plural voting proposal is compatible with his strong anti-paternalism.

NOTES

1. Of course, Mill finds paternalism justified when we deal with children and adults who lack capacity to make the relevant decisions.

2. Of course, there may be many other reasons to reject some of Mill's filtering mechanisms. For example, David Estlund famously argues that Mill's plural voting proposal violates the liberal principle of legitimacy since it is subject to a demographic objection and can thus be reasonably rejected (Estlund 2003, see also Cerovac 2020). These objections extend well beyond the scope of this book. I discuss the paternalism objection since it targets not only a few specific ideas but the very consistency of Mill's political thought.

3. This is a well-known discussion and can be found in numerous publications. However, it goes beyond the scope of this chapter or even this book. For additional

information on censorship and harm to others see Anschutz (1969), Baccarini (1993), Berger (1984), Gaus (2009) and Gray (1983).

4. Both conditions have to be met in order to legitimately exercise coercion over individual whose actions affect no one but himself. Action has to be both harmful for the individual *and* we should reasonable believe he lacks some relevant information or is in a state of (temporarily or permanently) diminished intellectual capacities. First condition alone (i.e., the fact that the action is harmful for the agent) is not enough for justify coercive action by the state. Second condition (i.e., our reasonable belief that the agent lacks some relevant information) is also not enough to support coercion. People often act while lacking some relevant information, and it is the potential serious harm of their actions that justifies coercion in some cases.

5. There is also a third, nowadays less relevant type of cases, including slavery contracts and other agreements individuals can use to permanently renounce their liberties. Mill is, of course, convinced such contracts should be prohibited (Mill 1977d, 299–301). For additional information, see Strasser (1988), Archard (1990) and Schwan (2013).

6. Plural voting proposal, of course, regards unequal distribution of political influence while electing political representatives, not while making or authorizing political decisions.

7. One can argue that Mill values education on instrumental grounds, since it enables citizens to recognize, pursue and acquire higher pleasures. Government thus has an additional task: not only to help citizens pursue their interests, but also to improve the quality of these interests (see Macpherson 2012). Higher pleasures are thus considered intrinsically valuable, while improving citizens' intellectual and moral capacities represents nothing more than a useful instrument for acquiring higher pleasures. However, while this interpretation characterizes education as only instrumentally valuable, it does not help escape Arneson's critique. In fact, it only seems to strengthen the paternalist reading.

8. We should distinguish between the harm inflicted upon moral, religious or aesthetic feelings of other individuals caused by our exercise of freedom of speech and the harm inflicted upon others' well-being caused by the exercise of our voting privileges. Laws and public policies, including those from the department of state (defense and security, internal affairs, public administration) as well as those related to economy or social security have a strong effect on citizens' lives and can harm them in a substantively different way than the exercise of freedom of speech.

9. Of course, as a utilitarian philosopher Mill puts a strong emphasis on citizens' well-being. Having read my interpretation, some might argue that the second criterion remains paternalistic since it endorses the promotion of citizens' education in order to improve citizens' well-being. However, this does not seem right. We can similarly (and inaccurately) characterize Mill's harm principle as paternalistic, since it endorses restrictions of citizens' liberties in order to inhibit and prevent actions that might harm citizens. In both cases, the citizens cannot be seen as a homogeneous group of people—there are some non-consenting individuals who are being harmed by actions performed by others. This is, for example, the case of uneducated citizens voting in

the elections and making laws (or electing representatives who will make laws) that affect all citizens, and not only themselves.

10. Mill does not explicitly highlight his argument focusing on education (and discussed earlier in this chapter) as an additional reason for plural voting proposal, and the same applies for his argument focusing on justice. However, these arguments are clearly presented (Mill 1977a, 474–480) and, following some contemporary scholars (Miller 2015), should be discussed separately since they cannot be simply reduced to the other two (preventing class legislation and introducing competence in decision-making process).

11. For additional information on the strictly consequentialist interpretation of Mill's political thought see Estlund (2003), Wolff (2016), Cerovac (2016b) and Peter (2017).

12. Estlund uses his famous garage-cleaning example. Suppose Alf helped Betty clean her garage on numerous occasions, putting himself under her authority during such cleaning process. It seems that Betty now (when asked to) has a moral duty help Alf clean his garage, putting herself under Alf's authority during that process. If Betty does not want to help Alf and rejects his request for assistance, we can say that her non-consent is null. She still has a moral duty to help Alf clean his garage (and to temporarily put herself under his authority), and this duty does not simply disappear due to her lack of consent. Of course, this does not imply that Alf (who has moral authority over Betty despite her non-consent) can legitimately coerce her to help him clean his garage, yet we can still argue that, by refusing to help, Betty violates a duty she has towards Alf. For a more detailed analysis of this example see Estlund (2008, 10), and for additional information on normative consent see Estlund (2005 and 2018), Koltonski (2013), Huseby (2014), Peter (2017) and Cerovac (2020).

13. This is the well-known expert-boss fallacy, introduced by David Estlund (2008, 22, 40) and later discussed by many scholars, including Quong (2010), Caplan (2012), Zelič (2012), Brennan (2016) and Peter (2019).

14. Sometimes referred to as "scholocracy," the rule of the educated. See Estlund (2003, 57) and Cerovac (2020, 128).

15. James Mill (1992) and Jeremy Bentham (1834b), for example, take a different view and argue that a democratic procedure characterized by equal distribution of political influence represents the best instrument for making (and authorizing) optimal political decisions, those that promote the interests of the majority and prevent politicians from making public decisions pursing only their personal interests. Mill (1977a, see also Anschutz 1969) disagrees: the majority can be mistaken regarding its own long-term interests. However, his argument against egalitarian distribution of political influence does not rest (only) upon a desire to save the majority from pursuing things which are not in its long-term interest—an important epistemic argument for filtered democracy builds upon our duty not to harm others or, to be more precise, our duty to follow epistemically most reliable procedure and thus make optimal political decisions. Unlike his father and Jeremy Bentham, John Stuart Mill does not think that egalitarian democracy has adequate (instrumental) epistemic value.

16. This is the well-known invidious comparisons objection, where the citizens agree that the experts should rule, but cannot agree on who the experts are. For additional information see Estlund (1997) and Peter (2017).

Conclusion

Mill's moral and political philosophy covers a vast area and has been thoroughly discussed by numerous authors. Although it refers to many contemporary scholars who write about Mill's political thought, this book does not present a comprehensive overview of the discussion. It instead aims to critically evaluate some of the existing interpretations and provide a novel contribution to the ongoing debate by attributing unity to Mill's political thought by interpreting it around the unifying concept of epistemic democracy. Furthermore, it aims to evaluate some of Mill's more contested proposals and to analyze their potential for application within contemporary debates on epistemic and political values in the process of public justification.

My central hypothesis is that we can (and should) read Mill as an early epistemic democrat. To properly situate his account, I have characterized him as a democratic instrumentalist and demonstrated how this classification follows from Mill's consequentialist (utilitarian) background. We evaluate forms of government (and decision-authorization procedures) by assessing the quality of their long-term results, i.e., their ability to produce beneficial consequences—to promote higher pleasures and "the permanent interests of man as a progressive being" (Mill 1977d: 224). Mill believes democracy, characterized by citizens' political participation and almost universal suffrage, represents the best instrument for producing these desirable ends. However, to attain this instrumental epistemic value, democracy must be properly realized in representative institutions that will help filter the public will, thus protecting it from incompetence, vehemence and negligence. The justification Mill provides to support representative institutions in general, and filtering mechanisms such as open ballot, division of epistemic and political labor, plural voting and partisan associations in particular, is profoundly epistemic. These practices are helpful because they help us improve the quality of political outcomes and create correct, efficient and just laws, policies and political decisions. A detailed analysis of these mechanisms, with a particular focus on the roles Mill ascribes to representative institutions (e.g., the parliament) and expert commissions (e.g., the executive branch of government) in collective decision-making and decision-authorization process, takes a central place in this book.

Since Mill holds that democracy, characterized by these filtering mechanisms, represents epistemically the best (or the most reliable) procedure for authorizing political decisions, he argues that we have a moral duty towards others to abide by democratic procedures and to endorse their results when we make decisions that affect other people and not only ourselves. This duty helps us unify Mill's political thought and reject alleged paternalism in his work on representative democracy and mechanisms used to filter the public will. However, to recognize this duty, we have to interpret Mill as a political instrumentalist and an epistemic democrat.

Bibliography

Anderson, Elizabeth. 1990. "The Ethical Limitations of the Market." *Economics and Philosophy* 6(2): 179–205.
Anderson, Elisabeth. 1991. "John Stuart Mill and Experiments in Living." *Ethics* 102(1): 4–26.
Annan, Noel. 1968. "John Stuart Mill." In *Mill: A Collection of Critical Essays*, edited by J. B. Schneewind, 22–45. London: Palgrave Macmillan.
Anschutz, Richard P. 1969. *The Philosophy of J. S. Mill*. London: Clarendon Press.
Applbaum, Arthur. 2007. "Forcing a People to Be Free." *Philosophy & Public Affairs* 35(4): 359–401.
Archard, David. 1990. "Freedom Not to be Free: The Case of the Slavery Contract in J. S. Mill's On Liberty." *The Philosophical Quarterly* 40(161): 453–465.
Arendt, Hannah. 1967. "Truth in Politics." In *Philosophy, Politics and Society*, edited by P. Laslett and W. G. Runciman, 104–133. Oxford: Blackwell.
Arneson, Richard J. 1980. "Mill versus Paternalism." *Ethics* 90(4): 470–489.
Arneson, Richard J. 1982. "Democracy and Liberty in Mill's Theory of Government." *Journal of the History of Philosophy* 2(1): 43–64.
Arneson, Richard J. 2003. "Defending the Purely Instrumental Account of Democratic Legitimacy." *Journal of Political Philosophy* 11(1): 122–132.
Arrow, Kenneth. 1963. *Social Choice and Individual Values*. New Haven: Yale University Press.
Atchison, Thomas. 2012. "Distrusting Climate Science: A Problem in Practical Epistemology for Citizens." In *Between Scientists and Citizens*, edited by J. Goodwin, 61–73. Iowa City: Great Plains Society for the Study of Argumentation.
Austin, John. 2015. *A Plea For The Constitution*. New York: Andesite Press.
Baccarini, Elvio. 1993. *Sloboda, demokracija, pravednost–Filozofija politike J. S. Milla* [Freedom, Democracy, Justice—Political Philosophy of J. S. Mill]. Rijeka: Hrvatski kulturni dom.
Baccarini, Elvio. 2013. "John Stuart Mill." In *Moderna politička teorija* [Modern Political Theory], edited by E. Kulenović, 291–330. Zagreb: Biblioteka Politička misao.
Baccarini, Elvio and Viktor Ivanković. 2015. "Mill's Case for Plural Voting and the Need for Balanced Public Decisions." *Prolegomena* 14(2): 137–156.

Baccarini, Elvio. 2021. "Epistemic Democracy, Political Legitimacy and Reasonable Pluralism." *Etica & Politica / Ethics & Politics* 23(1): 375–386.

Ball, Terence. 1995. *Reappraising Political Theory: Revisionist Studies in the History of Political Thought*. Oxford: Clarendon Press.

Ball, Terence. 2004. "History and the Interpretation of Texts." In *Handbook of Political Theory*, edited by G. Gaus and C. Kukathas, 18–30. London: SAGE Publications.

Barker, Chris. 2015. "Mass and elite politics in Mill's considerations on representative Government." *History of European Ideas* 41(8): 1143–1163.

Barry, Brian. 2001. *Culture and Equality: An Egalitarian Critique of Multiculturalism*. Cambridge: Harvard University Press.

Bell, Duncan. 2010. "John Stuart Mill on Colonies." *Political Theory* 38(1): 34–64.

Bell, Melina C. 2020. "John Stuart Mill's Harm Principle and Free Speech: Expanding the Notion of Harm." *Utilitas*. 1–18.

Bentham, Jeremy. 1843a. "Political Tactics." In *The Works of Jeremy Bentham, Vol. 2*, edited by J. Bowring, 299–375. Edinburgh: William Tait.

Bentham, Jeremy. 1843b. "Plan of Parliamentary Reform." In *The Works of Jeremy Bentham, Vol. 3*, edited by J. Bowring, 433–557. Edinburgh: William Tait.

Bentham, Jeremy. 1843c. "Constitutional Code." In *The Works of Jeremy Bentham, Vol. 9*, edited by J. Bowring, 1–646. Edinburgh: William Tait.

Bentham, Jeremy. 1907. *An Introduction to the Principles of Morals and Legislation*. Oxford: Clarendon Press.

Berger, Fred R. 1984. *Happiness, Justice and Freedom. The Moral and Political Philosophy of John Stuart Mill*. Berkeley: University of California Press.

Berlin, Isaiah. 1969. *Four Essays on Liberty*. London: Oxford University Press.

Bester, Keren. 2010. "Justifying Democracy—Proceduralism versus Instrumentalism." *Rerum Causae* 2(1): 33–42.

Biezen, Ingrid and Michael Saward. 2008. "Democratic Theorists and Party Scholars: Why They Don't Talk to Each Other, and Why They Should." *Perspectives on Politics* 6(1): 21–35.

Binmore, Ken. 2000. "A Utilitarian Theory of Legitimacy." In *Economics, Values, and Organization*, edited by A. Ben-Ner and L. G. Putterman, 101–132. Cambridge: Cambridge University Press.

Blau, Adrian. 2017. "Interpreting Texts." In *Methods in Analytical Political Theory*, edited by A. Blau, 243–269. Cambridge: Cambridge University Press.

Blau, Adrian. 2019. "Textual context in the history of political thought and intellectual history." *History of European Ideas* 45(8): 1191–1210.

Brady, D. W., Ferejohn, J. and Harbridge, L. 2008. "Polarization and Public Policy: A General Assessment." In *Red and blue nation? Volume One: characteristics and causes of America's polarized politics*, edited by P. S. Nivola and D. W. Brady, 185–2016. Washington: Brookings Institution.

Brennan, Jason. 2012. *The Ethics of Voting*. Princeton: Princeton University Press.

Brennan, Jason. 2016. *Against Democracy*. Princeton: Princeton University Press.

Brilhante, Atila A. and Francisco J. Rocha. 2013. "Democracy and Plural Voting in John Stuart Mill's Political Thought." *Ethic@* 12(1): 53–65.

Brink, David. 2013. *Mill's Progressive Principles*. Oxford: Oxford University Press.
Brink, David. 2018. "Mill's Moral and Political Philosophy." In *The Stanford Encyclopedia of Philosophy* (Summer 2018 Edition), edited by Edward N. Zalta.
Brooker, Paul. 2010. *Leadership in Democracy*. London: Palgrave Macmillan.
Brown, David M. 1973. "What is Mill's Principle of Utility?" *Canadian Journal of Philosophy* 3: 1–12.
Brown, David M. 2003. "Sauvé and Prisoners' Voting Rights: The Death of the Good Citizen." *The Supreme Court Law Review: Osgoode's Annual Constitutional Cases Conference* 20: 297–346.
Burns, James H. 1957. "J. S. Mill and Democracy, 1829–61: II." *Political Studies* 5(3): 281–294.
Caplan, Bryan. 2012. "The Myth of the Rational Voter and Political Theory." In *Collective Wisdom: Principles and Mechanisms*, edited by H. Landemore and J. Elster, 319–337. New York: Cambridge University Press.
Carter, Ian. 2016. "Positive and Negative Liberty." In *The Stanford Encyclopedia of Philosophy* (Summer 2016 Edition), edited by Edward N. Zalta.
Cassam, Quassim. 2016. "Vice Epistemology." *The Monist* 99(2): 159–180.
Cerovac, Ivan. 2014. "Egalitarian Democracy Between Elitism and Populism." *Journal of Education, Culture and Society* 5(2): 31–42.
Cerovac, Ivan. 2016a. "Epistemic Value of Public Deliberation in a Democratic Decision-Making Process." *Philosophical Alternatives* 25(4): 5–16.
Cerovac, Ivan. 2016b. "Plural Voting and Mill's Account of Democratic Legitimacy." *Croatian Journal of Philosophy* 16(46): 91–106.
Cerovac, Ivan. 2017a. "Antipaternalizam i višestruko pravo glasa u Millovoj političkoj filozofiji [Antipaternalism and Plural Voting Proposal in Mill's Political Thought]." *Političke perspektive* 7(1–2): 43–60.
Cerovac, Ivan. 2017b. "Guest Editor's Preface." *Etica & Politica / Ethics & Politics* 19(2): 161–168.
Cerovac, Ivan. 2017c. "Elite Decision Making." In *The SAGE Encyclopedia of Political Behavior*, edited by F. Moghaddam, 238–239. Thousand Oaks: SAGE Publications.
Cerovac, Ivan. 2018. "Epistemic Liberalism." *Prolegomena* 17(1): 81–95.
Cerovac, Ivan. 2019. "The Epistemic Value of Partisanship." *Croatian Journal of Philosophy* 18(55): 99–117.
Cerovac, Ivan. 2020. *Epistemic Democracy and Political Legitimacy*. London: Palgrave MacMillan.
Chambers, Simone. 2003. "Deliberative Democratic Theory." *Annual Review of Political Science* 6: 307–326.
Chiu, Yvonne and Robert S. Taylor. 2011. "The Self-Extinguishing Despot: Millian Democratization." *The Journal of Politics* 73(4): 1239–1250.
Christiano, Thomas. 2004. "The Authority of Democracy." *Journal of Political Philosophy* 11(2): 266–290.
Christiano, Thomas. 2008. *The Constitution of Equality*. Oxford: Oxford University Press.

Christiano, Thomas. 2012. "Rational deliberation among experts and citizens." In *Deliberative Systems: Deliberative Democracy at the Large Scale*, edited by J. Parkinson, 27–51. Cambridge: Cambridge University Press.

Claassen, Rutger. 2018. *Capabilities in a Just Society: A Theory of Navigational Agency*. Cambridge: Cambridge University Press.

Claeys, Gregory. 2013. *Mill and Paternalism*. Cambridge: Cambridge University Press.

Coady, David. 2010. "Two Concepts of Epistemic Injustice." *Episteme* 7(2): 101–113.

Cohen, Howard D. 2000. "The Many Sides of John Stuart Mill's Political and Ethical Thought." PhD diss., University of Toronto.

Cohen, Joshua. 1986. "An Epistemic Conception of Democracy." *Ethics* 97(1): 26–38.

Cohen, Joshua. 1997. "Deliberation and Democratic Legitimacy." In *Deliberative Democracy: Essays on Reason and Politics*, edited by James Bohman and William Rehg, 67–92. Cambridge: The MIT Press.

Cohen, Joshua. 2009. *Philosophy, Politics, Democracy: Selected Essays*. Cambridge: Harvard University Press.

Cohen-Almagor, Raphael. 2012. "Between Autonomy and State Regulation: J.S. Mill's Elastic Paternalism." *Philosophy* 87(342): 557–582.

Collini, Stefan. 1984. "Introduction." In *Collected Works of John Stuart Mill, Vol. 21*, edited by John M. Robson, vii-lvi. Toronto: University of Toronto Press.

Colomer, Josep M. 2007. "On the Origins of Electoral Systems and Political Parties." *Electoral Studies* 26(2): 262–273.

Condorcet, Marquis de. 1994. *Foundations of Social Choice and Political Theory*. Northampton: Edward Elgar Publishing.

Constant, Benjamin. 1993. "O slobodi u antičko i moderno doba [The Liberty of Ancients Compared with that of Moderns]." In *Načela politike i drugi spisi*, edited by Radule Knežević, 161–182. Zagreb: Politička kultura.

Conti, Gregory. 2019. *Parliament the Mirror of the Nation: Representation, Deliberation and Democracy in Victorian Britain*. Cambridge: Cambridge University Press.

Cowling, Maurice. 1990. *Mill and Liberalism*. Cambridge: Cambridge University Press.

Craig, Frederick W. S. 1977. *British Electoral Facts, 1832–1987*. London: The Macmillan Press.

Cressati, Claudio. 1988. *La libertà e le sue garanzie. Il pensiero politico di John Stuart Mill* [Liberty and Its Guarantees: Political Thought of John Stuart Mill]. Bologna: Il Mulino.

Dahl, Robert A. 1989. *Democracy and Its Critics*. New Haven: Yale University Press.

Dalaqua, Gustavo H. 2018a. "Representation, Epistemic Democracy and Political Parties in John Stuart Mill and Jose de Alencar." *Brazilian Political Science Review* 12(2): 1–28.

Dalaqua, Gustavo H. 2018b. "Conflict, Consensus and Liberty in J.S. Mill's Representative Democracy." *British Journal of the History of Philosophy* 26(1): 110–130.

Dalaqua, Gustavo H. 2019. "Representative Democracy, Conflict and Consensus in J. S. Mill." PhD diss., University of Sao Paolo.

Destri, Chiara. 2017. "Right or Wrong, It's Democracy. Legitimacy, Justification and the Independent Criterion." *Etica & Politica / Ethics & Politics* 19(2): 169–190.

Donner, Wendy. 2007. "John Stuart Mill on Education and Democracy." In *J. S. Mill's Political Thought: A Bicentennial Reassessment*, edited by N. Urbinati and A. Zakaras, 250–274. Cambridge: Cambridge University Press.

Dryzek, John K. 2000. *Deliberative Democracy and Beyond: Liberals, Critics, Contestation*. Oxford: Oxford University Press.

Dworkin, Gerald. 1988. *The Theory and Practice of Autonomy*. Cambridge: Cambridge University Press.

Dworkin, Ronald. 1988. "What is Equality—Part 4: Political Equality." *University of San Francisco Law Review* 22(1): 1–30.

Ellerman, David. 2010. "Workplace Democracy and Human Development." *The Journal of Speculative Philosophy* 24(4): 333–353.

Elliott, John E. 1994. "Joseph A. Schumpeter and The Theory of Democracy." *Review of Social Economy* 52(4): 280–300.

Estlund, David. 1997. "Beyond Fairness and Deliberation: The Epistemic Dimension of Democratic Authority." In *Deliberative Democracy: Essays on Reason and Politics*, edited by J. Bohman and W. Rehg, 173–204. Cambridge: The MIT Press.

Estlund, David. 2003. "Why not Epistocracy?" In *Desire, Identity And Existence: Essays In Honor Of T.M. Penner*, edited by N. Reshotko, 53–69. Kelowna: Academic Printing and Publishing.

Estlund, David. 2005. "Political Authority and the Tyranny of Non-Consent." *Philosophical Issues* 15(1): 351–367.

Estlund, David. 2008. *Democratic Authority*. Princeton: Princeton University Press.

Estlund, David. 2018. "Normative Consent and Authority." In *The Routledge Handbook of the Ethics of Consent*, edited by A. Müller and P. Schaber, 359–371. Abingdon: Routledge.

Feinberg, Joel. 1987. *The Moral Limits of the Criminal Law, Vol. 1: Harm to Others*. New York: Oxford University Press.

Feinberg, Joel. 1988. *The Moral Limits of the Criminal Law, Vol. 2: Offense to Others*. New York: Oxford University Press.

Festenstein, Matthew. 2009. "Truth and Trust in Democratic Epistemology." In *Does Truth Matter? Democracy and Public Space*, edited by R. Tinnevelt and R. Geenens, 69–79. Dordrecht: Springer.

Freeman, Samuel. 2003. "Introduction: John Rawls—An Overview." In *The Cambridge Companion to Rawls*, edited by M. Freeman, 1–61. New York: Cambridge University Press.

Fricker, Miranda. 2007. *Epistemic Injustice: Power and the Ethics of Knowing*. Oxford: Oxford University Press.

Galston, William. 1989. "Civic Education in the Liberal State." In *Liberalism and the Moral Life*, edited by N. L. Rosenblum, 89–101. Cambridge: Harvard University Press.

Garforth, Francis W. 1980. *Educative Democracy: John Stuart Mill on Education in Society*. New York: Oxford University Press.

Gaus, Gerald. 1996. *Justificatory Liberalism: An Essay on Epistemology and Political Theory.* New York: Oxford University Press.

Gaus, Gerald. 2008. "Is the Public Incompetent? Compared to Whom? About What?" *Critical Review: A Journal of Politics and Society* 20(3): 291–311.

Gaus, Gerald. 2009. "State Neutrality and Controversial Values in *On Liberty*." In *Mill's On Liberty. A Critical Guide*, edited by C. L. Ten, 83–104. New York: Cambridge University Press.

Gaus, Gerald. 2011. *The Order of Public Reason*. Cambridge: Cambridge University Press.

Gray, John. 1983. *Mill on Liberty. A Defense*. London: Routledge.

Green, Thomas H. 2003. *Prolegomena to Ethics*. Oxford: Clarendon Press.

Gutmann, Amy. 1980. *Liberal Equality*. Cambridge: Cambridge University Press.

Gutmann, Amy and Dennis Thompson. 2014. *The Spirit of Compromise: Why Governing Demands It and Campaigning Undermines It*. Princeton: Princeton University Press.

Habermas, Jürgen. 1996. *Between Facts and Norms: Contributions to a Discursive Theory of Law and Democracy*. Cambridge: MIT Press.

Halliday, John R. 2004. *Political Thinkers: John Stuart Mill*. London: Routledge.

Hamburger, Joseph. 1965. *Intellectuals in Politics: John Stuart Mill and the Philosophic Radicals*. New Haven: Yale University Press.

Hamburger, Joseph. 1999. *John Stuart Mill on Liberty and Control*. Princeton: Princeton University Press.

Hansen, Herman M. 1999. *The Athenian Democracy in the Age of Demosthenes*. Cambridge: University of Oklahoma Press.

Hare, Thomas. 2015. *A Treatise On the Election of Representatives, Parliamentary and Municipal*. London: Sagwan Press.

Hart, Jenifer. 1992. *Proportional Representation: Critics of the British Electoral System 1820–1945*. Oxford: Clarendon Press.

Hayek, Friedrich A. 2012a. *Individualism and Economic Order*. Chicago: The University of Chicago Press.

Hayek, Friedrich A. 2012b. *Law, Legislation and Liberty*. London: Routledge.

Hayek, Friedrich A. 2015. "John Stuart Mill and Harriet Taylor." In *The Collected Works of F. A. Hayek, Vol. 16*, edited by S. J. Peart, 5–272. Chicago: University of Chicago Press.

Hayward, Allison. 2010. "Bentham & Ballots: Tradeoffs Between Secrecy and Accountability in How We Vote." *Journal of Law & Politics* 39: 45–55.

Hollander, Samuel. 2015. *John Stuart Mill: Political Economist.* Singapore: World Scientific Publishing.

Holmes, Stephen. 1988. "Precommitment and the Paradox of Democracy." In *Constitutionalism and Democracy*, edited by J. Elster and R. Slagstad, 195–240. Cambridge: Cambridge University Press.

Holmes, Stephen. 1995. *Passions and Constraint: On the Theory of Liberal Democracy*. Chicago: University of Chicago Press.

Holmes, Stephen. 2007. "Making Sense of Liberal Imperialism." In *J. S. Mill's Political Thought: A Bicentennial Reassessment*, edited by N. Urbinati and A. Zakaras, 319–346. Cambridge: Cambridge University Press.
Honohan, Iseult. 2002. *Civic Republicanism*. New York: Routledge.
Hoppen, Theodore K. 2000. *The Mid-Victorian Generation 1846–1886*. Oxford: Oxford University Press.
Hudlin, Charles W. 1985. "Antipaternalism and John Stuart Mill." PhD diss., The University of Oklahoma.
Huseby, Robert. 2014. "Normative Consent and the Scope of Democratic Authority." *Politics* 34(4): 334–344.
Irwin, Terence H. 2006. "Mill and the Classical World." In *The Cambridge Companion to Mill*, edited by J. Skorupski, 423–463. Cambridge: Cambridge University Press.
James, Michael. 1981. "Public Interest and Majority Rule in Bentham's Democratic Theory." *Political Theory* 9(1): 49–64.
Justman, Stewart. 1990. *The Hidden Text of Mill's Liberty*. Lanham: Rowman and Littlefield.
Kelly, Paul. 2006. "Liberalism and Epistemic Diversity: Mill's Skeptical Legacy." *Episteme* 3(3): 248–265.
Kendall, Willmoore and George W. Carey. 1968. "The Roster Device: J. S. Mill and Contemporary Elitism." *Western Political Quarterly* 21(1): 20–39.
Kern, Paul B. 1998. "Universal Suffrage Without Democracy: Thomas Hare and John Stuart Mill." In *John Stuart Mill's Social and Political Thought, Vol. 3*, edited by G. W. Smith, 165–179. London: Routledge.
Kidd, Ian J., Heather Battaly and Quassim Cassam. 2020. *Vice Epistemology*. London: Routledge.
Kinzer, Bruce L. 1981. "J.S. Mill and the Problem of Party." *Journal of British Studies* 21(1): 106–122.
Kitcher, Philip. 2011. *Science in a Democratic Society*. New York: Prometheus Books.
Knight, Jack et al. 2016. "Roundtable on Epistemic Democracy and Its Critics." *Critical Review* 28(2): 137–170.
Koltonski, Daniel. 2013. "Normative Consent and Authority." *Journal of Moral Philosophy* 10(3): 255–275.
Kregar, Josip. 1998. "Alexis de Tocqueville i lokalna demokracija u Americi [Alexis de Tocqueville and Local Democracy in the United States of America]. In *Alexis de Tocqueville o američkoj povijesti*, edited by D. Roksandić and M. Brkljačić, 100–114. Zagreb: United States Information Service.
Kristol, Irvin. 1995. *Neoconservatism: The Autobiography of an Idea*. New York: Simon and Schuster.
Krouse, Richard W. 1982. "Two Concepts of Democratic Representation: James and John Stuart Mill." *The Journal of Politics* 44(2): 509–537.
Kukathas, Chandran. 2003. *The Liberal Archipelago: A Theory of Diversity and Freedom*. Oxford: Oxford University Press.
Kukathas, Chandran. 1997. "Cultural Toleration." In *Ethnicity and Group Rights*, edited by I. Shapiro and W. Kymlicka, 60–104. New York: New York University Press.

Kumar, Sujith S. 2006. "Reassessing J. S. Mill's Liberalism: The influence of Auguste Comte, Jeremy Bentham, and Wilhelm von Humboldt." PhD diss., London School of Economics and Political Science.

Kurer, Oskar. 1989. "John Start Mill on Democratic Representation and Centralization." *Utilitas* 1(2): 290–299.

Kurfirst, Robert. 1996. "J. S. Mill on Oriental Despotism, Including its British Variant." *Utilitas* 8(1): 73–87.

Landemore, Helene. 2017. *Democratic Reason: Politics, Collective Intelligence, and the Rule of the Many*. Princeton: Princeton University Press.

Latimer, Trevor. 2018. "Plural Voting and Political Equality: A Thought Experiment in Democratic Theory." *European Journal of Political Theory* 17(1): 65–86.

Lawson, Kay. 1988. "When Linkage Fails." In *When Parties Fail: Emerging Alternative Organizations*, edited by K. Lawson and P. Merkl, 13–38. Princeton: Princeton University Press.

Layman, G. C., T. M. Carsey and J. M. Horowitz. 2006. "Party Polarization in American Politics: Characteristics, Causes, and Consequences." *Annual Review of Political Science* 9: 83–110.

Lincoln, Abraham. 2000. "The Gettysburg Address." In *The Life and Writings of Abraham Lincoln*, edited by P. Van Doren Stern. New York: Modern Library.

Lister, Andrew. 2014. "The Challenge of Moderate Epistocracy." *IPSA World Congress of Political Science—New Directions in Democratic Theory*. Montreal, July 2014.

Locke, John. 1990. *Second Treatise on Civil Government*. Indianapolis: Hackett.

Loizides, Antis. 2013. *John Stuart Mill's Platonic Heritage: Happiness through Character*. New York: Lexington Books.

Lorimer, James. 2017. *Political Progress Not Necessarily Democratic: Or Relative Equality the True Foundation of Liberty*. London: Forgotten Books.

Lukes, Steven. 2006. *Individualism*. Colchester: ECPR Press.

Lustig, Doreen and Eyal Benvenisti. 2014. "The Multinational Corporation as the Good Despot: The Democratic Costs of Privatization in Global Settings." *Theoretical Inquiries in Law* 15(1): 125–157.

Mackie, Gerry. 2012. "Rational Ignorance and Beyond." In *Collective Wisdom: Principles and Mechanisms*, edited by H. Landemore and J. Elster, 290–318. Cambridge: Cambridge University Press.

Macleod, Christopher. 2016. "John Stuart Mill." In *The Stanford Encyclopedia of Philosophy* (Summer 2016 Edition), edited by Edward N. Zalta.

Macpherson, Crawford B. 2012. *The Life and Times of Liberal Democracy*. New York: Oxford University Press.

Manza, Jeff and Christopher Uggen. 2004. "Punishment and Democracy: Disenfranchisement of Nonincarcerated Felons in the United State." *Perspectives on Politics* 2(3): 491–505.

Manza, Jeff and Christopher Uggen. 2008. *Locked Out: Felon Disenfranchisement and American Democracy*. Oxford: Oxford University Press.

Marti, Jose L. 2006. "The Epistemic Conception of Deliberative Democracy Defended: Reasons, Rightness and Equal Political Autonomy." In *Deliberative*

Democracy and Its Discontents, edited by Jose L. Marti and Samantha Besson, 27–56. Hampshire: Ashgate Publishing.

McCloskey, Henry J. 1965. "A non-utilitarianapproach to punishment." *Inquiry: An Interdisciplinary Journal of Philosophy* 8(1–4): 249–263.

Meade, James E. 1964. *Efficiency, Equality, and the Ownership of Property*. London: G. Allen and Unwin.

Medina, Jose. 2013. *The Epistemology of Resistance*. Oxford: Oxford University Press.

Michelman, Frank I. 2003. "Rawls on Constitutionalism and Constitutional Law." In *The Cambridge Companion to Rawls*, edited by M. Freeman, 394–425. New York: Cambridge University Press.

Mill, James. 1992. "Government." In *James Mill: Political Writings*, edited by T. Ball, 491–505. Cambridge: Cambridge University Press.

Mill, John S. 1859a. *On Liberty*. London: John W. Parker and Son, West Strand.

Mill, John S. 1859b. *Thoughts on Parliamentary Reform*. London: John W. Parker and Son, West Strand.

Mill, John S. 1861. *Considerations on Representative Government. Second Edition.* London: Parker, Son, and Bourn, West Strand.

Mill, John S. 1965a. "The Principles of Political Economy with Some of Their Applications to Social Philosophy (Books I–II)." In *The Collected Works of John Stuart Mill, Vol. 2*, edited by John M. Robson, 3–454. Toronto: University of Toronto Press.

Mill, John S. 1965b. "The Principles of Political Economy with Some of Their Applications to Social Philosophy (Books III–IV)." In *The Collected Works of John Stuart Mill, Vol. 3*, edited by John M. Robson, 455–798. Toronto: University of Toronto Press.

Mill, John S. 1972. "Mill to Hare, 5th February 1860. Letters of John Stuart Mill." In *Collected Works of John Stuart Mill, Vol. 15*, edited by Francis E. Mineka and Dwight N. Lindley, 672. Toronto: University of Toronto Press.

Mill, John S. 1974. "A System of Logic (Books IV–VI)." In *Collected Works of John Stuart Mill, Vol. 8*, edited by John M. Robson, 641–1251. Toronto: University of Toronto Press.

Mill, John S. 1977a. "Considerations of Representative Government." In *Collected Works of John Stuart Mill, Vol. 19*, edited by John M. Robson, 371–578. Toronto: University of Toronto Press.

Mill, John S. 1977b. "Thoughts on Parliamentary Reform." In *Collected Works of John Stuart Mill, Vol. 19*, edited by John M. Robson, 311–340. Toronto: University of Toronto Press.

Mill, John S. 1977c. "Recent Writers on Reform." In *Collected Works of John Stuart Mill, Vol. 19*, edited by John M. Robson, 341–370. Toronto: University of Toronto Press.

Mill, John S. 1977d. "On Liberty." In *Collected Works of John Stuart Mill, Vol. 18*, edited by John M. Robson, 213–310. Toronto: University of Toronto Press.

Mill, John S. 1977e. "De Tocqueville on Democracy in America [II]." In *Collected Works of John Stuart Mill, Vol. 18*, edited by John M. Robson, 153–204. Toronto: University of Toronto Press.

Mill, John S. 1977f. "De Tocqueville on Democracy in America [I]." In *Collected Works of John Stuart Mill, Vol. 18*, edited by John M. Robson, 47–90. Toronto: University of Toronto Press.

Mill, John S. 1981a. "Autobiography." In *Collected Works of John Stuart Mill, Vol. 1*, edited by John M. Robson, 1–290. Toronto: University of Toronto Press.

Mill, John S. 1981b. "Periodical Literature: Edinburgh Review." In *Collected Works of John Stuart Mill, Vol. 1*, edited by John M. Robson, 291–326. Toronto: University of Toronto Press.

Mill, John S. 1982a. "Notes on the Newspapers." In *Collected Works of John Stuart Mill, Vol. 6*, edited by John M. Robson, 149–280. Toronto: University of Toronto Press.

Mill, John S. 1982b. "Fonblanque's England Under Seven Administrations." In *Collected Works of John Stuart Mill, Vol. 6*, edited by John M. Robson, 349–380. Toronto: University of Toronto Press.

Mill, John S. 1982c. "Reorganization of the Reform Party." In *Collected Works of John Stuart Mill, Vol. 6*, edited by John M. Robson, 465–496. Toronto: University of Toronto Press.

Mill, John S. 1984a. "Educational Endowments." In *Collected Works of John Stuart Mill, Vol. 21*, edited by John M. Robson, 207–214. Toronto: University of Toronto Press.

Mill, John S. 1984b. "The Subjection of Women." In *Collected Works of John Stuart Mill, Vol. 21*, edited by John M. Robson, 260–340. Toronto: University of Toronto Press.

Mill, John S. 1984c. "Reform in Education." In *Collected Works of John Stuart Mill, Vol. 21*, edited by John M. Robson, 61–74. Toronto: University of Toronto Press.

Mill, John S. 1984d. "Inaugural Address Delivered to the University of St Andrews." In *Collected Works of John Stuart Mill, Vol. 21*, edited by John M. Robson, 215–258. Toronto: University of Toronto Press.

Mill, John S. 1985a. "Utilitarianism." In *Collected Works of John Stuart Mill, Vol. 10*, edited by John M. Robson, 203–260. Toronto: University of Toronto Press.

Mill, John S. 1985b. "Remarks on Bentham's Philosophy." In *Collected Works of John Stuart Mill, Vol. 10*, edited by John M. Robson, 3–18. Toronto: University of Toronto Press.

Mill, John S. 1988a. "Morning Star, 6th July 1965." In *Collected Works of John Stuart Mill, Vol. 28*, edited by John M. Robson and Bruce L. Kinzer, 28–31. Toronto: University of Toronto Press.

Mill, John S. 1988b. "The Westminster Election of 1865. Daily Telegraph. 10th June 1865." In *Collected Works of John Stuart Mill, Vol. 28*, edited by John M. Robson and Bruce L. Kinzer, 31–40. Toronto: University of Toronto Press.

Mill, John S. 1988c. "Representation of the People [2]. 13th April 1866." In *Collected Works of John Stuart Mill, Vol. 28*, edited by John M. Robson and Bruce L. Kinzer, 67. Toronto: University of Toronto Press.

Milbrath, Lester W. 1981. "Political Participation." In: *The Handbook of Political Behavior*, edited by S. L. Long, 197–240. Boston: Springer.

Miller, Dale E. 1999. "Public Spirit and Liberal Democracy: John Stuart Mill's Civic Liberalism." PhD diss., University of Pittsburgh.

Miller, Dale E. 2005. "Moral Expertise: A Millian Perspective." In: *Ethics Expertise: History, Contemporary Perspectives, and Applications*, edited by L. M. Rasmussen, 73–87. New York: Springer.

Miller, Dale E. 2010. *J. S. Mill: Moral, Social and Political Thought*. Cambridge: Polity.

Miller, Dale E. 2015. "The Place of Plural Voting in Mill's Conception of Representative Government." *The Review of Politics* 77: 399–423.

Miller, Joseph J. 2003. "J.S. Mill on Plural Voting, Competence and Participation." *History of Political Thought* 24(4): 647–667.

Misak, Cheryl. 2000. *Truth, Morality, Politics: Pragmatism and Deliberation*. New York: Routledge.

Mladenović, Ivan. 2019. *Javni um i deliberativna demokratija* [Public Reason and Deliberative Democracy]. Belgrade: Institut za filozofiju i društvenu teoriju.

Mouffe, Chantal. 2009. *The Democratic Paradox*. London: Verso.

Murata, Minami. 2017. "John Stuart Mill and Political Reform." *Revue d'études benthamiennesis* 16: 1–17.

Nozick, Robert. 1974. *Anarchy, State, and Utopia*. Oxford: Blackwell.

Nussbaum, Martha C. 2000. *Women and Human Development*. New York: Cambridge University Press.

Nussbaum, Martha C. 2004. "Mill between Aristotle & Bentham." *Daedalus* 133(2): 60–68.

Oh, Eunseong. 2016. "Mill on Paternalism." *Journal of Political Inquiry* 2016(2): 1–9.

O'Neill, Martin. 2012. "Free (and Fair) Markets Without Capitalism: Political Values, Principles of Justice and Property-Owning Democracy." In *Property-Owning Democracy: Rawls and Beyond*, edited by M. O'Neill and T. Williamson, 75–100. Oxford: Wiley-Blackwell.

Pedersen, Johannes T. 1982. "On the Educational Function of Political Participation: A Comparative Analysis of John Stuart Mill's Theory and Contemporary Survey Research Findings." *Political Studies* 30(4): 557–568.

Peter, Fabienne. 2011. *Democratic Legitimacy*. London: Routledge.

Peter, Fabienne. 2012. "The Procedural Epistemic Value of Deliberation." *Synthese* 190(7): 1253–1266.

Peter, Fabienne. 2016. "The Epistemic Circumstances of Democracy." In *The Epistemic Life of Groups*, edited by M. Fricker and M. Brady, 133–149. Oxford: Oxford University Press.

Peter, Fabienne. 2017. "Political Legitimacy." In *The Stanford Encyclopedia of Philosophy* (Spring 2017 Edition), edited by Edward N. Zalta.

Peter, Fabienne. 2019. "Legitimate Political Authority and Expertise." In *Legitimacy: The State and Beyond*, edited by W. Sadurski, M. Sevel and K. Walton, 32–42. Oxford: Oxford University Press.

Pettit, Philip. 1999. *Republicanism: A Theory of Freedom and Government.* New York: Oxford University Press.
Pettit, Philip. 2012. *On the People's Terms.* Cambridge: Cambridge University Press.
Pitkin, Hanna F. 1967. *The Concept of Representation.* Berkeley: University of California Press.
Planinc, Zdravko. 1987. "Should Imprisoned Criminals Have a Constitutional Right to Vote?" *Canadian Journal of Law and Society* 2: 153–164.
Plato. 2000. *The Republic.* Cambridge: Cambridge University Press.
Poulter, Sebastian. 1999. *Ethnicity, Law and Human Rights. The English Experience.* Oxford: Oxford University Press.
Pratt, Cranford R. 1955. "The Benthamite Theory of Democracy." *The Canadian Journal of Economics and Political Science* 21(1): 20–29.
Prijić-Samaržija, Snježana. 2011. "Trusting Experts: Trust, Testimony and Evidence." *Acta Histriae* 19(1–2): 249–262.
Prijić-Samaržija, Snježana. 2018. *Democracy and Truth. The Conflict Between Political and Epistemic Virtues.* Udine: Mimesis International.
Primorac, Igor. 1986. "Millova obrana slobode [Mill's Defense of Liberty]." *Filozofska istraživanja* 16(2): 549–565.
Quinault, Roland. 2011. *British Prime Ministers and Democracy.* London: Continuum International Publishing.
Quong, Jonathan. 2010. "The Distribution of Authority." *Representation* 46(1): 35–52.
Ranciere, Jacques. 1998. *Disagreement: Politics and Philosophy.* Minneapolis: University of Minnesota Press.
Rawls, John. 2001. *Justice as Fairness: A Restatement.* Cambridge: The Belknap Press of Harvard University Press.
Rawls, John. 2005. *Political Liberalism.* New York: Columbia University Press.
Riley, Jonathan. 2015. "An Extraordinary Maximizing Utilitarianism." In *Individual and Social Choice and Social Welfare: Essays in Honor of Nick Baigent*, edited by C. Binder at al., 309–334. Berlin: Springer-Verlag.
Riley, Jonathan. 2007. "Mill's Neo-Athenian Model of Liberal Democracy." In *J. S. Mill's Political Thought: A Bicentennial Reassessment*, edited by N. Urbinati and A. Zakaras, 221–249. Cambridge: Cambridge University Press.
Roberts, John M. 2004. "John Stuart Mill, Free Speech and the Public Sphere." *The Sociology Review* 52(1): 67–87.
Robson, John M. 1968. *The Improvement of Mankind: The Social and Political Thought of John Stuart Mill.* Toronto: University of Toronto Press.
Rosanvallon, Pierre. 2008. *Counter-Democracy: Politics in an Age of Distrust.* Cambridge: Cambridge University Press.
Rosenblum, Nancy. 2000. "Political Parties as Membership Groups." *Columbia Law Review* 100(3): 813–844.
Rosenblum, Nancy. 2008. *On the Side of the Angels: An Appreciation of Parties and Partisanship.* Princeton: Princeton University Press.

Rousseau, Jean-Jacques. 1997. "Of the Social Contract." In *The Social Contract and Other Later Political Writings*, edited by V. Gourevitch, 39–152. Cambridge: Cambridge University Press.

Ryan, Alan. 1972. "Utilitarianism and Bureaucracy: The Views of J. S. Mill." In *Studies in the Growth of Nineteenth-Century Government*, edited by G. Southerland, 33–62. London: Routledge.

Ryan, Alan. 2011. "J. S. Mill on Education." *Oxford Review of Education* 37(5): 653–667.

Ryan, Alan. 2016. *J. S. Mill*. London: Routledge and Kegan Paul.

Sandel, Michael J. 2010. *Justice: What Is the Right Thing to Do?* New York: Farrar, Straus and Giroux.

Schmitt, Carl. 2007. *The Concept of the Political*. Chicago: University of Chicago Press.

Schumpeter, Joseph A. 2008. *Capitalism, Socialism, and Democracy*. New York: Harper Perennial Modern Classics.

Schwan, David. 2013. "J. S. Mill on Coolie Labour and Voluntary Slavery." *British Journal for the History of Philosophy* 21(4): 754–766.

Schwartz, Justin. 2012. "Where Did Mill Go Wrong? Why the Capital-Managed Rather than the Labor-Managed Enterprise is the Predominant Organizational Form in Market Economies." *Ohio State Law Journal* 73(2): 219–285.

Schwartzberg, Melissa. 2015. "Epistemic Democracy and Its Challenges." *Annual Review of Political Science* 18: 187–203.

Schweizer, Steven L. 1995. "Participation, Workplace Democracy, and the Problem of Representative Government." *Polity* 27(3): 359–377.

Selinger, William. 2019. *Parliamentarism: From Burke to Weber*. Cambridge: Cambridge University Press.

Sen, Amartya. 1984. *Resources, Values, and Development*. Cambridge: Harvard University Press.

Sen, Amartya. 1992. *Inequality Re-Examined*. Oxford: Clarendon Press.

Sen, Amartya. 1995. "Gender Inequality and Theories of Justice." In: *Women, Culture, and Development*, edited by M. Nussbaum and J. Glover, 153–198. Oxford: Clarendon Press.

Sidgwick, Henry. 2012. *The Elements of Politics*. New York: Cambridge University Press.

Siegel, Jonah A. 2011. "Felon Disenfranchisement and the Fight for Universal Suffrage." *Social Work* 56(1): 89–91.

Simmons, John A. 2001. *Justification and Legitimacy: Essays on Rights and Obligations*. Cambridge: Cambridge University Press.

Skorupski, John. 2006. *Why Read Mill Today*. London: Routledge.

Stevenson, Heyley. 2016. "The Wisdom of the Many in Global Governance: An Epistemic-Democratic Defense of Diversity and Inclusion." *International Studies Quarterly* 60: 400–412.

Strasser, Mark. 1988. "Mill on Voluntary Self-Enslavement." *Philosophical Papers* 17(3): 171–183.

Sturgis, Daniel. 2005. "Is Voting a Private Matter?" *The Journal of Social Philosophy* 36(1): 18–30.

Sullivan, Eileen P. 1983. "Liberalism and Imperialism: J. S. Mill's Defense of the British Empire." *Journal of the History of Ideas* 44(4): 599–617.

Sunstein, Cass R. 2011. *Going to Extremes: How Like Minds Unite and Divide*. Oxford: Oxford University Press.

Swift, Adam. 2006. *Political Philosophy*. London: Polity.

Talisse, Robert B. 2009. *Democracy and Moral Conflict*. New York: Cambridge University Press.

Taylor, Robert S. Forthcoming. "Reading Rawls Rightly: A Theory of Justice at 50." *Polity* 53(4): Forthcoming.

Tebble, Adam J. 2016. *Epistemic Liberalism: A Defense*. London: Routledge.

Ten, Chin L. 2012. "Justice for Barbarians." In: *Mill on Justice*, edited by L. Kahn, 184–197. Hampshire: Palgrave Macmillan.

Ten, Chin L. 1980. *Mill on Liberty*. Oxford: Clarendon Press.

Teorell, Jan. 1999. A Deliberative Defense of Intra-Party Democracy. *Party Politics* 5(3): 363–382.

Theuns, Tom. 2017. "Jeremy Bentham, John Stuart Mill and the Secret Ballot: Insights from Nineteenth Century Democratic Theory." *Australian Journal of Politics and History* 63(4): 493–507.

Thompson, Dennis F. 1976. *John Stuart Mill and Representative Government*. Princeton: Princeton University Press.

Thorley, John. 2005. *Athenian Democracy*. New York: Routledge.

Timmons, Mark. 2013. *Moral Theory: An Introduction*. New York: Rowman & Littlefield.

Tinnevelt, Ronald. 2015. "The Social Function of Agonism. A General Outline of a Deliberative Theory of Political Parties." *ECPR Joint Sessions 2015*.

Tocqueville, Alexis de. 2000. *Democracy in America*. Chicago: University of Chicago Press.

Urbinati, Nadia. 2000. "Representation as Advocacy." *Political Theory* 28(6): 758–786.

Urbinati, Nadia. 2002. *Mill on Democracy: From the Athenian Polis to Representative Government*. Chicago: Chicago University Press.

Urbinati, Nadia. 2007. "The Many Heads of the Hydra: J. S. Mill on Despotism." In *J. S. Mill's Political Thought: A Bicentennial Reassessment*, edited by N. Urbinati and A. Zakaras, 66–97. New York: Cambridge University Press.

Urbinati, Nadia. 2014. *Democracy Disfigured: Opinion, Truth and the People*. Cambridge: Harvard University Press.

Urdanoz, Jorge. 2019. "John Stuart Mill and proportional representation. A misunderstanding." *Political Science* 71(2): 158–171.

Van Parijs, Philippe. 1996. "Is democracy compatible with justice?" *The Journal of Political Philosophy* 4: 101–117.

Varouxakis, Georgios. 2008. "Cosmopolitan Patriotism in J. S. Mill's Political Thought and Activism." *Revue D'études Benthamiennes* 4.

Wall, Steven. 2007. "Democracy and Equality." *The Philosophical Quarterly* 57(228): 416–438.

Walzer, Michael. 1999. "Deliberation, and what else?" In *Deliberative Politics: Essays on Democracy and Disagreement*, edited by Stephen Macedo, 58–69. Oxford University Press.

Warner, Beth E. 2001. "John Stuart Mill's Theory of Bureaucracy within Representative Government: Balancing Competence and Participation." *Public Administration Review* 64(1): 403–413.

Weithman, Paul. 2004. "Political Republicanism and Perfectionist Republicanism." *The Review of Politics* 66(2): 285–312.

Wellman, Christopher. 1996. "Liberalism, Samaritanism, and Political Legitimacy." *Philosophy and Public Affairs* 25(3): 211–237.

West, Edwin G. 1965. "Liberty and Education: John Stuart Mill's Dilemma." *Philosophy* 40(152): 129–142.

Wolfe, Joel D. 1985. "A Defense of Participatory Democracy." *The Review of Politics* 47(3): 370–389.

Wolff, Jonathan. 2006. *An Introduction to Political Philosophy*. New York: Oxford University Press.

Wright, Erik O. 2010. *Envisioning Real Utopias*. London: Verso.

Wrigley, Edward A. and Ronald Schofield. 1981. *The Population History of England, 1541–1871: A Reconstruction*. Cambridge: Cambridge University Press.

Yenor, Scott. 2015. "Resisting the Seduction of John Stuart Mill." *Modern Age: A Conservative Review* Spring 2015: 28–35.

Young, Iris M. 2000. *Inclusion and Democracy*. Oxford: Oxford University Press.

Ypi, Lea and Jonathan White. 2010. "Rethinking the Modern Prince: Partisanship and the Democratic Ethos." *Political Studies* 58(4): 809–828.

Ypi, Lea and Jonathan White. 2016. *The Meaning of Partisanship*. Oxford: Oxford University Press.

Zakaras, Alex. 2009. *Individuality and Mass Democracy: Mill, Emerson, and the Burdens of Citizenship*. Oxford: Oxford University Press.

Zelič, Nebojša. 2012. "The Idea of Public Reason." PhD diss., University of Rijeka.

Index

Page references for figures are italicized.

administration, 30–31, 85–90, 104–106, 145;
  local, 104;
  public, 30–31, 68, 88–90, 175, 178n8;
  two levels of, 30
agonism, 42–45, 51, 68, 75, 89, 95, 124–27, 129, 135n18, 142, 157;
  deliberative, 12, 41–2;
  epistemic value of, 43–44, 49, 57, 93, 122, 152
Anschutz, Richard P., 1, 69, 178n3, 179n15
Aristotle, 125–26
Arneson, Richard, 7, 25, 56, 58, 61–64, 77n3, 161, 165–170, 172, 177, 178n7
authority, 4, 13, 14n4, 21, 24, 30, 105–107, 126–27, 134n8, 176, 179n12;
  and consent, 3, 173;
  moral, 174, 179n12;
  political, 4, 18, 33–35, 67, 95, 111n25, 173
authority tenet, 8–10, 35, 126
autonomy, 22–23, 52n7, 83, 88, 128, 135n20, 143, 165;
  of local government, 13, 82, 103–106;
  of political representatives, 97–99, 143–45, 153

Baccarini, Elvio, 34, 45, 70, 103–104, 108n7, 109n9, 111n24, 118, 125, 130, 132, 133n4, 163, 165, 178n3
Bentham, Jeremy, 3, 24, 37n11, 80n24, 94;
  on democracy, 73–75, 179n15;
  on education, 24, 37n11;
  on utilitarianism, 47, 59–60
Brennan, Jason, 5, 27, 34, 55, 104, 115, 175, 179n13
Brink, David, 7, 19, 25, 35n2, 77n5, 79n21, 128, 161, 165–66, 177
bureaucracy, 31, 35, 108n7

campaign promises. *See* pledges
censorship, 43–48, 52n4, 163–64, 178n3
centralization, 24, 103–104, 106, 111n25.
See also decentralization
character, 25–26, 29, 32, 69–70, 88, 90–91, 101, 120;
  active, 26, 36n4, 70;

individual, 18, 79n21, 90, 103;
    passive, 37n14, 68, 70;
    national, 127
Christiano, Thomas, 5, 20, 30, 52n8, 56–57, 80, 108, 114, 130–32, 134n8, 139, 148, 154–55
class, 48, 90, 96, 109n11, 123–25, 141;
    and representation, 88, 93, 100, 109n9, 126–27, 135n16, 147–51, 158n6;
    class interests, 50, 75, 109n9, 123–24, 143;
    class legislation, 12, 50, 76, 82–83, 93, 109n9, 113–14, 119, 123–25, 127–29, 166, 170–71, 177;
    working class, 88, 100, 109n9
coercion, 94, 163–64, 172–74, 178n4
competence, 1, 7, 9, 12–13, 17–18, 29–30, 33, 66, 84, 88, 97, 114, 128, 148, 166, 174;
    and participation, 1, 91–92, 108n7, 120, 118, 120–21;
    in local government, 103–104;
    moral, 30, 32–33, 102;
    principle of, 17, 104, 141, 147;
    technical, 31–33.
    See also experts
compromise, 75, 86, 99, 153, 156, 170;
    spirit of, 155–58, 159n11
conflict, 57, 68, 74–77, 80n26, 90, 107n5, 123–25, 138, 143, 152–54;
    epistemic value of, 41–43, 46–50, 52n5, 75–76, 91, 126, 139–41, 149, 153, 157;
    of interests, 43, 75, 123, 157;
    political, 8, 12, 41–43, 46–51, 52n6, 75, 124–25, 138–40, 146, 152–53
conscience, 3, 144, 176
consensus, 7, 41–43
consent, 3–4, 14n1, 51n2, 77n1, 162, 166, 173, 176;
    non–consent, 162–63, 168–69, 173–74, 179n12;
    normative, 162, 173, 179n12

consequentialism, 6, 45, 55, 170, 179, 181
Conservative Party, 32, 88, 142
correctness standard, 56, 61–64, 77n3

Dalaqua, Gustavo H., 7, 27, 42–43, 46–49, 52, 70, 87–88, 91, 107n2, 108nn5–6, 139, 148, 151–153, 156
debates, 2, 10, 65, 121, 128, 135n15, 161, 181;
    in the informal political sphere, 47, 91, 99, 155;
    parliamentary, 10, 27, 49, 84, 91, 99, 107n3, 125, 155, 159n10
decentralization, 103, 105.
    See also centralization
delegate conception of representation, 98–99.
    See also representation
democracy, 2–14, 27–28, 34, 51, 55–57, 61–63, 69–76, 81–84, 99–109, 110n16, 113–116, 129, 139, 161, 175–76;
    aggregative, 12, 27, 46, 59, 74–76, 81–83, 125, 139, 170;
    Athenian, 71, 83, 87, 135n11;
    deliberative, 6, 27, 43, 52n7, 56, 59, 76, 83, 138–39, 158n1;
    direct, 12, 50, 71–72, 83, 86–87, 90–93, 98, 106, 131;
    epistemic, 1–9, 11, 15n9, 20, 38, 42, 51n2, 56–57, 63, 176, 181;
    false, 93, 109n9;
    participative, 12, 18, 27, 113;
    representative, 7, 12, 20, 33–34, 73–74, 86–90, 98, 110n14, 139;
    Schumpeterian, 27, 83, 107n4
democratic government, 5, 26, 55, 59, 66, 73, 82, 108, 156;
    defects of, 12, 129–30
despotism, 6, 23, 28, 36n3, 37n14, 55–56, 61, 65–71, 119
discipline, 61, 72, 144–45

education, 18–29, 64, 90–92, 98–102, 147–49, 166–70;
and plural voting, 121, 123, 127–129, 176;
compulsory, 22–23, 36n3;
formal, 17–18, 21–24, 28, 31–32, 88, 123;
informal, 17, 24–25, 28–29, 37n11, 88, 148;
in despotism, 36n3, 69, 120;
in local government, 26, 91, 103–106
elections, 82, 84–85, 94–95, 106, 107nn4–5, 116, 121, 125, 169
electoral rights, 70, 100;
as privileges, 102–03, 116–117, 135n11
electoral system, 57, 93, 120, 142
elitism, 34, 39n22
epistemic injustice, 47, 108n9 150.
See also Fricker, Miranda
epistemology, 7, 80n23;
crippled epistemology, 27, 139, 151, 156
epistocracy, 3, 9, 34, 93, 125.
See also Plato
equality, 28–29, 117–18, 129, 133, 134n8, 176;
at workplace, 24, 26–28, 38n17;
gender, 28, 74, 91, 111n20, 120, 150
Estlund, David, 3, 6–8, 52n7, 63, 78n11, 113, 126, 173, 179nn11–14
experts, 6, 8, 55, 85–90, 114, 130–32, 152–56, 166, 172, 174–75;
moral experts, 32–33, 35, 126;
technical experts, 4, 33–35.
See also competence

fairness, 58–59
filtering mechanisms, 7–9, 13–14, 27, 81–82, 95, 100, 102–107, 113, 119, 140–41, 161;
epistemic justification of, 9, 12, 92, 166–67, 175, 177, 182;
and paternalism, 14, 161–62
franchise, 80, 100–102, 118, 120.

See also electoral rights
freedom, 3, 22, 30, 115, 162–66, 168–171, 173–74, 177;
effect on character, 70, 120;
of action, 168;
of expression, 41, 43–47;
of press, 125, 163, 171
free market, 6, 28, 38n18
Fricker, Miranda, 47, 108n9, 150.
See also epistemic injustice

Gaus, Gerald, 3, 58, 130, 178n3
government, 2–9, 11–13, 17, 22–26, 33, 55–63, 66, 68–69, 81, 117, 119–120, 129, 142, 167, 181;
democratic, 5, 12, 27, 55, 59, 66, 129–30, 156;
executive, 13, 30–31, 34–35, 82, 86, 89–90, 152–54, 175;
local, 24, 30, 73, 82, 91, 103–106, 113;
popular, 69, 71, 73, 76;
representative, 4, 17, 30, 71, 129, 142, 175;
two criteria of good government, 12, 71, 141
Gutmann, Amy, 128, 159n11

happiness, 3, 19–20, 22, 25, 58–59, 74, 79n21, 128, 163
Hare, Thomas, 57, 87, 100–101, 103, 110n17, 142–45, 157
harm, 115, 163–65, 168–69, 173–74, 178nn8–9
harm principle, 163, 178n9,
Hayek, Friedrick, 7, 38n18, 78n16, 150
hedonism, 19, 36, 74
Holmes, Steven, 80n26, 108n8
human nature, 24, 32

inconsistency objection, 13, 161–62
instrumentalism, 2, 56–58, 61, 63–64
interest, 31, 33, 44–45, 50, 59, 64, 70, 73–75, 86–87, 95–96, 99, 104–105, 120–27, 149;

class, 75, 124, 127, 132;
common, 62, 67;
general, 26–27, 30, 97–98, 105;
of man as a progressive being, 7, 44, 56, 80n25, 101, 111n20, 181

justice, 35, 64, 70, 101, 105, 126–27:
sentiment of, 4, 123, 176

Kinzer, Bruce L., 32, 139–40, 142, 144–47, 149, 157
Kitcher, Philip, 108n7, 114, 132
Kurer, Oscar, 73, 91, 103, 105–106
knowledge, 5–9, 17–18, 20–35, 68–70, 80n22, 84–86, 89–91, 126–27, 130, 147–49, 151–56, 164, 175.
See also expertise
knowledge tenet, 8–9, 29, 35, 126

Landemore, Hélène, 7, 43–44, 68, 76
Liberal Party, 142, 144
liberalism, 44, 47, 51, 65, 67, 115, 133, 138, 146, 176;
epistemic liberalism, 6–7, 11, 41
Legislative Commission, 30–31, 38n20
legislature, 50, 105, 125
legitimacy, 3–6, 34, 56–61, 77nn1–2, 99, 155–56, 176
liberty, 43, 67, 90, 95–96, 169, 171;
and education 21, 36n7, 166;
individual, 7, 41, 43, 115, 126, 163–66, 168, 161, 174;
negative, 13, 114, 117–118, 125;
positive, 13, 114, 117–118, 125
liberty principle. See harm principle

majority rule, 12, 27, 46, 73, 82, 165
Mill, James, 24, 59–60, 73–75, 80, 179n15
Mill, John S., 1–3, 6–10, 17–18, 41–42, 55–57, 81–82, 113–15, 137–39, 161–63, 181–82;
on Bentham, 37n11;
on education, 18–21, 23, 36n3, 111n25, 167;
on liberty, 21–25, 43–46, 68, 76, 79n21, 103, 127, 149, 163, 161n9, 174, 178n5;
on parliamentary reform, 49–50, 52n8, 70–73, 75, 88, 92–96, 102, 105, 114–18, 121–22, 126, 133n5, 135n14;
on political economy, 24–25, 28, 37, 67, 101, 163;
on representative government, 2, 4, 8–9, 14n4, 26, 30–33, 35, 37n12, 38n17, 47, 52n8, 60–73, 76, 78n10, 85, 89–91, 100–102, 104, 108n6–7, 116, 123–132, 133n4, 135n12, 148, 156, 171, 175–77;
on Tocqueville, 90, 97, 104, 166;
on utilitarianism, 19, 30, 32, 64, 79n21, 134n8;
on women, 27–29, 110n20
Miller, Dale, 29, 77n6, 101, 126–28, 134n7, 179n10
morality, 19, 43, 66, 103, 130, 165, 169

newspapers, 49, 108, 148, 150
Nussbaum, M., 25, 36n2, 79n21, 110

oligarchy, 35, 97
open ballot, 7–8, 72, 94–96, 113, 116, 166, 181

parents, 21–23, 28, 37n10, 101
Parliament, 20, 33–34, 49–50, 52n8, 72–73, 75, 79n22, 84–92, 96–99, 118, 124–25, 130–32, 142–44, 175.
See also government, representative
participation 1, 22, 24–29, 71–73, 90–91, 103, 141, 148–49, 168–69, 175, 181;
and education, 29, 93, 100–102, 111n24;
direct, 86, 93, 116, 153;
indirect, 86;
principle of, 17, 95, 103, 114, 142, 147
partisanship, 13, 138–58, 159n9;

Index

epistemic value of, 46, 108n5, 138, 147, 151–52.
See also filtering mechanisms; Conservative Party; Liberal Party
paternalism, 11, 161–65, 167–173, 177n1, 182
Peter, Fabienne, 4, 6–8, 14n1, 47, 51n1, 58–60, 63, 77n1, 130, 176, 180n16
Pettit, Philip, 3, 128
Plato, 5, 109n10, 125
pleasure, 19, 80n24;
  higher, 19–20, 25, 32, 35n2, 79n21, 131, 134, 178n7, 181
pledges, 49, 96–99, 103, 106, 113, 165–66
plural voting proposal, 7, 9, 11, 50, 103, 106–107, 113–16, 118, 121–130, 161–66, 169–177, 179n10
political sphere, 72, 86;
  formal, 9, 33, 49–50, 72, 75, 84–85, 90, 99, 107n3, 119–127, 133n2, 138, 149, 165, 176;
  informal, 24, 27–28, 33, 49, 72, 82, *86*, 91, 98, 108n6, 128, 138, 149–155
poor relief, 101, 104–105
proceduralism, 52n7, 56–59
progress, 29, 47, 76, 102, 142
public opinion, 37n15, 62, 73, 91–92, 139, 153

Rawls, John, 3, 5, 37n8, 38n18, 48, 65
representation, 8, 49–51, 71–76, 82–83, 87–88, 107n5, 109n9, 137–39, 153, 157;
  and political conflict, 49–51;
  epistemic value of, 71–73, 75, 97;
  of interests, 50, 74–75;
  of opinions, 50, 75;
  proportional, 49–50, 75, 83, 93, 107n5;
  two conceptions of, 83.
See also filtering mechanisms; government, representative

representative assembly, 34, 50, 72, 87, 92–93, 108n8, 125, 144, 148
Rousseau, Jean–Jacques, 86, 139
Ryan, Alan, 18, 20, 23–24, 31, 37n10, 101, 111n24

scholocracy, 34, 95, 113, 133n2, 179n14
Schumpeter, Joseph, 27, 83, 85, 107n4
secret ballot, 50, 57, 76, 94–96, 103, 106, 116
slavery, 66–67, 78, 178n5
suffrage, 64, 102, 115–17, 119, 123, 129–130, 133nn4–5, 169, 171;
  and education, 64;
  and women 28, 74, 91, 120;
  universal, 1, 25, 38n17, 55, 100–102, 106, 109n10, 113, 118–19, 123, 181.
See also electoral rights

Talisse, Robert, 6, 14n6, 27, 58, 63, 137, 159n9
Thompson, Dennis F., 1, 17, 24, 26, 29–30, 35n1, 37n12, 69, 79n19, 91, 103, 107n5, 114, 133n4, 139–142, 145, 159n11
Tocqueville, Alexis de, 96, 104, 166
trade unions, 28, 138, 148
truth tenet, 8, 126
tyranny of the majority, 12, 27, 93, 123–24, 128, 149, 170.
See also majority rule

Urbinati, Nadia, 7, 34, 43, 51n2, 59, 67, 73–74, 82–83, 85–89, 91, 97, 108n5, 128
utilitarianism, 19, 59, 64, 134n8, 163.
See also consequentialism
utility, 25, 46–47, 58–60, 64, 74, 80n24, 127;
  calculus, 44, 74, 80n24;
  maximization, 19, 46, 58, 77n1, 80n24;
  principle of, 19, 36n2

value, 5–14, 41–51, 100, 114;
  epistemic, 5–9, 35–37, 41–51, 57–58,
    70–73, 76, 82–83, 100, 105–106,
    108n5, 116, 125, 130–33, 140–41,
    146–49, 152, 175;
  instrumental, 6, 13, 34–35, 36n2,
    45–46, 52n6, 58–63, 114, 138,
    151, 175–76;
  intrinsic, 52n6, 58–59, 134n8, 167;
  political, 2, 130, 143, 150,
    153–55, 181;
  moral, 5, 14n6, 30–31, 35,
    52n6, 58, 69

voting 27, 46, 80n26, 83–84, *86*–87,
  94–95, 114, 116, 169;
  as a moral act 104, 115, 117, 126–27.
  See also elections; electoral rights;
    plural voting proposal

well-being, 19, 25, 59–60, 64, 70, 74,
  80n24, 81, 161–63, 165–67, 168–
  69, 178nn8–9
White, Jonathan, 47, 139, 147,
  151–53, 158n8

Ypi, Lea, 47, 139, 147, 151–53, 158n8

About the Author

Ivan Cerovac is research fellow at the Faculty of Humanities and Social Sciences, University of Rijeka (Croatia). He holds two PhDs in philosophy, one from the University of Trieste and another from the University of Rijeka. He writes and teaches a range of topics in ethics and political philosophy, including political legitimacy, social justice, and democratic theory. Cerovac is the author of *Epistemic Democracy and Political Legitimacy* (Palgrave Macmillan 2020).

www.ingramcontent.com/pod-product-compliance
Lightning Source LLC
Chambersburg PA
CBHW061714300426
44115CB00014B/2677